SEE INTERNATIONAL ~~Man~~
Richard D.
Basic Manage
Congress. 67-11817   1967.

Holt/Rinehart/winst

Govd on Policy Towards T. unions
    Decision making Process
    Relationships & Strategies

Managing the Multinational Enterprise

Managing
the Multinational
Enterprise

*Organization
of the Firm
and Ownership
of the Subsidiaries*

John M. Stopford
and
Louis T. Wells, Jr.

Longman

LONGMAN GROUP LIMITED
London
Associated companies, branches and representatives throughout the world

© 1972 by Basic Books

First published in the U.K. 1972 by Longman Group Ltd.

ISBN 0582 45001 2

Printed in Great Britain by Lowe & Brydone (Printers) Ltd., London

To
Karena and Robin,
both multinational enterprises

PREFACE

This book has been produced as a part of Harvard's Multinational Enterprise Project, a large-scale study that has been going on since 1965. It is the second of the four volumes that will present the project's main results.

In a project of this sort, involving a number of researchers concerned with overlapping problems, it becomes very difficult to attribute ideas to particular individuals. All our colleagues will recognize ideas that we have borrowed. In only a few cases were we able to acknowledge their contributions. To both Raymond Vernon and Lawrence E. Fouraker we owe an immense debt; their contributions have been so pervasive that we cannot possibly acknowledge them all. Professor Vernon, general coordinator of the project, has been our indispensable source of fresh intellectual insights when we became mired in the petty details of the research. Without his usually gentle and always subtle prodding, we would probably still be processing data and rewriting manuscripts. Dean Fouraker was initially involved in the study of organizational structure. He continued to offer us his wisdom and encouragement after he was promoted out of the project. And his intellectual imprint remains on the study. Lawrence G. Franko, who wrote his doctoral dissertation in conjunction with the research on ownership policies, provided us with several concepts, for which we are grateful.

We benefited from the centralized data collection effort that was undertaken for the use of all the researchers on the project. This work was ably managed by Joan P. Curhan and James W. Vaupel. Many students, who were supported mainly by the Federal College Work-Study Program, helped us extensively in handling the vast amount of data underlying this study. Among them, Ann Barcher, Joseph Bailey, Christopher Hartley, Charles Kokesh, and George Pijewsky made particularly important contributions.

The initial work on organizational structure was done by John M. Stopford as a part of his doctoral dissertation, which received financial support from the Ford Foundation. Continuation of this work and the study of ownership policies by Louis T. Wells, Jr. were financed in part by a grant that the Ford Foundation made to the Multinational Enterprise Project and in part by funds generously made available by the Division of Research at the Harvard Business School.

To the many businessmen whom we interviewed and who gave us access to their files we are especially grateful. Without their cooperation and willingness to spend hours of their time improving our knowledge of their organizations, this study could not have been undertaken.

Two cheerful secretaries, Elizabeth Greenleaf and Jeannie Didrichsen, learned by painful experience that our repeated claims of "final drafts" usually did not mean what we intended.

JOHN M. STOPFORD
LOUIS T. WELLS, JR.

Boston
1972

CONTENTS

Appendices

FIGURES

TABLES

Managing the Multinational Enterprise

ONE / Introduction: The Management of Size and Diversity

The rapid growth of American-based multinational enterprises has created difficult problems for their managers and for the governments of the countries in which the firms operate. The challenges presented by the spread of these enterprises vary widely, and the appropriate responses by the managers and the governments involved are necessarily of a complex nature. No one set of policies, instituted by managers or by governments, can be equally effective for all types of multinational enterprise. Managing such enterprises requires a thorough understanding on the part of both businessmen and government officials of how these complex organizations behave.

What are the challenges that these enterprises present to their own managers? Few organizations in the past have equalled today's multinational enterprises in sheer size and complexity. In part, the challenges to management stem from the fact that multinational enterprises are caught up in a web of powerful and opposing forces. Managing such organizations requires a response to the constant pull away from the center of units at the periphery. In many of the firms, units producing similar products tend to collude against control from the center; in some, units within a distant region join to resist direction from corporate headquarters. Furthermore, the governments of those countries in which subsidiaries are located introduce pressures, such as requirements for joint ventures, that make the units on the periphery even harder to bind to the center. Nevertheless, businessmen have found ways of organizing the multinational enterprise that enable them to control and coordinate the activities of the various units. For some multinational enterprises, however, continued growth is reducing the effectiveness of past solutions to the problems of control and coordination. New forms of organizational structure are being developed. Whether they will enable the manager to overcome the problems of the largest and most complex multinational firms is not yet certain.

What are the challenges to national policies? Enterprises with subsidiaries scattered around the globe have the potential to evade many of the pol-

icies of individual countries in which they operate. As will become clear
in this study, multinational enterprises differ dramatically in their ability
to move products, money, technology, and managers around the world in a
manner consistent with the objectives of the enterprise. However, faced
with the threat to their sovereignty, governments are responding to the
challenges. Sometimes, their responses are shaped by frustration.

The primary purpose of this study is to explore a few of the choices that
businessmen have been making in dealing with the challenges posed by the
multinational enterprises, the difficulties that they have encountered with
these choices, and the directions in which they are moving.

We have selected two particularly important issues as the subjects of
this study.

The first part of the study deals with the ways in which multinational
enterprises have altered their structures as they have developed new and
more complex strategies. The focus is on how the duties of the senior officers of the firms have been allocated, where decisions are made, and how
communications flow within the enterprise. For the manager, organizational structure is important in determining the ability of the enterprise to
coordinate the various units, to overcome the diseconomies of scale, and to
apply successfully a set of special skills in many different countries. For
the government official, the organizational structure of the enterprise is
equally important. If the individual subsidiaries act as autonomous national entities, they pose little challenge to the policies of the individual
nation. If they can be coordinated from the center to respond to suprana-
tional goals, the multinational enterprise is indeed a challenge to the concept of sovereignty.

The second part of the study deals with decisions about the inclusion of
local partners in the foreign operations of the firm. Governments and multinational enterprises have held different views about joint ventures for
some time. Governments typically look to joint ventures as a way of increasing local control over the actions of the multinational firm. Some multinational enterprises have actively sought out joint ventures, even in the
absence of government pressures; others have strictly avoided joint ventures, to the extent of not investing in countries that insist on them. We
will show that having joint venture partners has seemed to make sense for
some enterprises at certain stages of their development; for others, or at
different times, they would have been very costly. Similarly, for governments, exerting pressure on the multinational enterprises to take in a local
partner makes good sense under certain conditions, but not under others.

There is, of course, no generally accepted definition of "multinational
enterprise." What we and a number of other authors include under the ru-
bric are those large firms that have subsidiaries in a number of countries

and that, at least to some extent, attempt to coordinate and control these units in accordance with a common strategy.

This study focuses on multinational enterprises that began as American firms. To select firms that were large and had manufacturing units in a number of countries, we took those that were on *Fortune*'s list of the 500 largest manufacturing enterprises in the United States in 1963 or 1964, and that held 25 percent or more of the equity in manufacturing facilities in six or more foreign countries at the end of 1963.

The resulting list of 187 firms forms the basis of this study. Thorough searches of published sources, interviews with the managers, and responses to questionnaires enabled us to learn a great deal about the activities of these firms since 1900.[1]

A few numbers drive home the scale and complexity of these multinational enterprises. The smallest of the enterprises had annual worldwide sales of $115 million in 1966. The median worldwide sales of the 187 firms was close to $500 million annually. The median number of countries in which these enterprises had manufacturing operations in 1964 was ten. One of the firms had manufacturing subsidiaries in twenty-nine countries.

Along with large size and geographical dispersion, many of the firms had highly diverse product lines. For example, one firm manufactured products in forty-one different industries. The median enterprise in our study manufactured products in ten industries.[2]

Not only are these firms especially large, diversified, and geographically dispersed, they also differ from the typical American enterprise in other ways. For example, many spend an unusually large portion of their sales either on research and development, or on advertising, or on both. It is, of course, on the special skills in areas such as technology or marketing that these firms have relied for much of their multinational strength.[3]

Some have expanded abroad by building on their new research-based products that were developed to serve the high-income American market. Others have relied on their marketing skills gained in the mass market of the United States. Still others were attracted abroad early in their life in order to gain access to raw materials, and, once abroad, turned to foreign markets to provide outlets for the raw materials that they controlled.[4]

The strategy chosen by the multinational enterprise has been closely connected with the design of the organization and the ownership of the subsidiaries established to implement it. We found that a close tie between strategy and structure exists regardless of what industry the firm is in; managers in enterprises following similar strategies in quite different industries have developed similar organizational structures and ownership policies.

Once set up, the organizational structure almost certainly influences the choice of strategy of the multinational firm. The relationship between strategy and organization is clearly not the simple one in which strategy is determined first and then a structure established to implement it. The costs of reorganizing and the resistance of established interest groups within the firm to changes in the structure no doubt inhibit the introduction of strategies that require changes in the existing organization.

Until very recently, the strategies of most multinational enterprises have been relatively simple. For most firms, even an outsider could confidently identify one strength that was of prime importance. This strength might be marketing, technology, or control of raw materials. The firm tended to organize itself in a relatively simple form that allowed it to draw on this particular strength. This structure, however, entailed the sacrifice of some abilities to control or communicate efficiently along other lines within the firm.

Some multinational enterprises have continued to follow a simple strategy, even as they grew larger. These firms have had to adjust their management procedures in order to cope with problems of increasing scale and to retain control of their foreign subsidiaries.

In recent years, however, other multinational enterprises have undertaken more complex strategies. Increases in the complexity of the business, as for example when a new product line is added, have posed difficult problems of adjustment. Whereas greater size may often be accommodated with an existing structure by the addition of a few new procedures, greater complexity has typically required major changes not only in established procedure, but also in the organizational structure.

Today the very large and complex multinational enterprises do not rely on a single predominant strength. Some spend much effort on developing new products; at the same time, they exercise considerable energies in marketing their more mature lines. For managers of such enterprises, choosing one strength around which to build the organization is exceedingly difficult. But, at the same time, deciding to create an organization around multiple skills runs the risk that the structure will be so cumbersome that communication will be slow and controls ineffectual. The greatest management challenges exist in these enterprises. And it is in them that some of the most exciting innovation is occurring.

Part I
MULTINATIONAL STRUCTURE AND MULTINATIONAL STRATEGY

TWO / Developing an Organization for Multinational Business

Firms attempting to grow in foreign markets have followed a number of different strategic routes. Many firms, such as John Deere and Scott Paper, have concentrated their efforts on expanding the volume of manufacturing and sales abroad of the single line of closely related products in which they have the greatest expertise and experience. But many firms have diversified their foreign product lines to include products in which they have less experience. Sperry Rand and Dow Chemical, for example, manufacture abroad widely diversified product lines that include products they have manufactured in the United States for decades and also products only recently developed. Some firms have concentrated their efforts in a few carefully selected foreign markets; others have attempted no such geographical concentration.

The organizational structures that U.S. manufacturing firms use for the administration of their foreign activities are as diverse as the strategies they have followed. Most firms, including General Motors, assign responsibility for all the foreign activities to a single senior executive, who heads what is normally called the international division. But in a large and growing number of firms, such as Celanese Corporation, the responsibility is shared among several senior executives, each of whom manages only one component of the foreign operations. In these firms the foreign operations are divided in ways that reduce the distinction between domestic and overseas activities.

Some simplification of what we mean by strategy and structure is needed in order to make direct comparisons between firms. The strategy of every firm can be specified in terms of an enormous number of variables, many of which are unique to the firm's particular set of products, markets, and resources. The organizational structure can be described at all levels of the hierarchy, in terms of an almost limitless number of considerations. Descriptions at too great a level of detail may obscure the existence of factors common to many firms.

B*

The strategy of any enterprise, according to one definition, is "the determination of long-term goals and objectives of an enterprise, and the adoption of courses of action and the allocation of resources necessary for carrying out these goals." [1] The crucial dimensions of strategy are the volume of activities, the geographical dispersion of the effort, research, and product diversification. Senior managers in the firm are responsible for making decisions about these strategic dimensions of the firm and for allocating their resources accordingly. They provide the overall direction for the firm and set the scene for more detailed decision making carried out at lower levels of the hierarchy by men who are concerned with translating gross specifications into detailed plans of action. In this book, the dimensions of strategy considered are those of primary concern to senior managers.

Structure can be considered as the design of the organization through which the enterprise is administered. The design has three major aspects: first, the authority and responsibility of each executive; second, the kinds of information that flow along the lines of communication among executives; and third, the procedures established for channeling and processing the information.[2] In this study, the analysis of structure is limited to the level of those senior managers who report directly to the president's office. Because there are relatively few different ways of allocating responsibility among these senior managers, the number of structural alternatives considered is small.

This treatment of structure excludes any recognition of the legal or statutory features of an enterprise. But the legal structure is designed, in accordance with government regulations, for cash-flow and tax purposes; it seldom reflects the way in which the enterprise is managed. Because this book is concerned with managerial practice, the legal structure can be ignored.

The organizational structure of a firm can be thought of as evolving in a series of stages. Each stage is a modification or adaptation of the structure in the previous stage. The expertise and experience of the enterprise with one structure provide the building blocks for future structures. The strategy of the firm undergoes a similar process. There are often leads and lags in the relative changes of structure and strategy, as management does not always recognize the needs for change until operational difficulties occur. But over the long run firms attempt to reduce the inconsistencies that leads and lags introduce in the organization. In this chapter, attention is focused primarily on the associations that exist between strategy and structure rather than on the process by which the associations are developed.

The purpose of this chapter is to describe the evolution of the organizational structures that U.S. firms have developed during the course of their expansion abroad. This process closely parallels the structural developments that generally accompany growth and diversification at home. The changes at home are examined first, because most firms duplicate abroad what they have previously accomplished in the United States.

A Choice of Structures

All business enterprises have some form of hierarchy of authority and responsibility. This hierarchical attribute of structure is so widespread that it is generally accepted as an inevitable fact of business life. Yet, for the purposes of understanding the structural development experienced by firms as they expand abroad, an examination of the general reasons for building different types of hierarchy is helpful. The basic problems of choice are the same, regardless of the geographical location of the business. In order to simplify the analysis, only two types of organization are explored here: functional departments and quasi-autonomous divisions. A hierarchy of functional departments is normally used by firms that have a single product line in a single country. Quasi-autonomous divisions are generally established by firms as they begin to add new product lines or to enter new national markets.

THE FUNCTIONAL STRUCTURE

Some observers see the development and expansion of any business organization as occurring in three stages.

In Stage 1, an enterprise is usually small enough to be administered by a single man, typically the owner and founder. There is virtually no delegation of management tasks, and the success of the enterprise depends heavily upon the abilities and personality of the president. But success and growth in the volume of activity in this entrepreneur-centered enterprise soon generate the need for delegation; the single manager cannot cope with the increasing demands on his time.

The response is the establishment of functional departments, such as sales, production, and finance, each headed by a company officer reporting directly to the president. This change is considered to mark the emergence of the second stage in the development of an organization.[3] At the point of transition, the firm is generally small and producing only a single product or a single line of closely related products, and the spread of operations may not have reached even national dimensions. The Stage 2 structure is capable, however, of accommodating considerable growth, provided that growth is achieved by producing more of the product in the same national market.

To deal with simple growth of this sort each departmental manager can add junior managers who supervise the activities of one part of the department. For example, the manager of the sales department might have subordinates responsible for the salesmen in different regions of the country. As the volume of sales and the number of salesmen increase, the sales manager can choose to increase the number of his immediate subordinates and thereby to increase his span of control. Alternatively, he can keep his span of control constant and increase the number of levels of supervision in the department by appointing managers of subregions reporting to the regional managers. Similar choices are faced by the heads of the other departments. Either procedure represents merely an amplification of the basic functional structure and does not disturb the established methods of conducting the business.

The major parts of the Stage 2 structure are the functional departments and the office of the president. Each department is responsible for one specialized part of the firm's activities, and each is composed of subunits that are even more specialized. The heads of these departments have the difficult tasks of administering their subunits, but it remains for their activities to be coordinated by the office of the president. In effect, the Stage 2 structure, like all structures, is a system of interacting parts, each of which has management activities and a structure in its own right.[4]

If a large, complex organization tried to operate without a hierarchical system, the difficulties of managing the communication requirements of the system would be immense. Even in medium-sized firms the number of channels needed to allow each unit of the firm to communicate directly with all the other units is prohibitively large.[5] The hierarchy provides a system of channeling the flows of information among the units through a series of coordinators. For instance, the vice president of sales is the coordinator for the regional sales managers. These coordinators reduce the number of channels well below that required for direct communication among all the units.

Developing a hierarchy also increases the capacity of the system to absorb shock.[6] Because the complex tasks of the total system are broken down into simplified elements, each managed by a separate subunit, the effects of most disturbances are not transmitted throughout the whole organization.

These advantages of a hierarchy are achieved at the cost of imposing some barriers to the communication flows across the boundaries separating the specialized activities. The evidence shows that communication among the subunits of the marketing department occurs more readily than, for example, communication between marketing and production departments. Each department develops a coding system with which to order its world. This coding scheme enhances the efficiency of communication within the department, but it can reduce the efficiency of communication with other departments that have a different coding scheme.[7] The need for communication across the boundaries established by the functional departments, each with its own code, and the difficulties of achieving adequate communication must be taken into consideration by designers of the departmental boundaries.

The hierarchical structure incurs further costs. Communications have to be relayed by coordinators at each level. But each coordinator introduces delays and distortions in the messages handled. In large systems the organizational "distance" between two subunits can be so great that a message in any form passed from one to the other becomes lost in the "noise" introduced by the successive actions of the coordinators. A story from World War I illustrates this point. Word-of-mouth communication along the trenches in the British sector during a period when the field telephone was out of order is reputed to have resulted in the message "Send reinforcements: we are going to advance" from the front line being relayed to headquarters as "Send three-and-fourpence: we are going to a dance."

Inappropriate responses to change are another source of costs of a hierarchy. The shock of a change is absorbed by containing the effects of that change within those units directly affected. Corrective action that is not in the best interests of the whole system may be induced in those units. These costs are likely to increase as the number of levels in the hierarchy increases: the greater the number of levels, the greater is the possibility of suboptimal response.[8]

The costs of delays and distortion in communication and of suboptimization can be reduced by reducing the number of levels in the hierarchy. To do so, however, requires a widening of the span of control of the coordinator at each level. But there is a constraint on how wide the span of control can become; a single coordinator or decision maker has only a limited ability to absorb and to process information.[9]

The expansion of each functional department in a Stage 2 structure is controlled by the conflicting benefits and costs of increasing the span of control and of increasing the number of levels in the departmental hierarchy. It has been argued that expansion of such hierarchies is severely limited because constraints soon appear in the form of loss of control.[10] In practice, however, the functional departments of some enterprises have grown to enormous proportions without appearing to suffer from undue diseconomies of scale. In these large departments the activities are primarily of a routine nature and the interactions of the various units can be handled by standardized procedures and programmed responses to change without serious loss of control. Large Stage 2 structures are relatively common in the steel and paper industries, for example, where the rate of change both in the markets served and in technology is slow. Research into the behavior of different types of communication networks has shown that centralized networks resembling the functional departments were the most efficient for the performance of routine tasks in a stable environment.[11]

The president of the Stage 2 enterprise coordinates the functional departments and allocates resources among the departments. If the activities of the department are stable, the communication and coordination functions are relatively routine, leaving some time for the president to devote himself to strategic questions. But if there are changes in the departments or conflicts between them requiring prolonged attention, the strategic questions tend to be ignored because the president has only a limited capacity to process information.

Firms with Stage 2 structures often have only a single line of products, and maintain to some degree the stability of the activities. This strategy helps them to avoid overloading the limited decision-making capacity at the top of the hierarchy. These firms typically acquire new resources by means of vertical integration, as in the case of a steel company buying into ore mining. Acquiring such new resources does not disturb the arrangements of the established functional departments.

The Stage 2 structure can be enormously efficient in the rational use of resources and in the coordination of functional activities. Looking back on the performance of such structures, however, one observer noted a basic weakness.

A very few men were . . . entrusted with a great number of complex decisions. The executives in the central office were usually the president with one or two assistants, sometimes the chairman of the board, and the vice presidents who headed the various departments. The latter were often too busy with the administration of the particular function to devote much time to the affairs of the enterprise as a whole. Their training proved a still more serious defect. Because these administrators had spent most of their business careers within a single functional activity, they had little experience or interest in understanding the needs and problems of other departments or of the corporation as a whole.[12]

The shortage of general managers can prevent firms with Stage 2 structures from undertaking new directions of growth. Often the demands of the day-to-day administration of the enterprise are sufficient to tax the resources of the president's office, and large firms with Stage 2 structures commonly concentrate their attentions on a single product line without any conscious plan to continue doing so.

THE DIVISIONAL STRUCTURE

Adding new product lines or entering new markets disturbs the equilibrium of the system of functional departments in a Stage 2 structure. The functional departments are unable to absorb all the shock of learning how to manage the new activities and they throw the burden onto the shoulders of the president. The president is forced to institute fundamental changes in the structure to manage the new complexities of the system. This new structure is dubbed Stage 3 in the sequence of organizational development of an enterprise.

Merely enlarging the Stage 2 structure to include new businesses is costly. If each established functional department in a Stage 2 structure were to be expanded to include the activities of a new product line, the number of coordinating and communication linkages would be more than doubled. Procedures developed to cope with the original product line seldom apply to the new line. Furthermore, the heads of the functional departments are likely to devote their attention to familiar problems and ignore new ones. The result of attempting to contain diversity within a functional structure is a serious loss of control and efficiency. Attempts of this nature by such early pioneers of product diversity as Du Pont and Standard Oil of New Jersey illustrate the difficulties.[13]

The challenge is to find a new structure that is capable of "decoupling" some of the communication and coordination linkages.[14] Decoupling may be achieved by building subsystems composed of units that have strong interactions and by reducing the number of links needed to connect such subsystems. These subsystems appear in the form of product or area divisions, each headed by a general manager who performs most of the duties of the president of a Stage 2 structure. Provided that the interactions among the subsystems are weak compared to the interactions within each subsystem, the decoupling effect normally increases the internal efficiency of the subsystem. The subsystem managers are free to devote their energies to managing the internal interactions without being distracted by having to cope with other interactions that have little effect on the success of the subsystem.

Elimination of all the linkages between the subsystems provides independence for the subsystems at the cost of fragmentation and loss of control. The nearest approach to such complete decoupling in practice is a holding company, and it is debatable whether a holding company is a system at all. It is more like a collection of independent systems.

Most diversified firms, however, have some interactions among the divisions. These interactions must be provided for somewhere in the overall system. Such provision requires people and money. Control systems also cost money. There is, therefore, a trade-off to be made between the relative advantages and costs of coordination and independence in decoupled systems. The design of the decoupled system appropriate for a diversified firm must take into account these considerations. The Stage 3 structure tries to strike a balance between central coordination and independence for each subsystem.

The differences between the Stage 3 structure and the Stage 2 structure are illustrated in Figure 2-1. There are several important aspects of these differences. First, each division in the Stage 3 structure resembles the functional hierarchy of the Stage 2 structure, except that finance is removed from the divisional system and administered in the central office. Second, each division is a profit center, so that its economic performance may be evaluated separately from that of the enterprise as a whole. Third, the role of the president in the Stage 3 structure is more that of determining strategy and of achieving a balance among the various divisions and less that of day-to-day coordination of functional departments. Fourth, the boundaries of the activities of each division are drawn on the basis of product differences, whereas the prime determinants of the subsystem boundaries in the Stage 2 structure are functional differences. Fifth, the Stage 3 structure includes some staff groups that simply channel information, monitor the interactions among the divisions, and provide advice. These groups do not have any direct role in the short-term administration of the operations.

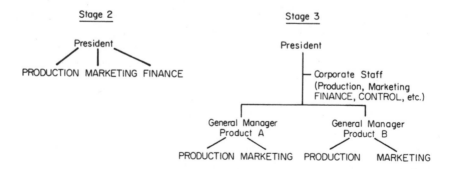

Figure 2–1   *Simplified Versions of Stage 2 and Stage 3 Structures*

NOTE: The functions shown in capital letters indicate operating responsibility; those in lower-cased letters indicate advisory and coordinating roles. See the text for a discussion of the operating role of the financial and control groups.

The divisional subsystems and the central office of the Stage 3 structure are linked together by three major processes. These linkages provide both constraints on the actions of the divisional general managers and controls necessary to avoid an undesirable fragmentation of the overall system.

The most important linkage is the control function. It acts to monitor the performance of each division and to signal the need for corrective action if targets are not met. Control over the actions of each division is also exercised by procedures for allocating funds. In accordance with the needs of the strategy of the overall system, any division can be expanded or starved of funds somewhat independently from the other divisions. New businesses may be entered and old ones eliminated with little or no effect on the rest of the organization. Both the financial and the control groups generate much of the data necessary for making strategic allocation decisions. They have, therefore, a much more direct impact on activities within the divisions than do the other staff groups in the central office.

The planning process forges another type of linkage among the divisions. Strategic plans for the enterprise as a whole are transmitted to the divisions with the purpose of making the organization behave as a coordinated system. These plans are generally formulated on the basis of information provided by the divisions and the financial group.[15] In many firms, separate staff groups in the central office add further inputs to the planning process by formulating long-range plans, by doing market research, and by searching for new opportunities outside the scope of the existing businesses. Communication among the divisions is stimulated to some extent by the exchanges of information in the various stages of the planning process. The actions of each division are constrained within the framework of the overall strategy and the actions of other divisions.

Other staff groups in the central office provide still another type of linkage between the divisions. These groups coordinate the direct interactions between the divisions. Direct interactions may be internal to the corporate system, as in the transfer of semifinished goods between divisions. They may also be external to the system, as in selling the output of several divisions through the same channels of distribution. Staff groups are also involved in dealing with some of the issues common to all the divisions. For example, legal questions or corporate advertising are generally handled centrally, on the assumption that the benefits of consistent behavior are not offset by the losses that come from reducing the autonomy of the divisions.

A system of quasi-autonomous divisions and central staff groups permits the management task to be divided on the basis of different time horizons. The president is concerned with long-range issues and the divisional general managers concentrate on short-term action. The short-term orientation of the divisional managers allows them to coordinate the functional

departments inside their divisions without too much distraction from strategic issues. But the different time horizons of the president and his immediate subordinates can cause problems for the coordination of the overall
effort. The staff groups act as processors of the information needed to reduce these problems and to help resolve the conflicts that inevitably
emerge.[16]

Highly skilled general managers are indispensable to the success of a
Stage 3 structure. They must adapt the divisional activities to the needs of
the corporate system without impairing the independent performance of
the divisions. They must resolve the conflicts of pressures for centralization and independence, of long-term goals and short-term needs, and they
must develop the coordinating systems necessary to support the heteroge-
neous activities in the most effective manner possible. Without able general managers acting as linch pins [17] the elaborate system of interdepen-
dent actions and control would be inefficient.

A firm choosing to diversify, either by adding new products or by
expanding abroad, is faced with problems that cannot be adequately managed by the hierarchical system of the Stage 2 structure. A new system
must be developed to provide the necessary management. More general
managers are required in the shift to this new system, because the Stage 2
structure economizes on this critical resource by requiring a single general
manager as president of the enterprise. The firm may reach outside for
able men who have gained experience in general management elsewhere,
or it may choose to train men already employed. In either event, decisions
to change the strategy are often delayed by the difficulties of finding good
men, or by the problems of providing effective training.

Training new general managers is accomplished primarily by exposing
men experienced in a single function to the problems of running a multi-
functional business. The Stage 3 structure provides an ideal proving
ground for new general managers, a fact that many firms discovered only
after they had set the new structure in place.[18] The end result of the
changes in procedures for handling information and in the delegation of
responsibilities to general managers is a body of experience or learning
about the running of a new type of management system.

Expansion Abroad and Structural Change

Expansion abroad adds complexities to the management task that are
similar in some respects to the complexities introduced by the decision to
enter a new product line. In both cases, the organization must learn new

skills and must develop new procedures before it can successfully merge the new activities into the overall system. There are, however, differences between the structural developments that accompany expansion abroad and those that accompany mere product diversification. Entry into foreign markets does not lead directly to the development of a Stage 3 structure. Instead, firms generally go through an initial period when all their new foreign subsidiaries, in the manner of a holding company, are tied to the parent firm by loose financial links.

This initial period of autonomy for the foreign subsidiaries may be considered the first phase in the growth of a firm's foreign activities. The second phase is a period of organizational consolidation when an international division is developed. The international division is typically considered an independent part of the enterprise and not subject to the same strategic planning that guides the domestic activities. In the third phase, strategic planning is carried out on a consistent and worldwide basis and the structure of the foreign activities is altered to provide closer links with the rest of the structure.

AUTONOMOUS SUBSIDIARIES

The initial autonomy of the first few foreign subsidiaries reflects the fact that most U.S. manufacturing firms stumbled into manufacturing abroad without much design. The early investments in foreign manufacturing made by most firms were defensive reactions against the threat of losing markets that in the first place had been acquired almost accidentally. Only later did conscious strategies for growth on a global scale emerge.

The high income level and high labor costs in the United States have led many firms to develop new products. These new products provide a promising base for exports.[19] As the demand for these new products increases abroad, unsolicited orders are often placed with American firms. The export business prospers. But the easy life that results from the monopoly position in foreign markets does not last indefinitely. Enterprises in other countries learn how to make the products and, as their markets become large enough to support a plant capable of producing the products at costs competitive to the prices of the imports, the American export market is threatened. Even if the export business grew in a haphazard fashion, however, it has become a significant source of revenue for the firm and is not lightly abandoned. The threat of losing an export market to a competitor often leads managers to decide that the firm should build its own plant abroad to maintain its competitive position. The firm has taken the first step towards becoming multinational without having had an explicit plan for so doing.

There are many other reasons that lead firms to initiate production abroad. Most of them are also defensive in nature. For example, some firms have constructed plants abroad without having first developed any significant exports in cases where their domestic markets have been threatened by low-cost imports from foreign companies or even from their domestic competitors with plants abroad. Purely noneconomic reasoning sometimes influences managers. The rush to invest in Europe during the late 1950's undoubtedly induced some managers to follow suit because they did not want to be judged old-fashioned.[20]

The men who are sent out to manage these fledgling subsidiaries are generally allowed virtually unlimited powers of decision and action, at least at first. Sometimes the only contact the subsidiary has with the parent company is no more than that involved in remitting dividends. The financial tie between the subsidiary and the parent company is often formalized in these early years by charging the senior financial officer in the enterprise with responsibility for foreign investments. In other cases, the formal reporting relationship may be to the office of the president if he happens to have a personal interest in international activities. In neither case, however, is the relationship active; reports that are sent to the central office are seldom used as the basis for decision making and action.

The autonomy initially accorded to each manager of foreign subsidiaries is the result of a combination of factors. The first few foreign investments are small and not critical to the success of the enterprise. They are often regarded as portfolio gambles, because the managers in the central office do not have any clear concept of the criteria that should be applied to the new operation. These gambles provide a form of insurance in situations where the potential penalties of not making the investment are impossible to calculate with any confidence. The gambling attitude normally persists after the investment has been made, since there are few executives with experience in managing operations abroad. It is difficult to employ any control system until a knowledge has been acquired of what constitutes a reasonable level of performance under the conditions prevailing for the subsidiary. In effect, the need for learning exceeds the desire for control. In such circumstances the subsidiary manager is in a strong position to behave as he pleases.

The subsidiary manager values his autonomy highly and is likely to behave in ways that delay for as long as possible the imposition of controls from the central office. By maintaining a profitable and growing operation and by using the local capital market for his borrowing requirements, he can minimize or perhaps eliminate the dependence of the subsidiary on the parent.

The enterprise can tolerate this unstructured system for a while. If the subsidiaries remain small and insignificant parts of the system, there is little pressure to introduce controls provided that the financial results remain satisfactory. But if the subsidiaries grow rapidly and accumulate resources, pressures to introduce controls begin to emerge in the central office.

The transitory nature of autonomy is clear. The first phase of expansion, involving autonomous foreign subsidiaries, is likely to give way rapidly to a new phase when controls and organization are introduced. Among the 170 firms for which organizational histories were developed in this study, over 60 percent developed international divisions before they had acquired their fifth foreign subsidiary. By the end of 1966, all 170 firms had passed out of the phase of autonomy of their expansion abroad.

FORMING THE INTERNATIONAL DIVISION

The international division provides an "umbrella" covering all the foreign activities of the enterprise. The managers of the foreign subsidiaries report to a general manager or divisional vice president, who is usually a senior corporate officer responsible directly to the president. Apart from that fact, however, there is great variety, both in the administration of the divisional activities and in the maintenance of links with the domestic side of the enterprise.

When the international division is formed, the initial effect on the activities of the subsidiaries is likely to be small. The man who is assigned to the new job usually has a great deal to learn about managing international activities. For example, the man promoted to head the division is often the manager of the export department. He has experience in selling the firm's products abroad, but he has no prior experience in production and other functions of the subsidiaries for which he is responsible. Consequently, controls tend to be introduced only slowly.

One task of the international division is to coordinate the activities of the subsidiaries. The coordination is directed toward raising the overall performance above the level that would be possible if each subsidiary behaved autonomously. In cases where there are transfers of goods and services among the subsidiaries, the total taxes may often be reduced by adjusting the transfer prices. Such adjustments reduce the profits of some of the subsidiaries and are unlikely to be instituted without central control. In other cases, central control is needed to designate those facilities that are to produce for export. Without control, each foreign manufacturing subsidiary is likely to attempt to utilize its spare capacity for exports even though the marginal costs of production may be lower in other parts of the enterprise. Raising capital for the overseas subsidiaries is another activity that can sometimes be performed more efficiently by central coordination than by each subsidiary relying solely on local capital markets. The international division can take many other actions to improve the overall performance. The possibilities of economic gain from coordination of the foreign subsidiaries provide pressure for centralizing decision making within the international division.

Nevertheless, the ability of the division to go far toward centralization is severely constrained. The variety of local conditions in different foreign countries is so vast that information covering the subject cannot readily be processed by the division. Some policies and procedures such as accounting can be standardized; but others, such as marketing policies, require careful tailoring to the needs of each subsidiary. Managers of the subsidiaries are often best placed to make many of the necessary decisions. Besides, there are inevitable delays in transmitting information to the divisional office, evaluating the information and making the appropriate decisions, and informing the local manager of those decisions. In many situations, a rapid response to change is essential to keep the subsidiary competitive, which can best be achieved by autonomous action on the part of the local manager.

Pressures for and against centralization within the international division vary among firms. They also vary over time in any one division. As the divisional manager gains experience, and as managers of the subsidiaries learn how to operate effectively under the control of a divisional office, some movement toward centralization generally occurs. The speed with which the movement occurs and the extent of its impact on the administration of the division are influenced by the nature of the product line. If firms produce narrow lines of products in foreign countries, and if those lines involve mature goods and stable technologies, the move in the direction of centralization tends to be greater than in firms expanding into diversified lines of new products and rapidly changing technologies and markets.

The early developments within the international divisions are seldom closely monitored by the central office of the enterprise. The relationship between the manager of the division and the rest of the enterprise is analogous to that existing between the autonomous subsidiaries and the president. Though reporting procedures are typically more elaborate than those in the first phase of expansion abroad, there is little attempt to build strong links between the domestic and the foreign parts of the activities. In part, this lack of close supervision of the division is due to the central office's lack of understanding when international problems arise. Responsibility for learning how to manage these problems has been delegated to the divisional manager, and short of disaster there is no immediate cause for interference. Furthermore, the central office may judge that the division is too small a part of the enterprise to be worth the effort of creating elaborate controls.

Figure 2-2 outlines the bare bones of a Stage 3 structure that includes an international division. Several features distinguish this structure from Stage 3 structures developed for purely domestic activities. The international division normally includes a staff group that has a role similar to that of the staff in the central office. This staff group assists the general manager of the division in developing the control procedures appropriate for the subsidiaries in different countries. In other words, the internal structure of the division is a mini version of a Stage 3 structure.

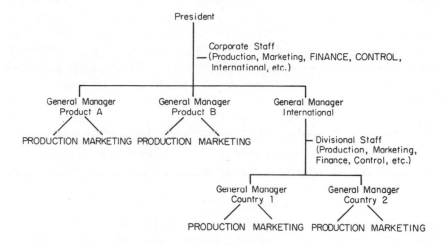

Figure 2–2   *The Stage 3 Structure with an International Division*

NOTE: The functions in capital letters indicate operating responsibility; those in lower-cased letters indicate advisory and coordinating roles.

A financial group is normally included in the divisional staff to coordinate closely with the financial staff in the central office. The task of this divisional staff changes as knowledge of how to deal with the specifically international aspects of money accumulates in the corporate office.[21] Initially, the divisional staff typically duplicates most of the functions of the corporate financial staff. In later years, many of the functions are administered centrally, leaving this staff group concerned primarily with the control of the foreign subsidiaries. This variation in the use of staff illustrates how management procedures change as experience of international business is gained.

An international division may be attached to a Stage 2 structure of functional departments as well as to a Stage 3 structure of product divisions; response to pressures for expansion abroad is not restricted to firms with Stage 3 structures. In fact, almost all the 170 firms for which organizational histories were available had Stage 2 structures when they first expanded abroad. In the majority of firms, however, the establishment of an international division to control the autonomous foreign subsidiaries was delayed until after a Stage 3 structure had been adopted for the domestic operations.

The development of a Stage 3 structure represents a significant investment in an information-processing system and in professional general management. The knowledge and skills acquired as a result of this investment provide the enterprise with a degree of flexibility in entering new areas of business that it did not possess before. Once firms have developed a Stage 3 structure for their domestic activities, therefore, they are more likely to enter new overseas businesses. Only 38 percent of the firms in this study established an international division when they had Stage 2 structures at home, and most of them soon thereafter moved to Stage 3 structures. A similar process of learning about international business occurs regardless of the sequence of structural changes, but the evidence suggests that moves to control the foreign activities through an international division are generally made after the enterprise has developed analogous divisional systems for managing diversity at home.

The international division does not have the same degree of autonomy as do the domestic product divisions, and depends more on the cooperation and assistance of the product divisions than they typically depend upon each other. Generally the products manufactured abroad by the international division are also manufactured at home by one of the product divisions. Without a flow of information about engineering, new technical developments, design, and so forth from the domestic division, the international division is likely to lose its competitive edge. The manager of the product division is normally reluctant, however, to provide the necessary information. Because he is judged against purely domestic measures of performance, he gains nothing by using his resources abroad. The separation of the domestic and foreign subsystems producing the same product raises a high barrier to communication. In response to the communication difficulties, a staff group in the central office is often formed to help the international division acquire information more readily.

Despite the development of procedures for channeling information and establishing some degree of central financial control, the international division remains a separate part of the enterprise. There are inherent conflicts in the structure. The overall management system is designed to control subsystems among which there are few interactions. By being dependent on a domestic product division, the international division creates pressures to expand the size of the coordinating staff groups. These pressures are reduced as men in the product division and the international division become familiar with the problems and devise ways of working together that avoid the lengthy formal channels of communication. Stability in the operations greatly reduces the barriers to communication, but it does not eliminate the conflicts.

The international division is the locus of all the international expertise of the firm and serves as a training ground for providing more managers with experience of management abroad. Pressures for continued involvement in international business develop as the firm accumulates more senior managers whose careers depend upon the success of the activities abroad. The manager of the international division plays a critical role in changing the status of the division from that of a gamble at the periphery of the system to that of an integral unit of the enterprise. He acts as a "champion" of the foreign activities by demanding the funds and support necessary for growth. A strong voice capable of commanding the respect and attention of senior managers in the central office is needed to generate the necessary commitments of resources to the overseas activities.[22] But these commitments are based on a strategy of growth determined at the divisional level, not at the top corporate level. If the central office wishes to integrate the domestic and foreign businesses, changes in the relationship with the division are necessary.

Not only has this relationship been changed in many firms, but also major structural alterations have been undertaken. Though international divisions were typical in large U.S. enterprises with foreign operations in the early 1960's, a large number of firms had by the mid-1960's abandoned or were in the process of abandoning their international divisions in favor of alternative structures.

DEVELOPING A GLOBAL STRUCTURE

As the international division increases in size, the same forces that led to its creation act to cause its dissolution. Managers may become aware, for example, that there are gains to be realized by coordinating production on a worldwide scale. It has been argued that the really decisive point in the transition to global enterprise occurs when top managers recognize that strategic planning and major policy decisions must be made in the central office so that a worldwide perspective on the interests of the total enterprise can be maintained.[23]

This new perspective generally leads to more comprehensive planning and control mechanisms. In some firms the additional planning effort is backed up by sending men from domestic locations to foreign subsidiaries so that they may learn more about the problems abroad. But the presence of the international division as a separate, autonomous unit acts as a constraint against the full integration of all the activities. Managers of divisions on either side of the domestic-foreign fault in the structure are not motivated to act in accordance with the worldwide interests of the enterprise, as they are normally judged on the performance they achieve in their separate parts of the enterprise.[24] Structural changes are needed.

Three major types of global structures emerged during the 1960's to replace the international divisions of many firms. Some firms, like Olin Mathieson, based their structure on product considerations and assigned worldwide responsibilities to the erstwhile domestic product divisions. Others, such as Corn Products, divided their organization into area divisions, each responsible for one geographical region of the world market. Still others, such as AMF Corporation, chose a combination of both product and area assignments in a mixed structure; some product lines were managed on a worldwide basis, and others were managed by several area divisions.

Decisions about which global structure a firm should adopt involve difficult choices. During the early phases of the growth abroad, the assumption had been that it was useful to separate the foreign from the domestic activities. Once that assumption is removed, the costs and benefits incurred in the possible alternative structures must be evaluated. But these costs and benefits are usually extremely hard to define for any one structure. It is even more difficult to assess the relative merits of all the alternatives in terms of what would be ideal for the particular set of products and markets concerned.

Even if one preferred global structure can be clearly identified, the problem of finding managers to carry out the new assignments remains. Men trained in the international division have skills that are not tailored to the needs of the new structures. Adopting any global structure, in fact, requires an increase in the number of international general managers. Before the reorganization, the vice president of the international division is the only general manager in the enterprise with responsibilities that cross national boundaries. In the case of a structure of area divisions, the number of international general managers required equals the number of world-partitioning area divisions that are established. Similarly, the manager of each worldwide product division has international responsibilities.

The shortage of adequate management is a major problem for firms un-

dertaking the transition to a global structure. Some firms have even delayed their transition until more managers with appropriate experience
have been trained. These men play a crucial role in the conduct of the
business by providing the integrative linkages between the dispersed parts
of the enterprise.

The structure that a firm creates to replace the international division is
almost certainly not the final phase of the development of a multinational
organization. Some firms have found that none of the. three global
structures—area divisions, worldwide product divisions, or a mixture of
product and area divisions—is entirely satisfactory. All three structures
are based on the principle of unity of command: one man has sole responsibility for a specified part of the business and is accountable to a single
superior officer. As a result, barriers to communication between divisions
are high, and coordination of the activities of foreign subsidiaries in different divisions is difficult.

In response to these difficulties, some firms have introduced staff groups
or management committees with responsibilities that cut across the formal
boundaries of the divisions. A few firms have attempted to go further and
to build new structures where managers operate with dual or multiple reporting relationships. Worldwide product divisions and area divisions are
established with shared jurisdiction over the foreign subsidiaries. The precise nature of this "grid" structure remains unclear, as the pioneering firms
are still in the process of experimentation. There is evidence that other
firms are likely to follow suit in the near future. A fourth phase of expansion abroad, in which global structures are replaced by new forms, may
thus be emerging.

Sequences of Structural Change

The three-phase pattern of expansion has been followed by most of the
firms studied. The precise nature of the structural changes they have undertaken has depended, however, on the timing of changes at home relative to those abroad. Most firms went through one of two major sequences
of structural change. Either they moved from a functional Stage 2 structure
to a divisional Stage 3 structure for their domestic businesses before adding an international division, or they added an international division to a
domestic Stage 2 structure and then later developed a domestic Stage 3
structure. Figure 2-3 shows the frequency with which these two sequences
of structural change have been followed by 170 firms. Figure 2-3 also
shows that forty-nine of the fifty-seven firms that replaced their interna-

tional divisions with global structures did so after they had developed Stage 3 structures for their domestic activities. The few firms that moved directly from a Stage 2 structure with an international division to a global system are exceptions to the general trend, and all of them adopted area divisions.

PHASES OF EXPANSION ABROAD

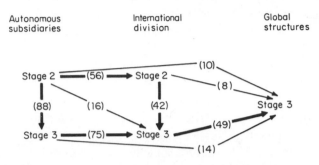

Figure 2–3   *Sequences of Structural Change*

NOTE: The numbers in the arrows indicate the number of firms out of 170 that had undertaken the structural change by the end of 1968. Six cases of structural change in directions opposite to those shown are excluded. The term "global structures" includes all the area division, worldwide product division, mixed, and grid forms.

Only twenty-four firms, or 14 percent of the 170 firms, have moved directly from the phase of autonomous subsidiaries to a global structure without ever using an international division. In almost every instance, these firms have expanded abroad primarily by acquisitions or mergers with other firms that had international interests.

Only six cases of firms reversing the directions of change shown in Figure 2-3 were observed. These reversals are associated with failures in the decentralized systems and with decisions to recentralize authority and to establish tighter controls.

Expansion abroad by a large number of firms has produced a few well-trodden paths of structural development. Yet these firms have been following widely differing strategies of expansion. Is structure independent of strategy after all? In most cases, the first few foreign investments that firms have made have been in product lines that were under pressure for some sort of defensive action. Later on, during the second phase of expansion, the manager of the international division is likely to continue this initial strategy; he has the freedom to determine the international strategy and usually chooses to restrict the divisional activities to the product line with which he is experienced. Thus, during the first two phases of expansion abroad, the strategies of firms are usually similar. Only during the third phase do firms begin to implement radically different types of strategy. Each strategy has its own set of managerial requirements. Management responsibilities are assigned according to the patterns of interaction among the various subunits of the enterprise, producing different versions of the global structure. The forces that lead firms to change their strategies and the effects that these changes have on structure are explored in subsequent chapters of the study.

THREE / Strategies of Product Diversification

When a firm decides to diversify its foreign product line it takes one step in the transition to the third phase of expansion abroad. The addition of new product lines introduces problems of complexity that are not easily resolved by an international division. Just as product diversification at home is associated with the move from a centralized Stage 2 to a decentralized Stage 3 structure, so product diversification abroad is associated with the move from an international division to a global structure. In this move each domestic product division is assigned responsibility for the worldwide activities in its product line. The problems of managing product diversity in any one subsystem are avoided in this structure. Managers in domestic and foreign locations communicate within each of the worldwide subsystems, and their communication is not impeded by the barriers that are raised by the presence of an international division.

Adoption of worldwide product divisions implies a management judgment that the benefits of product coordination on a global basis exceed the costs of impaired area coordination. Yet the difficulty of measuring with any degree of precision the benefits and costs of such crude concepts as coordination, centralization, and decentralization has led one observer to conclude: "It is difficult, if not impossible, in any given situation to demonstrate in rational terms how one particular organization structure yields a higher payoff than another." [1] Nevertheless, managers faced with similar structural choices in similar situations typically make the same choice. The behavior of these men suggests that they make similar assessments of the possible consequences of each of the available courses of action. The nature of these assessments is explored in this chapter and interpreted in terms of the concepts described in Chapter 2.

For a few firms, organizational structure is determined by noneconomic factors. For instance, the structure may reflect the presence of a dominant personality, as was the case in Ford before World War II.[2] In general, however, the design of a structure is based on economic considerations. Changes in structure can be interpreted as attempts to gain greater efficiency and to avoid diseconomies of scale.

Product Diversity at Home

Most firms limit their foreign businesses to those activities in which they have developed expertise in their domestic markets. Product diversity at home is generally, therefore, a necessary condition for product diversity abroad. But product diversity at home does not by itself guarantee the same condition abroad; firms must take the conscious decision to transfer abroad the manufacture of each line.

Firms often choose to diversify their product line at home as part of a reaction to threat. Changes occur as a product moves through its life cycle from introduction to the market to initial growth, maturity, and eventual decline. The managerial requirements and the costs of differentiating a product from those of its competitors vary at each stage of the life cycle.[3] Firms are threatened with extinction unless they respond adequately to these changes.

Initially, most new products are highly differentiated from a technical point of view.[4] For example, early automobiles had internal combustion, electric, or steam engines. These came in three-wheel and four-wheel varieties. The list of basic technical variations for early automobiles—and for most new products—goes on and on. The consumer finds it difficult to compare one model with another; he cannot easily use a single scale to determine which model is cheaper. As a result, an individual manufacturer sees less purpose in reducing his prices than he would if various lines were easy to compare. Moreover, for many products, the price sensitivity of the initial purchasers seems to be much less than that of others who will purchase the product later on.[5] Faced with a relatively inelastic demand for the product in general and for the output of his firm in particular, the manufacturer is not primarily concerned with reducing prices or costs. A more important problem is to develop a version of the product that will appeal to as many consumers as possible. Feedback of consumer desires and adjustment of the product to information gained from consumer response are critical. For the firm that can succeed in product development, profit margins are likely to be high.

However, as a product matures, marketing factors change. Competitors are able to copy the successful attributes of the products that have found consumer acceptance. The technology and design know-how are no longer held by a small number of firms. Consumers who are more sensitive to differences in price than the early experimenters become interested in the product. The result is that the demand for the product as a whole becomes more price elastic. Demand for the output of an individual firm may become very elastic as product differentiation in the industry decreases.

On the production side, changes are occurring also. Longer runs are becoming feasible. Specialized production equipment is developed for the product now that design is becoming stabilized and mass markets are available. With increasing competition and falling costs, prices may begin to decline. Profit margins may also decline as the high initial rates of growth of demand slacken and more firms are competing for market shares.

Business enterprises respond in a number of ways to the threat of falling profit margins and lower rates of growth. Three of the possible responses lead to product diversification, first in the United States and later abroad. The first is to develop new products. The second is to acquire going businesses with new products in other industries. The third is to expand abroad and to add new markets for the product line that is maturing in the domestic market. Growth in many firms is achieved through these strategies, separately or in some combination.

The response that is chosen has an impact on the management problems that a firm faces when it transfers the diversified lines abroad. The research effort of a firm is typically directed toward the development of products that either share a common technological base with the original product line, or are based on by-products from some intermediate stage of a vertically integrated production process. General Electric, for example, has diversified extensively from its technological base in electrical machinery. The entry of oil companies into the petrochemicals business was based on the use of gases that had originally been burned as waste. The products introduced by this type of diversification have a considerable degree of interaction with the original product line. In contrast, products acquired by buying other companies may have no such interactions. The diversification of Textron, for example, has been based on considerations that gave little or no weight to relationships with its existing lines.

There are differences in the ways in which firms manage these two types of diversification. A recent study has shown that firms with a diversified line of related products tend to build elaborate procedures and large staff groups to control the interactions among the divisions.[6] The autonomy of the divisional managers is constrained. When diversification takes place in unrelated products, however, divisional autonomy remains high, central staff groups are small, and financial controls are limited.

In cases of diversification into closely related products, firms are faced with the problem of deciding whether the differences between the products are more important than the similarities. For the reasons discussed in

Chapter 2, a Stage 3 structure tends to be more appropriate than a Stage 2 structure when the differences are judged to be more important than the similarities. Though many considerations are involved when a firm makes its choice of organizational structure, one of these is the degree of product differentiation in the firm.

A crude measure of product differentiation is provided by a count of the number of products manufactured by each firm. The 1967 Standard Industrial Classification (SIC) Code provides one measure of product differentiation.[7] This code classifies products into groups that reflect similarities in markets and in production characteristics. In some cases, the groups are also defined on the basis of the raw materials used.

Data were available for the products of each firm at a reasonably fine level of product classification, the so-called five-digit SIC categories.[8] The classification system is arranged to provide a progressively finer definition of each product group as the number of digits in the code increases. Thus, for example, SIC 36 covers all types of electrical machinery, but SIC 363 covers only household electrical appliances.[9]

By inspection of the counts for each firm, only those made at the gross two-digit level of aggregation provided any sharp distinction between the product diversity contained in Stage 2 and Stage 3 structures. Less than 40 percent of the firms with Stage 2 structures during 1966 had products in more than a single two-digit industry. The implication is that the diversified products within a single two-digit industry can be so closely related that a Stage 2 structure can be effective. In addition, only 10 percent of the Stage 3 firms had product lines entirely within a single two-digit industry. Products in different two-digit industries are likely therefore to have so few relationships that they cannot be contained within a Stage 2 structure except at the cost of loss of control.

A simple count of the number of industries does not, however, capture the full impact on structure that is generated by product diversity. The structure of the firm is sensitive to the relative proportion of the volume generated in different lines. For example, if a firm has 99 percent of its volume in one industry and only 1 percent in another, a Stage 2 structure might be used: the activities in one industry are so insignificant that senior managers are not directly concerned. In such cases, the management of the diversified activities is normally assigned to men of low status in the hierarchy. But if an activity grows to the point at which it accounts for a significant proportion of the total business, it begins to have its effect; if there are enough significant secondary activities, a Stage 3 structure is normally developed to allow the appropriate controls and resource allocation procedures to be exercised.

c

The proportion of the total sales generated outside the major two-digit industry provides a measure of the relative importance of the diversified products. But this measure by itself does not predict whether firms will use Stage 2 or Stage 3 structures. Only the combination of this measure with the count of the number of industries represented in the product line indicates how product diversity is related to structure.

Three categories of diversity were developed on the basis of this combined measure. Each category indicates different degrees of product diversity, and their boundaries may be considered as benchmarks placed at intervals along the continuum of complexity that ranges from an enterprise with a single product to the most highly diversified of firms with operations in dozens of different industries. On this continuum, firms operating entirely within a single two-digit industry are considered to have no product diversity; those with a dominant product line in one industry and less important activities in other industries are treated as having low product diversity; and firms with product lines in three or more industries, none of which is of dominating importance, are considered to be highly diversified.*

As it turned out, none of the firms with highly diverse product lines had a Stage 2 structure at the end of 1966. Five of the six firms with low product diversity that had Stage 2 structures in 1966 had adopted Stage 3 structures by the end of 1968. The evidence suggests that any Stage 2 firm diversifying into new two-digit industries is subject to pressures for reorganization, regardless of how related or unrelated the product lines may be.

The main direction of the diversification movement in the United States has been for firms to enter industries characterized by technological change, by introduction of new products, and by a growth rate higher than that of their primary activities.[10] That direction has posed a special challenge to Stage 2 firms, because they do not generally possess the highly specialized research and technical skills required in new industries.[11] Stage 2 firms diversifying into areas of new technology are, therefore, faced with learning how to manage research in addition to learning how to develop a Stage 3 structure. Once they have crossed the learning hurdle in the course of making their initial diversification moves, however, they may be expected to undertake further diversification. For example, the 3M Company remained for over forty years primarily dependent upon abrasives and related products. Not until after a Stage 3 structure had been developed, an event that occurred soon after World War II, were major moves into new products undertaken. Magnetic recording tapes were introduced by the

---

* The details of the procedure used to classify firms in the low and high categories of product diversity are described in Appendix A.

company in 1947 and products in the fields of copiers, medical products, photography, tape recorders, and many others followed in rapid succession. Most of the new products originated in 3M's research laboratories, suggesting that scale economies in research may have played a part in the pace of diversification. Nevertheless, the ability of the firm to move into many new markets simultaneously was critical to the success of the development effort.

There is a relationship between the Stage 3 structure on the one hand and product diversification, product innovation, and research on the other. This relationship is important for understanding the structure of multinational enterprises because the transfer of relatively new products to foreign markets is the principal means by which most firms diversify their international business. The Stage 3 structure provides a system for the coordination of activities with both long-range and short-range time horizons, and is well suited to the management of research efforts. Firms engaged in their own research efforts have the technical capabilities needed for entry to new areas of technology; they have been the most active diversifiers into new areas.[12]

The figures in Table 3-1 show the extent of the relationship between research and product diversity for the 102 multinational enterprises for which data on research expenditures were available. All but two of the firms with highly diverse product lines spent more than 1 percent of their sales revenues on research, and many of them spent 3 percent or more of sales on major research efforts. All these highly diverse firms had, as was indicated earlier, Stage 3 structures.

TABLE 3-1   *Multinational Enterprises, Classified by Domestic Product Diversity and by R&D Expenditures*

Domestic product diversity[a]	Total number of firms	Number of firms, classified by R&D expenditures (as % of sales)		
		1% or less	1.1-2.9%	3% or more
None	15	9	4	2
Low	40	13	12	15
High	47	2	23	22
Total	102	24	39	39

[a]"None" indicates that a firm has all its products in a single two-digit SIC industry; "low" indicates that a firm has products in more than one industry, but that one product line is of dominating importance; "high" indicates that a firm has products in many industries, and no dominant product line. See Appendix A for details of the classification procedures.

Sources: R&D expenditures from *News Front*, November 1965, January and February 1966, and annual reports of the firms.

Of course, firms diversify into new businesses even though they do not depend upon research and development (R&D) activities. Diversification is sometimes undertaken to capitalize on superior marketing skills. For example, Philip Morris could apply to another consumer product the marketing skills it developed in the tobacco business when it acquired Clark Chewing Gum. The data in Table 3-1 show, however, that only two firms with limited research efforts have diversified extensively.

Distortions in this association between research and product diversity are created by the directions of diversification undertaken by firms in high-technology and low-technology industries. A firm making prescription drugs, for example, may spend over 8 percent of its revenues from drugs on R&D, but if it diversifies heavily into proprietary medicines or toiletries, which require comparatively little research effort, the combined index of research activity based on the total sales drops well below 8 percent. At the other extreme of technological effort, firms in the food industry that have diversified into chemicals, such as Borden, have a greater research intensity than their nondiversified competitors in the food business. Such distortions probably account for the wide scattering of firms in the intermediate ranges of the variables shown in Table 3-1.

The extreme illustration of distortion in the measure is the petroleum industry—a traditional international business involving several different kinds of industry. All the major petroleum firms are engaged in exploration, transportation, refining, marketing, and petrochemicals. For them, aggregate measures for the firm are so distorted that they give useless signals. Consequently, petroleum firms have been excluded from most of the quantitative analysis in this study.[13]

Firms that have diversified extensively in the United States are likely to be leaders in innovation. They have generally developed procedures in their Stage 3 structures that allow new products to be transferred quickly from the laboratory to the market place. They are likely to be leaders in transferring new products to foreign markets. The extent and direction of the strategy of product diversification at home and the accompanying organizational developments are important determinants of the decisions that managers make abroad.

Managing Foreign Product Diversity

The first step in diversifying abroad is to transfer the manufacture of added product lines to foreign locations. The second involves the building of organizational structures that provide an efficient system for managing the diversified activities abroad. These two steps are closely interrelated: decisions to manufacture new products abroad usually take into account the existence of an adequate management system, or the need to build one.

TRANSFERRING NEW PRODUCTS ABROAD

The initial move abroad by U.S. firms has been described as a defensive reaction to changes in export markets. This initial reaction typically has involved only a single product line, even for firms that had diversified product lines in the United States. For more than 90 percent of the firms studied, the first three subsidiaries established abroad were engaged in the manufacture and sale of the major product line of the enterprise [14] (as measured at the three-digit SIC level of classification). Only after the first phase of international expansion have these firms begun to diversify abroad into their lesser product lines.

Table 3-2 indicates the extent to which the firms had diversified their foreign product lines by the end of 1966. On the whole, diversification was limited; over a third had not diversified abroad outside the primary two-digit industry of their U.S. operations. In no case were the foreign lines more diversified than those at home.

TABLE 3-2 *Multinational Enterprises, Classified by Domestic and Foreign Product Diversity*

Domestic product diversity[a]	Total number of firms	Number of firms, classified by foreign product diversity[a]		
		None	Low	High
None	26	26	0	0
Low	65	28	37	0
High	71	3	31	37
Total	162	57	68	37

[a] For definitions, see Table 3-1.

One explanation of this behavior is that senior managers have been unwilling to accept the initial gamble of expansion into foreign markets for more than one product line. These men have been making the judgment, explicitly or intuitively, that the necessary learning about international business can best be achieved by concentrating the effort in the business that they know best.

A more likely explanation of the investment behavior is provided by the relative positions of the various products in their life cycles. Because U.S.

firms typically diversify into areas of new technology, they are not generally under pressure to transfer abroad their diversified product lines immediately; the technology is unstable and not readily available to foreign competitors, and demand in foreign markets for the new products requires time to build up to levels compatible with economic foreign production. There is, therefore, likely to be a lag between the time when an enterprise diversifies at home into a new product and the time when it begins to manufacture that product abroad.

The response of a firm to external changes may be delayed and perhaps distorted by internal groups lobbying to preserve the status quo. But, as is so often the case, the tide of events eventually becomes so strong that no one can continue to swim against it. The fact that only three of our firms with highly diverse domestic product lines remained concentrated within a single industry abroad is indicative of how strong the economic forces are that push managers to duplicate internationally what has been accomplished at home.

In a few firms, pressures for foreign diversification have emerged internally before the external forces have gathered momentum. Some managers of international divisions have regarded diversification as a means of achieving greater growth and status. In some cases they have initiated proposals for diversification before they have felt threatened by a decrease in exports.

A few exceptional international managers, as in Phelps Dodge, have even initiated manufacture abroad of products that were not being produced in the United States. Products that are entirely new to the enterprise as a whole are not normally introduced abroad: the risks are usually too great and there is no way for the central office to exert control or to provide help and expertise. For Phelps Dodge the expertise was provided by foreign partners in the ventures, and the board of directors was presumably willing to back the judgment of a man with a strong record of accomplishment. Most firms, however, are not willing to behave in this fashion, preferring to diversify their foreign business in a series of orderly steps that begin in the familiar territory of their home market.

A critical intermediate step in this process is that of exporting the products concerned from the United States. Firms that manufacture abroad only one of their many domestic product lines often have a widely diversified export business; the diversified domestic lines generally include new research-based products, which have been the source of much of the export strength of the United States in manufactured goods.[15] These exports allow the firm to gain a detailed knowledge of the foreign markets before local manufacture is started.[16]

BUILDING WORLDWIDE PRODUCT DIVISIONS

Most firms with highly diverse foreign product lines have replaced their international divisions with global structures that divide their activities on a product basis; either worldwide responsibilities have been assigned to all the product divisions, or some worldwide product divisions exist in a mixed structure. For example, Eaton Yale and Towne, Inc., replaced its international division in 1967 with worldwide product divisions. The chairman summed up the reasons for the change: "With such a diverse product line, it was well-nigh impossible for one guy to ride shotgun over everything. Also having an international and domestic company leads to duplication of time and money." [17]

The formal structure in which all the product divisions have worldwide responsibilities is outlined in Figure 3-1. The managers of the domestic product divisions each assume part of the responsibilities that were previously exercised by the international division. The staff of the abandoned international division is assigned to new duties either in the corporate staff group or in one of the product divisions.

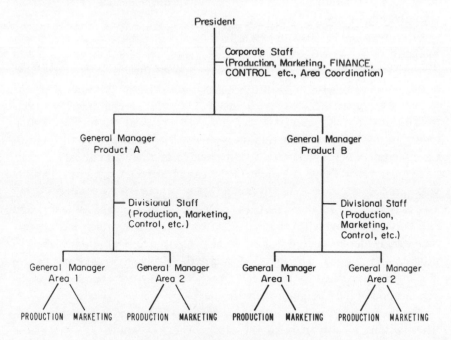

Figure 3–1   *Worldwide Product Divisions*
NOTE: The functions shown in capital letters indicate operating responsibility; those in lower-cased letters indicate mainly advisory and coordinating roles.

In order to cope with the increased demands on their time for coordinating the operations of their enlarged jurisdictions, the divisional managers generally build structures that are equivalent in most respects to either Stage 2 or Stage 3 structures. The needs for decoupling diverse activities discussed in Chapter 2 in terms of the enterprise as a whole also apply within each division. The form of the divisional structure depends upon the pattern of transactions among the subunits. Figure 3-1 shows only one of the many possible structures of a worldwide product division. If Area 1 in Figure 3-1 is treated as the United States and Area 2 as international, the divisional structure shown is equivalent to a Stage 2 structure with an international division. In other cases, where the product line of the division is diversified in the United States but not abroad, the divisional structure generally resembles a Stage 3 organization with an international division.

Most worldwide product divisions include a staff group for control purposes. This group services the divisional manager with information in addition to generating data required by the corporate financial and control groups. The divisions may use other staff groups; the staff assignments depend upon the requirements for coordinating the activities of the decoupled divisional units.

Few firms have a structure in which all the international activities are managed by worldwide product divisions. For example, Eaton Yale and Towne, Inc., has a marketing group, covering all the firm's products, that is responsible for sales in countries where the worldwide product divisions do not have manufacturing subsidiaries. Only the formal reporting relationships established among general managers responsible for the performance of the manufacturing and marketing subsidiaries abroad distinguish the structure of worldwide product divisions from other structures.*

The figures in Table 3-3 indicate the extent to which firms with worldwide product divisions had diversified their product lines abroad by the end of 1966. All of them had diversified outside a single industry, and two-thirds were highly diversified. The mixed structure, which has at least one worldwide product division, is also associated with highly diverse product lines abroad. The fact that international divisions were not generally highly diversified by product suggests that they are abandoned as diversification of the foreign product line develops.

The association between foreign product diversity and worldwide product divisions is only part of the story. The indications are that these divisions are generally used for the administration of relatively new prod-

---

* Appendix B describes the procedures that were used to classify structure. In all the tables that include classifications of structure, the classifications apply to the end of 1968, unless explicit mention is made of an alternative date.

TABLE 3-3 *Multinational Enterprises, Classified by Structure and by Foreign Product Diversity*

Structure	Total number of firms	Number of firms, classified by foreign product diversity[a]		
		None	Low	High
International divisions with:				
domestic Stage 2	8	7	1	0
domestic Stage 3	82	39	39	4
Area divisions	17	11	4	2
Worldwide product divisions	30	0	11	19
Mixed	22	0	13	9
Grid	3	0	0	3
Total	162	57	68	37

[a] For definitions, see Table 3-1.

ucts. New products impose great demands on the communication network between domestic and foreign locations. For any product line, the worldwide product division provides the shortest possible communication channels among the various locations. The delays and distortions in communicating product and technical data are likely therefore to be less within a worldwide product division than in any of the other organizational structures.

The fact that worldwide product divisions go with an emphasis on new products is suggested by the figures in Table 3-4. Many of the firms with worldwide product divisions spent over 3 percent of sales on R&D.

To be sure, many firms with other structures also underwrite major research efforts. Table 3-4 shows that over a third of the firms with international divisions spent more than 3 percent of sales on R&D. It was shown in Table 3-3, however, that very few international divisions had highly diverse product lines. Given the fact that most firms first expand abroad with their traditional product line, the data suggest that diversified research-based products have not generally been transferred to the international divisions. In the future, it is likely that decisions will be made to transfer the manufacture of these new products to foreign locations. When such decisions are made it is also likely that the international divisions will be replaced by worldwide product divisions.

When a product is at an early stage in its life cycle, production generally requires more management attention than does marketing. By the time that new research-based products are first transferred abroad, most of the basic technical problems of manufacture have been sorted out. In foreign markets, management is concerned with solving secondary technical prob-

c*

TABLE 3-4   *Multinational Enterprises, Classified by Structure and by R&D Expenditures*

Structure	Total number of firms	Number of firms, classified by R&D expenditures (as % of sales)		
		1% or less	1.1-2.9%	3% or more
International divisions with:				
domestic Stage 2	3	2	1	0
domestic Stage 3	49	14	18	17
Area divisions	10	6	3	1
Worldwide product divisions	19	2	8	9
Mixed	18	0	9	9
Grid	3	0	0	3
Total	102	24	39	39

Source: R&D Expenditures from *News Front*, November 1965, January and February 1966, and annual reports of the firms.

lems, such as those involved in adjusting to different scales of operation, different national standards of regulation, different requirements for labor force training, and so on. The production department in the U.S. division responsible for the original development effort must help the international managers. In the early stages, such help cannot be satisfactorily provided solely by assigning experts on a short-term basis to the foreign subsidiaries, and is generally required on a continuing basis. If the basic technology remains somewhat unstable and under further development, the demands for continued help can be extremely large.

The marketing function can also be improved in some cases by the development of technical information systems within worldwide product divisions. Where there is a high technical content in the marketing effort—in after-sales service, for example—the foreign subsidiaries benefit from close links with their domestic counterparts. The observation of one senior manager makes this point:

We are doing a much better job now than under one international division. Selling plastics to other manufacturers requires sitting down and pointing out the product advantages. It is end-use selling and it was difficult when we were centrally organized to have a high degree of technical know-how. Each division has now also been able to strengthen its export sales force.[18]

Although most of management's attention is focused on the problems of developing and maintaining systems for coordinating each product line on a global basis, coordination on a regional basis among the various worldwide product divisions is not completely ignored. There is often a central staff group in the structure (labelled Area Coordination in Figure 3-1) responsible for channeling the flows of information that the separate product divisions need if they attempt to coordinate their activities. This central staff group cannot, however, do much more than provide an intelligence function, as it does not have the power to resolve differences between the operating product divisions.

The innovative emphasis of most of the firms with worldwide product divisions indicates that there is little benefit to be gained by developing strong, formal systems for coordination by area: diverse new products typically have little in common in any area. Lacking area coordination, most firms with worldwide product divisions have duplicated the few common activities, such as finance and government relations, in those foreign countries where two or more product lines are manufactured. The cost of this duplication, however, is generally a small price to pay for the large benefits gained by ensuring close product coordination.

Once a structure of worldwide product divisions is set in place, it does not follow that it will remain appropriate forever. Each division is free to develop its own international business with few distractions or controls imposed from other parts of the enterprise. The advantages of allowing each division to act as an independent entity, however, may decline over time. As products age, the technology matures, marketing becomes the critical function, and potential benefits from area coordination increase. Furthermore, as each division allocates more of its resources to international business, the need for central coordination of the strategic investment decisions increases. Responses to these changes in the needs of the business are difficult to achieve without further structural adjustment.

A few of the firms with worldwide product divisions had begun, by 1968, to modify their formal structures in order to increase the degree of area coordination. Sperry Rand, for instance, has established a series of "umbrella companies" that foster regional coordination among the separate divisions in addition to providing legal and tax benefits. In other cases, the modifications have been in the form of creating ad hoc committees with regional responsibilities.

Most firms with worldwide product divisions, however, have not moved very far in the direction of providing coordination on a regional basis. At the end of 1966, these firms typically had less than 20 percent of their sales and assets outside the United States. Very few of them had product lines that shared common activities. They had not reached the stage where the benefits of introducing area coordination outweighed the costs of diluting their single-minded concentration on product coordination.

THE MIXED STRUCTURE

Some firms that have diversified their product lines abroad have developed a mixed structure: one part of the structure has the characteristics of a worldwide product division structure and the other part the characteristics of an international division. The two separate parts of the structure can develop entirely different types of management procedure, each suited to the particular needs of the products involved. The central office influences the strategy followed in either part of the structure primarily through the resource allocation process. Seldom does it directly coordinate the activities that are common to both parts. As in the case where all the product divisions have worldwide responsibilities, the absence of coordination in the mixed structure can entail serious costs when a significant proportion of the global business is conducted outside the United States.

One of many possible configurations of the mixed structure is sketched in simplified form in Figure 3-2. The domestic and foreign activities in Product *A* are managed by two separate divisions, while the activities in Product *B* are managed by a single worldwide product division. A staff group in the central office, labelled International, is normally required for the purposes of channeling communication flows between the two divisions responsible for Product *A*.

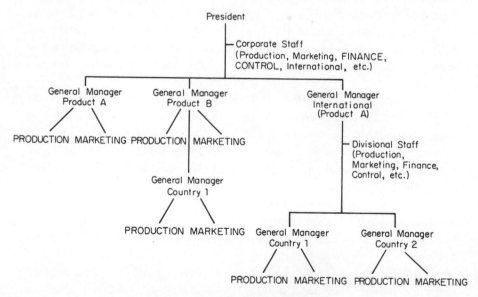

Figure 3–2   *The Mixed Structure*

NOTE: The functions shown in capital letters indicate operating responsibility; those in lower-cased letters indicate mainly advisory and coordinating roles.

Turning back to Table 3-4, one can see that all the firms with mixed structures spent more than 1 percent of sales on R&D. In most cases the product lines managed by the worldwide product divisions account for most of the research expenditures; they require a greater innovative effort than the product lines abroad managed by the international division. For example, international food companies that have established subsidiaries abroad for the manufacture of chemicals have generally developed a worldwide chemicals division and retained an international division for the food business.

There are, however, reasons other than technology for the existence of a mixed structure. In many firms, the mixed structure has emerged as the direct result of mergers and acquisitions. The foreign subsidiaries of the acquired firms were never attached to the international division, so that the international division did not have to face the problems of managing a diverse product line. For example, when the Ford Motor Company acquired Philco Corporation, Philco became a separate worldwide product division of Ford; the international division used for Ford's foreign automobile activities was not altered by the acquisition.

Historical factors also may explain why W. R. Grace has a Latin American Group that is diversified in many industries and managed separately from other worldwide groups in chemicals and consumer products. The firm originated in Latin America, and the long history of the relations with the local governments has led to the implementation of product strategies that were not appropriate elsewhere.[19]

There have also been cases in which the mixed structure has been used in the transition from an international division to a structure containing only worldwide product divisions. One product line abroad is detached from the international division and added to the jurisdiction of the appropriate domestic product division. The worldwide product division created by this move is charged with the responsibility for developing procedures for integrating the domestic and foreign parts of the division and for training managers capable of undertaking the new types of assignment. Once the procedures have been developed satisfactorily, they can be adapted for use by other divisions. By this means the international division can be slowly dismantled piece by piece without subjecting the whole organization to the shock generated by a sudden transition to a structure in which all the product divisions are worldwide.

An example of the use of a mixed structure in a gradual process of transition is provided by the case of a large firm that manufactures a wide variety of electrical and nonelectrical machinery and many types of consumer products. This firm established an international division in the early 1950's as part of a major reorganization to form product divisions in the

United States. The international division grew rapidly and became diversified in many of the products manufactured in the United States. But after ten years, the profits levelled off and then declined sharply. A variety of causes of the decline in profits were identified:

1. There was no consistent method of investment evaluation. The international division, in its haste to expand, had established numerous small and unprofitable plants.

2. There was little coordination between the foreign subsidiaries and their counterpart product divisions in the United States. Apart from creating barriers to the transfer of technology, this lack of coordination had led to situations where the foreign subsidiaries were competing with the United States product divisions for national markets that were small enough to be supplied economically by only one plant.

3. No control system had been established to enable the firm to meet international competition effectively.

The reaction to this situation was the resignation of the international vice president and a restructuring of the foreign operations. A mixed structure was adopted: one machinery division was given worldwide responsibilities, and the remainder of the foreign businesses were maintained within an international division. Since the foreign subsidiaries in the machinery group accounted for more than half of the foreign sales and almost all the profits abroad, most of the strength (in terms of people and profits) of the international division was thus removed.

For the machinery division, the change had important results. Previously, each subsidiary had maintained a design team that worked in isolation from other design teams concerned with similar problems. The new structure allowed the work of these teams to be more readily coordinated and the workload shared rather than duplicated.

The creation of only a single worldwide product division was in the nature of an experiment to determine whether the new structure would be beneficial in the special circumstances of the firm. Further changes in the same direction were planned if the experiment proved to be successful.[20]

Conclusion

As firms have diversified their foreign product lines, they have generally developed global structures in which worldwide product divisions are used for some or all of the different product lines. This is one more form of the general process of adaptation of structure to strategy. In this case, the adaptation is also one of the forms that increases the integration between the domestic and foreign activities in the enterprise. But, like all the other adaptations, it is only a temporary resting place until new problems of coordination and control arise.

FOUR / Strategies of Area Diversification

Some firms have developed global structures without diversifying the product line of their foreign business. They have chosen to concentrate effort on the development of skills in the production and marketing of a narrow line of products in a large number of national markets. As these firms have moved into more foreign markets, they have undertaken a series of reorganizations. These reorganizations have generated more elaborate structures for coordinating the activities of each subunit of the firm. First, an international division is attached to a domestic Stage 2 structure; second, regional groups are formed within the international division; and third, a number of divisions, each responsible for one geographical area of the firm's worldwide market, are established. The general managers of the area divisions are all at the same level in the hierarchy, each reporting directly to the president.

Firms that moved abroad without much product diversification were the exception in this study, not the rule. On the whole, these exceptional firms were marketing fairly mature products. But mature products have their own managerial requirements. For such products, the benefits of ensuring coordination on a regional basis within each area division generally outweigh by a large margin the costs of imperfect coordination among the various divisions.

Increasing Area Diversity and Structural Change

As the number of foreign subsidiaries increases, the manager of the international division is subjected to many of the same types of pressures that the president of a firm with a Stage 2 structure experiences as new product lines are added. Just as a Stage 2 structure is transformed into a Stage 3 structure, the international division is often transformed into a decoupled system of regional units. Procedures for controlling and coordinating the regional units are developed in the international headquarters. At later stages of the expansion abroad, some firms create area divisions and transfer the procedures developed in the international division to the corporate headquarters.

AREA MANAGEMENT IN THE INTERNATIONAL DIVISION

The control system developed in an international division depends largely on both the number of foreign subsidiaries and the nature of the transactions among the subsidiaries. In some divisions, each subsidiary serves a single national market and has little business contact with other subsidiaries. Subsidiaries of this type are common in the cement industry, for instance, where the costs of transportation are very high in relation to the value of the product. In other divisions, however, a few large manufacturing subsidiaries are established in major markets abroad to act as supply points for marketing subsidiaries in other countries. For example, until well after World War II, Singer Sewing Machine used only a few foreign plants to supply machines for sale in almost every country of the world. There are also cases where a few large subsidiaries supply semifinished goods for assembly, packaging, or further processing by a network of smaller subsidiaries located in local markets. Combinations of these and other methods of conducting business abroad are common, and each method generates different managerial needs and problems. If the product line is diversified, the problems are relatively greater than those for a single line of closely related products.

Other factors also influence the type of control system developed. Managers of each subsidiary make demands on the divisional headquarters that vary according to their needs and abilities. Experienced managers probably both desire and need less attention than recently appointed managers. Managers of small subsidiaries generally require the assistance of divisional specialists in expanding the subsidiary to a size large enough to support its own specialists. Furthermore, the divisional manager usually wants to know more about the operations of unprofitable subsidiaries than about the operations of profitable ones.

Some of the workload can be delegated to staff specialists appointed by the general manager of the international division. But much of the work, particularly on the strategic questions, cannot be delegated satisfactorily. As the complexities of the division and its control system increase beyond the limits of the general manager's capacity for decision making, control and coordination are likely to be impaired. Many firms, such as IBM or Rohm and Haas, have responded to these problems by appointing regional general managers, each responsible for the performance of one group of the foreign subsidiaries, and each reporting to divisional headquarters.

One indicator of the workload of the divisional manager is the number of manufacturing subsidiaries in the division. As the number grows, the manager's span of control widens. A recent study found that a strong correlation exists between the number of subsidiaries and the existence of regional general managers in the international division.[1] However, other indicators of workload, such as the total volume of business, do not appear to be related to the existence of regional managers in the international divisions examined in this study. The implication is that the degree of geographical dispersion of the activities is an important source of organizational stress in the international division.

Regional general managers are responsible for what amounts to smaller versions of the international division. Their tasks resemble in microcosm those that the divisional manager performed. Each region develops its own control system and, in many cases, its own staff groups. The relationships between the regional managers and the international headquarters resemble those existing between the international headquarters and the central office. After regional units have first been created, further growth is often accompanied by the creation of additional regional units. By continuously dividing the operations into units small enough to be managed by one man, the division is normally able to cope with the stresses that accompany geographical dispersion.

When regional offices have responsibility for the profits of a group of foreign subsidiaries, they are quite distinct from the regional centers of other types. For example, for many years a major firm in the paper industry maintained a large European office to perform the duties of little more than those of a glorified postman. Information was channeled through this office, but decisions were made elsewhere. The office was eventually disbanded when the manager of the international division became aware of the delays in communication and the needless expense incurred by the office. In other cases, small regional offices are maintained solely for legal and tax purposes.[2]

DEVELOPING AREA DIVISIONS

An international division cannot continue indefinitely to increase in size and to add more foreign subsidiaries. Constraints on further expansion eventually emerge. When their international divisions had grown to the point at which they accounted for a large proportion of the total business, some firms decided to build a global structure in the form of a series of area divisions.

Judging from data that were available for seventy-seven firms, there appears to be a constraint on the size of the international division which is determined by its relation to the size of each domestic division and not simply its relation to the size of the total business. Pressures for developing area divisions have typically resulted in action only when the international division has threatened to become the largest unit in the firm. Most of the firms that adopted area divisions did so when their international divisions were threatening to equal the size of the largest product division. In only four cases was reorganization delayed until after the international division had become the largest of the divisions. The view that the largest domestic division acts as a constraint on the growth of the international division is supported by additional evidence: only four of the international divisions existing in 1968 were the largest divisions in their firms.

The developments leading to area divisions have generally occurred free from the stresses that accompany the addition of new product lines in the international division.[3] The few U.S. firms that have expanded abroad to the point at which the size of the foreign operations exceeds the size of the largest domestic division have typically chosen to remain concentrated in a single industry; only two of the firms with area divisions have become highly diversified by product.

Pressures for reorganization stem from the costs that are incurred by a prolonged separation of the domestic and international parts of the enterprise. For instance, as a result of such prolonged separation, inconsistent criteria may be used for the evaluation of investment opportunities at home and abroad, because the locus of international expertise is the international division. Investments at home may be accorded higher priority than those abroad, simply because the decision makers in the central office are more familiar with the domestic environment. One senior executive commented soon after his firm had abandoned its international division: "We have missed the overseas opportunities of the past decade because of the way we were organized and because we have been too busy at home." [4]

One common result of such pressures is the development of a structure of area divisions. The significant feature of this structure is that the general manager responsible for the United States (or in some cases North America) has no greater status than the heads of the other area divisions. There is only one divisional voice in the executive committee arguing for U.S. investments. If the U.S. activities are organized by product divisions, the divisional managers do not report directly to the president as they would if the international division existed. Similarly, if the domestic structure is organized on Stage 2 lines, the heads of the functional departments do not have direct access to the president's office. This shift in the balance of power at the top reflects the shift in the geographical balance of the business that occurs as the foreign activities grow faster than those in the United States.

Figure 4-1 shows the structure of area divisions in a simplified and

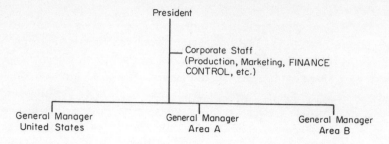

Figure 4–1   *Area Divisions*

NOTE: The functions shown in capital letters indicate operating responsibility; those in lower-cased letters indicate mainly advisory and coordinating roles. See text for a discussion of the different possible structures within each area division.

idealized form. The structure within each division is not included in Figure 4-1, because of the many possible variations. Some area divisions have regional general managers, whereas others have each foreign subsidiary reporting directly to the area general manager. There are also variations in the staff groups in each division. Furthermore, the U.S. division can have either a Stage 2 or a Stage 3 structure.

The change to a structure of area divisions does not greatly disturb the

TABLE 4-1   *Multinational Enterprises, Classified by Structure and by the Number of Foreign Countries in Which They Had Manufacturing Subsidiaries in 1966*

Structure	Total number of firms	Number of firms, classified by number of foreign countries in which they had manufacturing subsidiaries[a]			
		6-9	10-13	14-17	18 or more
International division with:					
domestic Stage 2	8	5	2	1	0
domestic Stage 3	82	22	19	26	15
Area divisions	17	6	3	2	6
Worldwide product divisions	30	4	14	4	8
Mixed	22	6	3	4	9
Grid	3	0	0	0	3
Total	162	43	41	37	41

[a]The figures include assembly or packaging operations, but exclude agricultural, mining, and other extractive operations.

system by which the foreign subsidiaries are managed; the change consists primarily of adding an extra level of senior general managers. Typically, the regional units of the international divisions become the area divisions. The control procedures developed in the international division are often transferred to the central office by merging the staff groups in the international and central offices.

Firms that have developed area divisions are no more diversified by area than firms with other types of structure. Table 4-1 shows that the number of foreign countries in which each firm had manufacturing subsidiaries in 1966 has no relationship with structure. A number of other measures of geographical dispersion, based on the location, age, size, and ownership of the subsidiaries, also failed to exhibit any relationship with structure. These data suggest that area diversity per se does not influence the decision to build area divisions.

Table 4-2 shows the percentages of total sales that were generated outside the United States in 1966 [5] for firms classified by structure. Of the firms that had more than 40 percent of their sales abroad, most had area divisions. Furthermore, none of the firms with area divisions had less than 25 percent of their sales abroad. These data, together with the data on the relative divisional size mentioned earlier, suggest that only changes in the geographical balance of the business are sufficient to lead to the development of area divisions.

TABLE 4-2 *Multinational Enterprises, Classified by Structure and by Relative Importance of Foreign Sales*

Structure	Total number of firms	Number of firms, classified by foreign sales (as % of total sales)[a]		
		0-20%	21-39%	over 39%
International division with:				
domestic Stage 2	8	6	2	0
domestic Stage 3	82	53	26	3
Area divisions	17	0	4	13
Worldwide product divisions	30	21	9	0
Mixed	22	6	14	2
Grid	3	0	2	1
Total	162	86	57	19

[a] Foreign sales include exports from the United States, but exclude sales of foreign licensees and foreign subsidiaries in which the parent firm owned less than 25 percent of the equity: includes estimates of foreign sales for a few firms.

Managing Extensive Area Diversity

Most of the problems of managing extensive area diversity are related to the general problems of managing mature products. Firms specializing in mature products generally emphasize the marketing function and many attempt to lower their production costs by following policies of product specialization in their manufacturing plants. On a global scale, the demands that these policies place on the managerial system of a firm are compatible with the characteristics of a structure of area divisions.

MARKETING ORIENTATION

At the onset of maturity in their principal domestic business, many firms have responded by attempting to generate in the purchaser's mind an image of differentiation.[6] If the firm is successful in this strategy, it can charge a price for its products that is sufficient to recoup the marketing costs and yield an added profit besides. The advertising component of marketing has been shown to have an important impact in raising profitability, at least for consumer products.[7]

Firms that emphasize marketing may be able to protect themselves by raising the price of entry to their markets. The initial expenditures required by a potential competitor to gain brand acceptance may be very high.[8] And the absolute amount of money spent on advertising is likely to be an important barrier to entry. The firm that can spread its expenditures on the creation of a brand image across a number of products may take advantage of scale economies. The large advertiser may get reduced rates that are an additional barrier to a new entrant.[9]

Allocating a high proportion of the available resources to marketing seldom leaves a firm with sufficient additional resources for entering new businesses. Of the firms that spent more than 6 percent of sales on advertising in 1965, almost 90 percent had confined their operations to a single industry.[10] In contrast, among the firms that spent less than 1 percent of sales on advertising, not a single one had concentrated its product lines within a single industry. Any measure of the intensity of the marketing effort, of course, has to take into account the basic differences between consumer and industrial markets. If one examines firms in consumer markets separately from those in industrial markets, the same inverse relationship exists between advertising expenditures and product diversity.

Firms that have chosen to concentrate on marketing have also devoted considerable attention to expansion abroad. Often the growth potential of mature products is higher abroad than at home: many products that have matured in the United States are at earlier stages in their life cycles in foreign markets. The numbers in Table 4-3 show that among those firms that spent 10 percent or more of sales on advertising—a group of sixteen highly marketing-oriented firms—only two had less than 20 percent of their total sales in foreign markets. Among the eighty-seven multinational firms for which advertising data were available, this small group of highly marketing-oriented firms accounted for half of those with over 40 percent of their business abroad. The implication is that strategies of foreign expansion are generally implemented more aggressively by firms that concentrate on marketing than is the case for firms following other strategies of growth.

TABLE 4-3 *Multinational Enterprises, Classified by Relative Importance of Foreign Sales and by Advertising Expenditures*

Foreign sales[a] (as % of total sales)	Total number of firms	Number of firms, classified by advertising expenditures (as % of total sales)		
		Less than 3%	3-9.9%	10% or more
0-20%	49	36	11	2
21-39%	28	12	7	9
over 39%	10	3	2	5
Total	87	51	20	16

[a] For a definition, see Table 4-2.

Source: Advertising expenditures from *News Front*, March 1966: includes all media expenditures in television, radio, magazines, newspapers, and direct mail.

In most cases, highly marketing-oriented firms do not devote much attention to research and development. Their developmental efforts are typically directed to the introduction of new brands of their mature products, such as a breakfast cereal, or to lower-cost production processes. Pharmaceutical firms are exceptions to this general rule; they are constantly introducing new drugs, but they also spend considerable sums of money on marketing the new drugs by using costly forces of detail men who sell directly to doctors.[11] In addition, many pharmaceutical firms have diversified heavily into consumer products, such as proprietary medicines; these are products that require large marketing expenditures but little research effort.[12]

Marketing is the principal competitive weapon available to managers of foreign subsidiaries when a mature product is first manufactured in a foreign country. At that stage, the production processes are standardized and probably freely available to local competitors. The marketing techniques of the parent firm, however, have to be adapted to local conditions. In cases where exports from the United States or from any other production location of the enterprise have preceded local manufacture, many of the necessary adaptations have already been made. But the increased volume produced by the local plant typically requires further adaptations; marketing policies suitable for a small share of the local market are seldom appropriate for a much larger market share. The skill of the manager in making the necessary adaptations is critical to the success of the subsidiary. Product policies, such as the choice of shades of lipstick, have to be matched to local preferences; prices, discount structures, channels of distribution, packaging, advertising, and other elements of the marketing mix have to be adjusted. The local subsidiary is normally allowed almost complete freedom of action to make the necessary adaptations, as marketing policies can seldom be successfully dictated from headquarters by men who do not know the foreign market conditions in detail.

Once several of them have been successfully established, however, there are pressures to reduce the autonomy of each marketing-oriented subsidiary, especially if they are located in areas that share common consumer preferences. As more and more people become internationally conscious, there are pressures for standardizing brand names and images. In Europe, particularly, where large sectors of the population are constantly being exposed to cross-border advertising on television and radio and in magazines, the demands for standardization among national markets are becoming stronger.

Regional coordination of the marketing effort allows the firm to respond to these demands. For example, the European subsidiaries of Chesebrough-Pond's at one time retained over fifty separate agencies, running dozens of different campaigns. When the firm established a European headquarters it found it could coordinate advertising policy more effectively than was possible before. The European division has reduced the number of agencies to six and standardized many of the campaigns.[13]

There are situations where advantages may be gained by coordinating other parts of the overall marketing effort for consumer products. One large food-processing firm, for example, considers that it could reduce costs considerably by developing one standard package for the prepared soup brand it sells in Europe. Such a move would have the added advantage of reducing the consumer confusion that has resulted from the use of eleven different packages in the various national markets.[14] A few firms have even gone to the extent of standardizing advertising on a worldwide basis. Pepsi-Cola sells exactly the same product in all its numerous national markets and uses the same advertising and promotional themes in all of them.[15] The transfer of marketing programs from one country to another is important in other marketing-oriented firms, though some adaptation to local conditions occurs.

Considerable savings in promotional expense can be gained by making marketing programs standard throughout the world, but relatively few firms have so far standardized more than one or two of the elements. Most firms judge that the potential savings are less than the expected costs that would result from not adapting to local conditions and that would come from impairing the freedom of each subsidiary to respond rapidly to competitors' actions.[16]

Industrial products are subject to additional pressures for regional coordination. Producers of many industrial products, such as fabricated metals, sell to large international buyers. These buyers often do business with many of the separate units of the selling firm and are in a strong position to demand uniform terms of sale and service on an international basis. To meet these demands, the seller must be able to coordinate the efforts of each of the national subsidiaries.

Mechanisms for providing adequate coordination of marketing on a regional basis can be developed fairly readily within area divisions and within regional units of an international division. Only occasionally are there requirements for coordinating the marketing efforts across the boundaries of area divisions. In addition, for mature products, transfers of technology among divisions are seldom necessary. As a result, the barriers to communication among divisions are of little consequence for most firms with area divisions.

NEW TECHNOLOGY AND AREA MANAGEMENT

Despite the strong association between area divisions and mature products, there is no intrinsic organizational reason why area divisions should not also be associated with new products, as long as the product line remains narrow. Firms that emphasize the development of new products, however, generally diversify their product lines to such an extent that product divisions are the logical structural forms. Area divisions, like Stage 2 structures, cannot easily cope with a diversified product line.

Only a few research-oriented firms that are concentrated in a single industry have adopted area divisions. Although the management of new products on an area basis is likely to be more costly and to generate more organizational stress than is the case for mature products, these firms have considered such costs to be less than the benefits of providing some degree of regional autonomy.

Several pharmaceutical firms are cases in point. The growth and profitability of these few firms in foreign markets have been above the average, both for industry as a whole and for the pharmaceutical industry in particular. Their record suggests that for them the problems of transferring new technology among area divisions are not insuperable and also that the costs of managing the transfers are not prohibitively large. They have devoted an appreciable proportion of their managerial resources to the building of communication systems designed to transmit messages with a high technological content, and to the training of managers capable of interpreting and processing the information. Because technical information is of critical importance to both the production and the marketing function in pharmaceutical firms, the technical communication system is inextricably mixed with the general business communication system. As a result, the costs of developing the technical system are probably not as great as they would be if a separate technical system had to be added.

Similar specialized systems for the transmission of new technology have been developed by some diversified firms. But these developments have occurred only within those few worldwide product divisions that have very large overseas activities. The structure of these few divisions is an array of regional subdivisions.

Although there have been instances where it has been clearly feasible for firms to manage new technology on an area basis (either by area divisions or by regional units within a division), such instances are likely to remain rare. For most products, the technology has matured by the time that the markets outside the United States have grown sufficiently to warrant the development of regional units. Thus, only those few products that face large international markets early in their life cycles warrant the expense of developing the systems necessary for disseminating new technology among regional units.

PRODUCTION RATIONALIZATION

Many firms with area divisions have attempted to lower their manufacturing costs by "rationalizing" production. In those industries where economies of scale are significant, such a strategy may lead to a specialization of plants abroad. The enterprise may use parts produced in a number of different countries to assemble its final product in a number of national locations; or it may assign a complete final product to a particular country, filling in the product line as necessary with models manufactured in other countries. The automobile and farm equipment industries provide examples of both kinds of production rationalization.[17] But this strategy is likely to increase profitability only when the technology is stable, the overall foreign production level high, and the products standardized to some extent in world markets.

Rationalizing or integrating production on an international scale lifts many policy decisions above the managers of subsidiaries to a higher level in the organization.[18] Someone above the subsidiary level must decide which country can best produce each product in the interests of the multinational system as a whole. Someone must decide what transfer prices are to govern shipments among subsidiaries of parts, components, and assembled products. And someone must allocate markets to each operation. Expansion of output in country B to supply country A usually means that the profits for the subsidiary in A are less than they would have been; but the results may be a lower cost and a higher profit for the system as a whole. Higher prices may be charged for the items shipped from country B to the subsidiary in A to transfer profits to a country with a lower tax rate; but the changes in price mean less profits for the subsidiary in A. An indication of the problems of planning the allocation of production and the complexities of the necessary coordination of the output of many plants in different countries is contained in a statement by the former chairman of General Motors:

If the South African assembly operation and its recently added manufacturing facilities are to function smoothly and efficiently, they must today receive a carefully controlled and coordinated flow of vehicle parts and components from West Germany, England, Canada, the United States, and even Australia. These must reach General Motors South Africa in the right volume and at the right time to allow an orderly scheduling of assembly without accumulating excessive inventories. This is a challenging assignment which must be made to work if the investment is to be a profitable one.[19]

The allocation decisions cannot be made satisfactorily by the subsidiary managers. The parochial perspective of these men is reinforced by the fact that they are typically responsible for and judged on the performance of their subsidiary as if it were an independent profit center, and not on the contribution of their subsidiary to the performance of the enterprise as a whole. If the disputes are of major importance, staff advice may be of little use in resolving differences; staff groups do not ordinarily have the authority to enforce policies against the opposition of the subsidiary managers. The disputes among these managers over such issues as transfer pricing and the allocation of production and markets, therefore, can occupy an undue amount of senior management time unless some organizational mechanism for controlling and resolving these disputes is developed.[20]

In cases where production has been extensively rationalized on a regional basis, the formation of regional management groups can be used to provide some of the necessary organizational mechanisms for coordination and control. Where possible, the boundaries of these regional groups are usually drawn to coincide with the boundaries of the integrated production flows, so that the disputes may be contained within organizational subunits of relatively low status. In many cases, these boundaries are drawn around economic blocs, such as the European Economic Community or the European Free Trade Area, where the removal of tariff and other barriers to trade has spurred many firms to integrate production.

The presence of a regional management center in the structure does not eliminate the problems of the disputes among managers of the subsidiaries; it merely provides a cut-off point in the structure above which the disputes are seldom carried. The subsidiary managers need to be motivated to act in the best interests of the region and to stop considering that national frontiers define the horizons of their activities. Some firms have developed control systems that allow the regional effect of action in each national subsidiary to be evaluated. Few firms, however, have gone as far as International Flavors and Fragrances. This firm eliminated the national profit center system in Europe after the regional office had been set up. By the late 1960's, each national unit was judged on its contribution towards the growth and profitability of the area. Controls on competition among the subsidiaries were made more effective without causing the loss in morale and incentive among subsidiary managers that often accompanies attempts to legislate policy from a central office.[21]

Greater control and a more far-reaching rationalization of production might be achieved if, instead of regional divisions, the organization had a Stage 2 structure in which each functional department had worldwide responsibilities. But this structural option is seldom adopted, even by firms with only a single product line. The marginal gains of increased rationalization of production and lower costs are normally judged to be more than offset by losses in marketing effectiveness. The functional departments centralize decision making in the corporate office and inhibit rapid responses to changes in the foreign markets; delays and distortions in information processing occur. Only under certain rare conditions can the worldwide functional structure be efficient. If the operations are relatively stable, standardized procedures and short cuts in the lines of communication can be developed to maintain control without loss of efficiency. The National Cash Register Company during the first half of this century is an example of the efficient and successful use of worldwide functional departments. And some European firms, such as SKF (Sweden), have also used this structure.

Firms with regional units have made more efforts to lower manufacturing costs by rationalizing production than have firms with other structures.

Only a few worldwide product divisions manufacture on a rationalized basis. Singer, for example, has developed a considerable degree of production specialization and cross-shipping of components for its sewing machine operations. In addition, Sperry Rand and some other firms with worldwide product divisions are in the throes of building specialized plants. But, in general, these firms have not developed a network of highly interrelated product flows as extensively as have firms with area management centers. In many cases, this lack of rationalization is probably due to the small proportion of the activities of the product division that are located overseas and the consequent relative lack of attention paid to international affairs by the divisional officers.[22]

Firms with area divisions have generally rationalized production only within each area division. Investment in production facilities that are rationalized on a global scale can be justified for only a few standard products. Consumer preferences for such standard items as the washing machine can vary so widely between different national markets that even regional standardization of the product is impossible. Hoover, for instance, had to invest considerable sums of money and management time during the 1960's before a washing machine for the European market could be developed. And even after the developmental effort, only some of the components could be standardized throughout this one region of Hoover's global market.[23] Hoover was able to make substantial savings in development costs, tooling, and unit production costs by regional coordination, but the savings would have been even larger had a greater degree of standardization been possible. For other products, such as automobiles, the problems of standardization are equally severe.

Where global rationalization of production has been achieved, firms face the problems of coordinating product flows across divisional boundaries. The conflicts cannot be contained within low-level units of the structure as they can when the rationalization is regional. There are formidable problems of deciding the precise dimensions of those activities that should be centralized or coordinated and those that should be delegated to the divisions. An example illustrates the severity of the problem. Massey-Ferguson developed area divisions as it expanded abroad and rationalized its production on a global scale. This firm was able to assemble in Detroit a machine for sale in Canada that included an engine from England, a transmission from France, and an axle from Mexico. The task of coordinating manufacturing, marketing, engineering, and the intersubsidiary movement of finished products and component parts posed huge problems. The president of Massey-Ferguson has outlined the principal bases of choice between these opposing methods of management:

. . . Marketing and manufacturing activities together with some supporting service function, should be organized in a way that would bring them as close as possible to the local market situation. On the other hand, the activities that determine the long-range character of the Company—such as control of product line, facilities, and money, and planning the strategy of reacting to changes in the patterns of international trade—should be handled on a centralized basis.[24]

But even these guidelines do not resolve the problems, and there are frequent negotiations as the markets change.

In spite of these inherent problems, firms that have built area divisions and have rationalized production through these structures have been successful in capturing major shares of the world market for their products. The potential costs of poor coordination of the product flows across the divisional boundaries can be held in check by developing planning committees and other organizational mechanisms that cut across the formal lines of responsibility. Provided that the tasks of coordination are relatively routine, the divisional managers or their representatives on the committees can learn how to act cooperatively without unduly restricting the autonomy of any one division. The structure of area divisions can be tailored to meet the conflicting requirements for centralized production and decentralized marketing.

FIVE / Structural Change Reviewed

To an outsider, replacing an international division with some form of global structure may appear a simple and logical affair. In practice, however, the process is enormously complex. Managers have conflicting views on the need for reorganization and on the form that the reorganization should take. These conflicts generally have to be resolved before any new structure can be set in place. As a result, there are often leads and lags in the timing of reorganizations relative to shifts in strategy.

The Timing of Structural Change

From its origin early in the development of a firm's foreign activities, an international division expands and diversifies until it begins to reach a limit. As the new products transferred abroad increase in number or when the foreign sales of a single product line begin to rival the U.S. market for the product, the pressure to reorganize is generally strong.

The "boundary" on the international division's permitted scope can be indicated graphically, as in Figure 5-1. Units are not indicated on the axis

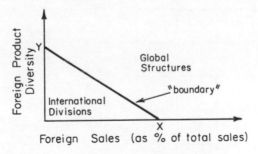

Figure 5–1   *Relationships between Strategy and Structure* (schematic diagram)

of foreign product diversity in Figure 5-1, because of the difficulty of providing the appropriate numerical measure. Point *Y* may, however, be viewed as being quite low, corresponding to the case where one product

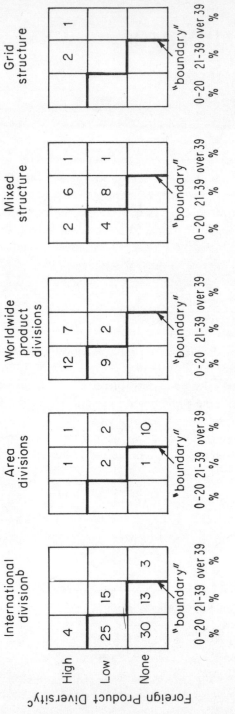

Figure 5-2 *Relationships between Strategy and Structure* (observed results)[a]

[a] The number in each cell of the matrices indicates the number of firms with each set of structural and strategic characteristics.

[b] Includes firms with Stage 2 and Stage 3 domestic structures.

[c] For definitions, see Table 3-1.

line accounts for a dominant share of the business. Point *X* on the axis of foreign sales corresponds to the case where the volume of foreign sales equals the volume of sales in the largest U.S. product division. The "boundary" drawn between the points on the two axes reflects the assumption that the problems of combining both types of complexity are additive.

Figure 5-2 shows, with a specific set of measurements, the concepts contained in Figure 5-1. Here, firms are classified according to both the diversity of their foreign product lines and the percentage of total sales that were generated abroad. Because the use of relative divisional size was proscribed by the absence of appropriate data for many firms, the representation of the boundary does not correspond precisely to that shown in Figure 5-1.

Twenty-two firms with international divisions lie outside the boundary in Figure 5-2. All the Stage 2 firms with international divisions, which are not distinguished from their Stage 3 counterparts, lie within the boundary. Fourteen firms with global structures are also inside the boundary. Because the boundary is only an approximate representation of the point of intolerable organizational stress, some boundary crossing is to be expected. But 75 percent of the international divisions lie inside and 80 percent of the global structures lie outside. The boundary as shown provides a reasonable indicator of the strategies normally contained within the international division.

Figure 5-2 provides a "snapshot" of growth and diversification abroad and the structure of each firm. The process of expansion that led to the positioning of each firm in Figure 5-2 can be portrayed as a path of increasing complexity in international business. Figure 5-3 shows two typical paths of growth and change in strategy abroad, together with the accompanying structural developments.

In Figure 5-3, one firm is represented as developing its foreign business

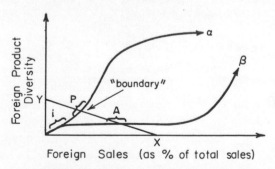

Figure 5–3   *Two Typical Paths Relating
Strategic Choice to Structural Change*

D

over an unspecified time period and making the strategic choices represented by line α. A period of rapid diversification of product lines in foreign markets is followed by a period of expansion in the sales of the products. This shift in emphasis in the strategy is represented by the shape of line α. An international division was established in the region under the bracket labeled i, and later replaced by worldwide product divisions in the region P.

The other firm started abroad in a similar fashion, but once the international division had been established, growth was along line ß. With an increasing share of the total sales being generated abroad, area divisions were developed in the region A. At some later time new products were added to the foreign businesses, as the shape of line ß indicates. Both firms are shown to be converging on a region where further structural adjustment is likely to be necessary.

The paths depicted in Figure 5-3 are a rough-and-ready method of viewing the dynamics of the associations between strategy and structure shown on a cross-sectional basis in Figure 5-2. As a predictive tool, the boundary has utility; the collective past experience of the firms on which the generalization is based is likely to be repeated in the future as others reach similar stages.

International divisions are not, of course, inevitably replaced by global structures: firms must choose to pursue strategies of growth abroad that push their international divisions out to the boundary before reorganization is worthwhile. Some firms have chosen to expand abroad less aggressively and have retained their international divisions for decades. In some cases, the most profitable new avenues for growth have been at home. In other cases, managers have been so busy fighting for survival at home that they have been unable to allocate their time or other resources to expansion of the international division. But, for most of the firms included in this study, growth in foreign markets is an important component of strategy. Many are likely to build global structures in the future.

LAGS IN STRUCTURAL CHANGE

In some cases structural change precedes the implementation of the strategy for which the new structure is best suited. However, the more common relationship appears to be a lag in structural change behind the strategy that induced it. Reorganization is often delayed until the difficulties of managing the new businesses threaten to break apart the old structure. Delays in reorganization, especially at senior levels where the managers are the organizational arbiters, are often caused by the unwillingness of executives to accept new managerial roles until there is overwhelming evidence of the need to change. In the firms studied here, the change from a Stage 2 to a Stage 3 structure has often been delayed for these reasons,[1] and the abandonment of international divisions has commonly been put off until after the retirement of key executives.

Figure 5-4 provides a reflection of the lag in abandoning the international division. Nineteen of the firms abandoned their international divisions during 1967 or 1968. Thirteen of these firms were already outside the boundary in 1966, and the other six had all diversified abroad to some extent. The lag between diversification abroad and abandoning the international division is not great in terms of the measures used in Figure 5-4; all but one of the nineteen firms reorganized close to the imputed boundary. In terms of time, however, the lag may be considerable, for many years can elapse after the boundary has been crossed and before the international division is finally abandoned.

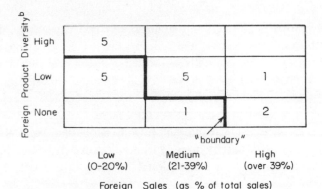

Figure 5–4   *Characteristics in 1966*
of Nineteen Multinational Enterprises
That Abandoned Their International Divisions
in 1967 or 1968[a]

[a] The number in each cell of the matrix indicates the number of firms with each set of characteristics.
[b] For definitions, see Table 3–1.

After a firm has adopted a global structure, it often finds itself shifting its strategy once again. As a result, as Figure 5-2 indicates, global structures sometimes exist in firms for which they are not appropriate. For example, two firms with area divisions transferred numerous new products abroad after they had established the area divisions. Both firms can be expected to adopt some other form of global structure in the future.

During the period of lag before the formal structure is changed in response to strategic changes, changes in the informal structure are likely.

The informal structure of communication can develop mechanisms separate from those of the formal structure as managers learn how to deal with new problems and to devise shortcuts through the formal procedures to ensure that necessary actions are taken sufficiently rapidly. These informal mechanisms become a source of pressure for change in the formal system if they are thought to be more efficient. The lag in response in the formal structure, therefore, does not rule out relatively timely informal changes. Once these changes occur, they speed the formal changes that are to follow.[2]

In Figure 5-2, the twenty-two firms with international divisions that are shown lying outside the boundary in 1968 are likely candidates for reorganization. Undoubtedly, many of them had undertaken informal changes prior to 1968 so that formal changes may be expected. Some, however, had characteristics which suggest that in their case reorganization may be slow in coming. Consider the four divisions with high-product diversity. Three of these have expanded and diversified almost exclusively by using joint venture partners. These foreign partners provided much of the necessary product and area expertise and relieved the divisional management of many of the stresses that normally accompany diversification. In addition, these international divisions may have been regarded as experiments that needed to be segregated from the main businesses, because they each accounted for only a very small part of the total firm.

Some of the other eighteen international divisions had been able to diversify both by product and by area. During an interview, one senior executive in a firm that used an international division to diversify for many years commented:

Our growth and diversification abroad increased *pari passu*, so that it was never clear whether we should go to your worldwide product divisions or area divisions. We continued with an international division and [the divisional vice president] eliminated the channels whereby the domestic men could get at him; that is, he duplicated the United States organization in his division. He pushed staff and even research activities out to the strong regional centers and even set up some product-based profit centers. It was only when serious problems developed in one of the major product lines that the empire was divided.

The confusion that results from rapid diversification in several directions simultaneously can act to delay structural change.

THE EFFECT OF POOR PERFORMANCE

The timing of decisions to reorganize can be influenced by the performance of the divisions. In some instances, where one or more divisions failed to meet a growth target or where they recorded a financial loss, reorganization has been undertaken earlier than might otherwise have been the case.

Poor performance in any firm with a Stage 3 structure affects the subtle relationships that exist between divisional managers and the central office. Many responsibilities are delegated to the divisional manager, allowing a degree of autonomy and discretion in his actions. But some responsibilities remain the preserve of the central office, and considerable ambiguity clouds the dividing line. The relationship involves a contradiction, but the maintenance of the contradiction in a purposeful manner is regarded by some observers as the essence of modern management.[3] The relationship is basically a bargaining one. If the environment in which the division does business is favorable, and if the division has the necessary resources, the divisional manager is likely to be given his head. But if the environment is threatening, or if the division performance has been poor, the central office is more likely to monitor decisions and to intervene. Intervention by the central office is analogous to the active participation of banks or shareholders in the management of firms that are in financial trouble.

Top management sometimes intervenes in the management of the international division. Consider the situation where an international division responsible for developing a second and unfamiliar product line has failed to do the job adequately. The managers of the division may not have been sufficiently interested in the new line to give it adequate attention. If the new line does not develop according to plan, attention in both the international and the central offices will be focused on the problem area. Pressures for improvement can force the firm to reorganize sooner than it wishes.

One senior manager in a firm that suffered from these pressures and adopted worldwide product divisions commented in an interview:

We tried to run them [the new diversified product lines] under the control of the international division but it didn't work out. We lost a lot of money. There had to be liaison between manufacturing and marketing in the United States since our competence is at the division level. Now we still don't have the people to run these businesses properly. They are small, so we cannot hire the best Europeans. We can send United States people to do the marketing, but it is with only great reluctance that the manufacturing people will go abroad. Even so, the operations have been tightened up and begin to show promise. We didn't want to do all this in such a great hurry but we had to get out of the hole somehow.

Adopting worldwide product divisions can, in effect, centralize responsibility for secondary lines that are unattended by the international division. Managers of operations that had previously been highly independent are subjected to close scrutiny by men from the divisional headquarters in the United States. Of course, the product division may not be greatly concerned with small and unprofitable foreign subsidiaries and may also ignore the problem. Decisions to reorganize in a hurry involve a gamble that the help necessary to alleviate the problem will be forthcoming.

At times, intervention by top management may be no more than a tightening of the control system. But sometimes poor performance has stimulated far-reaching reorganizations that have run counter to the general movement toward decentralization observed in this study. Several cases were observed in which the structure had become more decentralized than was necessary for the efficient management of the product lines, and top management decided to abandon the divisions altogether.

Crown Cork and Seal faced such a situation in its domestic business during the mid-1950's. The company had formed product divisions for the various lines in crowns and containers, and overheads had greatly increased. The firm was almost bankrupt before the advent of a new president who reorganized the firm on a functional, Stage 2 basis. Costs were reduced dramatically both by wholesale dismissals of senior officers and by changing many of the operating policies.[4] Because the product lines had so many similarities, they could be managed better on a centralized rather than a decentralized basis.

Three other cases of reversion to a Stage 2 from a Stage 3 structure were observed. In all three cases, there were large product flows between the divisions, each of which was responsible for one stage of a vertically integrated chain of production. The divisional managers were allowed little autonomy, but they were judged on performance that they could not control. This and other conflicts introduced by the divisional structure proved to be so sufficiently damaging to overall performance that the functional departments were reinstituted.

Recentralization of responsibility for international activities has also occurred. In two cases, an international division was established after the firms had had a number of years of experience with worldwide product divisions. One firm had grown and diversified by acquiring other U.S. firms with international activities, and each acquired firm became a worldwide product division. In most foreign markets, the products were all sold through the same retail outlets. The acquisition strategy had produced an extremely high rate of growth in sales. But while net earnings increased rapidly in the United States, increasing losses were recorded abroad. Each division had built up considerable staff support for the overlapping foreign businesses, and the resulting duplication of management had added a heavy overhead burden. The eventual formation of an international division allowed much of this fat to be cut off with no loss of market shares and a return to profitability. The other firm suffered from similar problems and used the same remedy. In neither case may recentralization be considered as the primary cause of the improved foreign performance, although it undoubtedly helped.

ABSOLUTE SIZE AND STRUCTURAL CHANGE

Structure, according to the arguments of earlier chapters, is associated with strategy. But all such statements court the risk that both are related to some third variable. In this case, one might be entitled to suspect that both the strategies and structures of large multinational enterprises were a function of their size. There are data, however, which suggest that size is not an important factor in determining structural change of the type discussed here.

To be sure, the transition from a Stage 1 to a Stage 2 structure in the early years of a firm's growth was attributed in Chapter 2 to growth in absolute size. As the volume of activity increases, the top executive is unable to coordinate the enterprise, and an increasing degree of task specialization is required. The transition from a Stage 2 structure to a Stage 3 structure, is, however, another story.

Table 5-1 shows that Stage 2 firms came in all sizes, as did those in Stage 3. In addition to the sales figures shown in Table 5-1, two other measures of size—net earnings and net assets—showed the same diffusion. The fact that four firms with over $1 billion in sales maintained Stage 2 structures suggests that irresistible pressures to adopt a Stage 3 structure are not generated by size alone.

The pressure to abandon an international division also seems unrelated to absolute size. Table 5-2 shows that both firms with international divi-

TABLE 5-1   *Multinational Enterprises with Domestic Stage 2 and Stage 3 Structures, Classified by Sales Volume, 1966*

| Structure | Total number of firms | Number of firms, classified by total sales (in $ millions)[a] | | | |
		Less than 300	300-599	600-999	1,000 and over
Stage 2	16	4	6	2	4
Stage 3	146	35	43	28	40
Total	162	39	49	30	44

[a]Sales data are for the consolidated worldwide operations of the firms.

TABLE 5-2 *Multinational Enterprises with International Divisions and Global Structures, Classified by Foreign Sales Volume, 1966*

Structure[a]	Total number of firms	Number of firms, classified by foreign sales (in $ millions)[b]			
		Less than 50	50-99	100-199	200 and over
International division	106	31	24	31	20
Global structure	56	12	9	15	20
Total	162	43	33	46	40

[a]International divisions are attached to both Stage 2 and Stage 3 domestic structures.
[b]For definitions, see Table 4-2.

sions and those with global structures existed over the same sales range. Indeed, General Motors' international division was the largest foreign operation of any U.S. firm in 1966. Other measures of size produced similar results.

Absolute size does, of course, influence the strategic decisions that firms take. For example, large firms are generally much more highly diversified than small firms; very few of the 500 largest U.S. manufacturing firms remain concentrated in a single industry.[5] The fact that most of these 500 largest firms have Stage 3 structures,[6] however, is not a result of their size but of their diversification; absolute size by itself does not have a direct relationship with structure.

Absolute size can also have an effect on the structures developed within a division. The building of regional units within the international division as the number of foreign subsidiaries increases is indicative of this effect. In addition, the operating policies for the conduct of the business can be influenced by size; questions of scale are important factors in the ability or willingness of general managers to sustain and justify the presence of specialists. There is evidence, for instance, that size is related to financial policies, and to the location of financial specialists in the firm.[7] At the top levels of the firm, however, the diversity of strategic issues appears to take precedence over absolute size in influencing structure.

Management Coalitions

Any change in the organizational structure of an enterprise is likely to be resisted.[8] When the effect of the change is to increase the power of some senior managers, those who lose power strongly resist the change.

An organization can be regarded as a network of power groups, each of which is centered on a major subsystem of the structure. The nature of each group reflects the structure of authority and control in situations where men work together on common tasks.[9] Managers with complementary interests tend to form a group and establish procedures that advance or protect their interests. The actions of these groups of managers are essentially efforts at securing and retaining effective power and control.[10]

The power of each group is, to some extent, based on how well it has performed in the past. There is evidence, for example, that requests for capital funds made by men who have built up strong "track records" are approved more readily than are requests from less successful men.[11] The manager of the largest, most profitable domestic division is likely, therefore, to be in a powerful position to influence the way in which the scarce resources of the firm are allocated. He is also likely to consider his power threatened by the growth of the international division. The fate of those international divisions that were broken into smaller, less threatening units when they approached the size of the largest domestic divisions may have been caused by domestic managers defending their positions of power.

The manager of the international division almost always loses power when a global structure is adopted and he almost always opposes the reorganization. In order to defend his position, he engages in a process of bargaining with other managers who do not share his perspective on the problem. This process is political in the sense that the vested interests of individuals play a large part in determining how differences and conflicts become resolved. The political strength of the international manager can influence how long he can successfully hold out against pressures to break up his division.

Conflicts over areas of responsibility tend to emerge in any organization. But these conflicts do not cause major difficulties in all situations. In the Stage 2 structure, the standard conflict is between marketing and production. The treasurer may mediate (or the president arbitrate) through the finance function, since the language of the debate is typically cast in terms of money. In the Stage 2 firm that has an international division, the conflicting groups may be arrayed on either side of the domestic-foreign fault in the structure. Whereas functional differences exist on the domestic front, area differences are likely to predominate in the international division. In the domestic Stage 3 firm, the conflicts between divisional managers and the functional staff groups are likely to require the regular attention of the top management. Yet, in all these situations, workable solutions that do not require structural change may be generated by means of orderly bargaining, negotiation, and mediation.

Intractable organizational problems appear, however, when all three

D*

types of differences—of products, of areas, and of functions—are contained in the structure. A firm that has domestic product divisions, an international division, and a central staff group of functional specialists faces the problem of managing conflicts among three groups, each of which has a different view of the problem. This state of affairs often leads to the appearance of multiple dotted-line relationships on the organizational chart. There may be no orderly or logical procedure that the firm can use to reconcile the differences between the groups or to provide agreement on common priorities.

So long as the international division remains small and relatively unimportant to the strategy of the enterprise, these problems are of little consequence. The "champion" of the new business is allowed freedom to experiment without undue interference from others and is rewarded according to his individual performance. But the separation of the international division during its early years can increase the difficulties later on, when efforts are made to introduce consistency of purpose throughout the whole enterprise.

Expansion of a fledgling international division generates a need for more managers. Promising executives in the company must be identified and given the choice of staying on the traditional main tracks or of branching out into new, largely unexplored territory. It is not an easy decision for the young able managers, since the main tracks usually have well defined schedules of promotion and the new activities seldom do. There is evidence that in the early years of a firm's foreign expansion these men typically make the risk-avoiding decision to stay at home.[12] How to identify, recruit, develop, and motivate men for the new assignments is a task for more than the personnel department. The manager of the international division looks upon the reproduction of his own kind as one of his most urgent and demanding jobs. His choices may lead to the formation of a group of men who share his perspectives, and who act to reinforce and perpetuate the lines of demarcation. It is difficult for these men to discard their sense of exclusivity when the international division is finally abandoned, and some of them have become less effective managers as they have attempted to adjust to a new role in a global structure.

Once the international division becomes critical to the strategy of the enterprise, attempts to introduce consistency of purpose generate stresses and conflicts. Managers may spend more time on internal disputes than they do on managing their businesses. Confronted with this situation of turmoil, top management might be tempted to restore stability by issuing detailed directives to the divisions. Such authoritarian intervention would, however, destroy much of the advantage of delegating authority. In any firm that is diversified along both product and geographical dimensions, there are simply too many operating decisions for a highly centralized management to make. To restrict delegation of decision making ultimately means a restriction in diversification. The alternative solution to the problem is to reorganize into a form that allows the conflicts to be resolved more easily and in a manner more consistent with the objectives of the firm.

In this reorganization, the interests of three groups are at stake: the international division is fighting for survival, and both the domestic divisions and the central staff face major realignments of the boundaries of their jurisdictions. In analyzing management's choice of a new structure, it is useful to view the problem from the perspective of each group. Although the choice of structure is ultimately the responsibility of top managers, they have the role of identifying a workable solution, persuading each group of its logic, and implementing the reorganization. The information available to top management is almost invariably biased according to the personal interests of those who provide it.[13] What appears, therefore, to top management as "workable" is largely a function of the perceptions of the adversary groups.

The perception of each group is indicated by the ordering of priorities among the three main dimensions—functions, products, and areas. The managers of the product divisions typically accord first priority to product differences. They are also likely to give least priority to area differences, since they do not have responsibility for any foreign business and tend to regard the domestic market as homogeneous.[14] They are familiar with the problems of coordinating the functions in their divisions and probably therefore accord second priority to functional differences. These managers are also likely to be eager for worldwide responsibilities if the foreign business is well established, profitable, and of significant proportions.

Managers in the international division are concerned primarily with area differences. Their secondary concern is likely to be with product differences, particularly if there have been moves to diversify the foreign product lines. Even in the absence of product diversification, the problems of adapting a single product line to the requirements of overseas markets are familiar to managers in the international office. Coordination of the functions is primarily the responsibility of the managers of each subsidiary and generally of least concern to the managers in the international headquarters.

Disputes confined to an exchange between the product divisions and the international division would most probably have led, in many instances, to the adoption of global structures quite different from those that were in fact adopted. But there is a third group involved in the dispute: the central staff. The interests of this third group then become critical to the outcome.

The central staff has several views of the problem. The priorities of the central staff are shaped by the nature and extent of the requirements for coordination of the divisional activities. These requirements appear to produce three distinctive staff views of the drama.

A. In firms producing interrelated products, there are groups in the central staff concerned with manufacturing and marketing problems.[15] The presence of these groups indicates that there are interactions among the product divisions in these two functions that require central coordination. Interrelated products may, for example, use common channels of distribution or common technologies in the manufacturing processes. The central staff groups are involved with those aspects of the functions that are common to the different products; the functional managers in the divisions look after those aspects that are different in each division. Men in the central staff are likely to consider themselves as being concerned primarily with differences among the functions, and pay much less attention to product differences. They are, however, concerned to some extent with area differences. In cases where the international division is small and has only a small divisional staff, men in the central staff have to communicate with the international division on aspects of their speciality in foreign countries. Under these circumstances, the imputed order of priority in the staff is: functions, areas, products.

B. Firms with unrelated products may have no interactions among the product divisions, either in manufacturing or in marketing functions. All the manufacturing and marketing staffs are assigned to the divisions in this case. The central staff is seldom engaged in coordinating interactions among the divisions. For the purposes of analysis, these central staffs may be considered as merely interested spectators in the disputes over divisional reorganization.

C. There are cases where large manufacturing and marketing staff groups exist in both the central and the international office. If the international division is large and composed of regional units, the international staff may even be as large as the central staff. Men in these large international staff groups often regard themselves as internationalists first and functional specialists second. The imputed ordering of priorities is: areas, functions, and, lastly, products.

Table 5-3 summarizes these classifications and the imputed orderings of priorities. The global structure that the firm eventually chooses accords first priority to only one of the three dimensions, so that one or more of the negotiating groups is forced to accept a solution other than the one it would prefer. It is assumed that consensus about the form of global structure is reached by the political process of coalition formation among the groups, rather than by the unilateral imposition of rules by top management. Quite possibly the structure is chosen by a coalition of two groups which together can out vote the third group. In some cases the coalition is a compromise agreement in which the accepted structural solution is based on the dimension of first priority in one group and second priority in the other. In such cases, side payments in terms of other agreements about policies or personal assignments may be made by the winning group to the losers.[16]

TABLE 5-3 *Priorities of Key Groups Prior to the Development of a Global Structure, for Three Types of Multinational Enterprise*

Type of multinational enterprise	Priorities arranged in descending order		
	Domestic product divisions	International division	Central staff
A: interrelated products and small international division	Products Functions Areas	Areas Products Functions	Functions Areas Products
B: unrelated products and either small or large international division	Products Functions Areas	Areas Products Functions	— — —
C: interrelated products and large international division	Products Functions Areas	Areas Products Functions	Areas Functions Products

In order to classify a firm according to the types of enterprise shown in Table 5-3, one has to know what the central staff does. Data on the central staff group assignments immediately prior to the development of a global structure were available for fifty firms. These data provide a means of examining how closely the above argument reflects actual behavior.

Firms that corresponded to type *A* in Table 5-3 faced a set of extremely difficult choices. The priorities of the three key groups form a profile that resembles what some observers have labelled the Latin Square problem of choice. The consensus among those who have examined the characteristics of the Latin Square problem is that there is no logical means for deriving a common group priority, and that there is no intrinsic reason for any two-group coalition to occur more readily than any other. For any coalition, there is always the possibility of a countercoalition that will act to break it.[17] Type *A* situations may, therefore, be expected to produce a scatter of management choices among all four global structures. Some preference might be accorded to the mixed and grid forms. In fact, of the fifteen firms classified as type *A,* three replaced their international divisions with worldwide product divisions, two firms chose area divisions, seven emerged with a mixed structure, and finally all three grid structures found their roots in this situation.

In the situation represented by type *B,* where the central staff is not involved, product differences are given the highest priority: first priority, as always, is accorded by the domestic product divisions to product differences; and second place is accorded to these differences by the international division. It would seem reasonable to expect that these priorities would lead to adoption of worldwide product divisions. There were twenty-three firms with divisional staff assignments that disbanded their international divisions. Fifteen of these firms did what they were expected to do, replacing the international division with worldwide product divisions; seven chose the mixed structure; and one opted for area divisions.

Type *C* implies two groups with initial first priority for the geographic distinction, so the consistent organization choice is the structure that partitions the world by area. All twelve general managers whose firms were in this category responded as suggested by this analysis.

These results are not independent of the hypothesis that choices of structure emerge from a process of group bargaining. The turbulence observed in the efforts of large corporations to organize their foreign activities suggested that conflicts were being resolved by bargaining rather than by rational analysis. The three-group conflict model, described in Table 5-3, was developed to represent the bargaining conditions observed in some of the firms. The model was formulated in 1967 using data for 1966. Thus, only those nineteen firms that abandoned their international divisions after 1966 provide an independent test of the hypothesis. The results for the nineteen firms were, however, similar to those for firms that undertook the structural change before 1966. Because of the similarity, both sets of results are presented here in combined form.

After 1967, some firms modified the form of global structure that they chose initially. These modifications provide additional support for the hypothesis. One of the two firms of type *A,* having first chosen area divisions, later moved to a mixed structure even though there was no change in strategy. By 1970, this firm had begun to develop management groups that cut across both product and area divisions, and it seemed likely that a grid structure would eventually emerge. Movement toward a grid structure was also occurring in two of the other members of the type *A* group: one by creating a European profit center in addition to its worldwide product divisions, and one by initiating worldwide management committees for both products and areas in addition to its present formal mixed structure. The mixed structures chosen by some of the firms in the type *B* group are probably transitional forms; by 1970 one firm had adopted worldwide product divisions for all its product lines, and others appeared likely to do the same. The one firm in the type *B* group that chose an area structure had not, by 1970, modified its formal structure in line with the model. Product coordination among the area divisions was, however, being facilitated by the presence of the domestic product division managers on the various boards of directors of the foreign area divisions.

These results are consistent with the view that the resolution of the internal conflicts generated by the growth and diversification of the international division takes place through bargaining among the groups of managers. But the results are also consistent with the view that change is a consequence of rational analysis. Some managers may analyze the problem in terms similar to those discussed here, and then impose a workable form that causes least disaffection among the groups. By negotiation, by rational analysis, or by both, firms make predictable choices.

Structure and Performance

With so many factors influencing structure and the timing of changes in structure, it is not surprising that we found firms using structures which did not appear to be appropriate for implementing their chosen strategies. On the whole, however, these firms seemed to perform less well than those whose structures seemed harmonious with their strategies.

Any analysis seeking to relate structure to performance is very difficult, because performance is an amalgam of many factors. Firms make trade-offs between risk and profit, between growth now and growth later on. Besides, even if one could decide how best to measure performance, one could never be sure that the results were influenced by the choice of structure.

Differences in reporting and accounting practices add further problems to the comparisons of performance in different firms. For example, different accounting treatments of certain expenses, such as R&D, affect both the reported net income and the yield on investment. Similarly, differences in the treatment of foreign subsidiaries in the consolidated accounts of the firms affect the reported growth of sales over any given period of time.

Measures of consolidated worldwide performance did not show important differences between the firms with well matched strategies and structures and those with mismatches. Mismatching in this context applies primarily to the foreign operations and in many cases marginal differences abroad had no appreciable impact on the consolidated results. Nevertheless, systematic differences in foreign performance existed between the two groups of firms, even though they were not very large.

The Stage 3 structure with an international division is not suited, we have argued, to a strategy of foreign product diversification. Nonetheless, of the eighty-two firms with this structure, forty-three had diversified the foreign product lines. These were considered as "mismatched." Four of these "mismatched" international divisions are considered in a separate subcategory of "extreme mismatching," because they had developed highly diverse product lines abroad. The median performance data of the three groups of firms are shown in Table 5-4.

TABLE 5-4   *Median Performance of Eighty-six Multinational Enterprises with an International Division, Classified by Strategy*

Performance	Thirty-nine firms with matched strategy	Forty-three firms with mismatched strategy	Four firms with extremely mismatched strategy
Growth of foreign sales 1961-1966[a]	13.4%	13.7%	9.7%
Foreign ROI, 1966[b]	11.8%	10.1%	Loss

[a]Growth is calculated as the annual compound percentage increase in sales volume abroad between 1961 and 1966, inclusively. Foreign sales include exports from the United States, but exclude sales of foreign licensees and foreign subsidiaries in which the parent firm owned less than 25 percent of the equity. Fiscal years were used for firms that did not report their results by calendar year.

[b]Foreign return on investment (ROI) is calculated as the net foreign income in 1966 expressed as a percentage of the average net assets located abroad during 1966. Fiscal years were used for firms that did not report their results by calendar year.

The international divisions with matched strategies had a slightly greater median profitability than those with mismatched strategies, but they exhibited no advantage in terms of growth. These data suggest that the international division can be adapted to cope satisfactorily with limited degrees of product diversity. The performance of the four divisions with highly mismatched strategies suggests, however, that such adaptability is limited. These four divisions were identified earlier as likely candidates for reorganization in the near future. Their poor performance records may well act to hasten reorganization by focusing the attention of top management on the problem areas abroad.

Area divisions are best suited, as Chapter 4 suggested, to the management of a single product line. But area divisions may be efficiently adapted to some strategies of foreign product diversification, provided that the diversified lines are relatively unimportant, and provided that they also share with the principal line some common functional facilities, such as channels of distribution. All but two of the firms with area divisions met these specifications. The exceptions are the two that had highly diverse product lines in each area. Both of these mismatched firms had performance records, in terms of growth and in terms of profitability, below that of the median for the matched firms.

Firms with either worldwide product divisions or a mixed structure were considered mismatched when they had more than 20 percent of their business located abroad. This figure was chosen on the assumption that the costs of impaired coordination on an area basis are likely to be high when a significant proportion of the business is outside the United States. Table 5-5 shows that the sixteen mismatched firms have not been inhibited by their structure in their growth abroad, but that they have taken a penalty in the form of reduced profitability. Indeed, each of the three firms with worldwide product divisions that reported losses on their foreign business in 1966 was in the mismatched category.

TABLE 5-5 *Median Performance of Fifty-two Multi-national Enterprises with either Worldwide Product Divisions or a Mixed Structure, Classified by Strategy*

Performance[a]	Thirty-six firms with matched strategy	Sixteen firms with mismatched strategy
Growth of foreign sales 1961-1966	14.5%	14.7%
Foreign ROI, 1966	10.8%	7.5%

[a] For definitions, see Table 5-4.

An alternative way of examining the effect on performance of a mismatch between strategy and structure is to look at firms classified by strategy. The figures in Table 5-6 show that firms with mismatched structures in each category of foreign product diversity had median performance levels lower than those of firms with matched structures.

To be sure, some firms with mismatched strategies and structure have grown faster and been more profitable abroad than those with matched strategies and structures. The analysis does not show that one structure is

TABLE 5-6 *Median Performance of Multinational Enterprises with Matched and Mismatched Structures, Classified by Foreign Product Diversity*

Foreign product diversity[a]	Number of firms	Growth of foreign sales, 1961-1966[b]		Foreign ROI 1966[b]	
		Matched structure	Mismatched structure	Matched structure	Mismatched structure
High	37	19.3%	13.5%	10.0%	7.5%
Low	68	14.9%	13.8%	11.3%	10.1%
None	57	12.0%	—	11.9%	—

[a] For definitions, see Table 3-1.
[b] For definitions, see Table 5-4.

necessarily better than another in all cases. Nevertheless, the data suggest that a match between strategy and structure gives a firm a slight advantage over others in which the characteristics of the structure are not well tailored to the managers' needs.

Differences in the size of the firms do not account for the differences in performance. Among all the firms taken together, a very small negative correlation existed between absolute size abroad and the profitability of the foreign operations.[18] For the consolidated worldwide operations of these firms there was a small positive correlation between size and profitability.[19] Furthermore, the correlation between growth in total sales (measured over the period 1951–1966) and profitability in 1966 was small but positive.[20] Clearly, large multinational enterprises have developed a capacity for maintaining highly profitable growth over long periods of time.

These results appear to contradict the predictions of some economists that diseconomies of scale will lead to declining profitability as firms grow large.[21] This contradiction may perhaps be explained in terms of the organizational structures that multinational enterprises have developed. The Stage 3 structures, used by all but eight of the firms in 1968, keep at bay many of the threats of diseconomies by dividing the enterprise into smaller business units. These decoupled structures allow rapid growth without an even faster increase in overhead costs. Also, economies, in the form of opportunities to spread research costs over larger sales volumes for instance, may appear during the course of a firm's expansion abroad. These economies may offset, or at least delay, the impact of the diseconomies of scale. In contrast, the Stage 2 structure, which appears to be the principal model in the traditional economic theory of the firm,[22] cannot generally expand into new areas of business without a relatively rapid growth in overhead and costs of coordination.

This critical difference between Stage 2 and Stage 3 structures is illustrated by the results of a recent analysis of the performance of 136 large U.S. firms.[23] All these firms were among the largest four in each of thirty-four industries, and many of them had neither diversified their product lines nor expanded abroad. The figures in Table 5-7 are taken from this study to show the enormous gap that existed in 1966 between the median levels of performance of domestic firms with Stage 2 structures and those of multinational firms with Stage 3 structures.

TABLE 5-7 *Median Performance of 136 Domestic and Multinational Enterprises,[a] Classified by Structure*

Structure	Type	Number of firms	ROI in 1966 (%)	Growth of sales 1951-1966 (%)
Stage 3	Multinational	52	12.6	9.4
Stage 3	Domestic	42	12.6	9.0
Stage 2	Domestic	42	7.5	3.9

[a]The 136 enterprises in the sample were all among the largest four in each of thirty-four industries. Those enterprises included in the analysis throughout this book are classified as multinational; the others are classified as domestic.

Source: ROI from Federal Trade Commission, *Rates of Return for Identical Companies in Selected Manufacturing Industries*, (Washington, D.C.: United States Government Printing Office, various issues). Growth in sales from annual reports of the firms; the sales figures apply to the reported worldwide sales of each firm; the growth rate is the annual compound percentage increase in sales over the period 1951-1966.

These figures, together with the fact that most multinational enterprises have developed Stage 3 structures, suggest that there is a basic mismatch between the Stage 2 structure and any strategy of expansion abroad. The development of procedures for controlling decentralized operations is critical to the successful management of foreign operations. The Stage 2 structure lacks such a system.

Conclusions

Firms make predictable choices of structure, but the processes by which they reach those choices vary. Once a new structure has been chosen there are often delays before the reorganization is undertaken. Such variations are to be expected, because managers behave differently.

Structural changes are generally designed to eliminate a mismatch between strategy and structure. Apparently such changes do have some such effect, though the influence on performance is not marked. This is not a surprising conclusion, as much of the success of an enterprise must inevitably depend upon the abilities and skills of its managers. Just as an exceptionally able manager can overcome the handicap of having an inappropriate structure for the purposes of implementing the chosen strategy, so a less able manager can fail to achieve good results no matter how well designed the structure. Nevertheless, the fact remains that appropriate structures are more associated with better performance than those that are not appropriate for the strategy.

SIX / New Responses to New Problems

Many multinational enterprises have found that none of the global structures discussed in previous chapters is an entirely satisfactory means of organization. In a structure of worldwide product divisions, for example, there are usually some benefits to be gained by ensuring a degree of area coordination at low levels in the hierarchy. Even though these potential benefits may be small compared to those yielded by global product coordination, firms seldom ignore them altogether. But attempts to coordinate subsidiaries in different divisions on a regional basis pose a dilemma: how to develop procedures that induce area coordination but that do not at the same time unduly restrict the autonomy of each division. A similar dilemma is faced by firms with area divisions that have added new products which need to be coordinated on a global basis.[1]

The problem is exacerbated by the fact that the organizational structure that is appropriate for, say, the European operations of a firm may be inappropriate for Africa; much depends on the mix of products and market requirements in each area. Although a uniform structure for all areas may not be appropriate, there are usually limits to the extent of the differences that can be introduced between areas. Managers have to strike a balance between uniformity and distinctiveness.

Innovations in structure have been occurring in response to these problems. These adaptations suggest the directions in which structures will develop as firms add new product lines and invest larger amounts in foreign markets.

Shared Responsibilities

Management in the United States has placed a high premium on the separation and specialization of managerial tasks. In purely domestic Stage 3 structures, this preference has led to the establishment of units inside each firm that were responsible for a single product in a single market. A product division in a domestic Stage 3 structure, for instance, has responsibility for a single line of closely related products in the United States. Coordination among the separate units has been accomplished with the help of staff groups. For multinational enterprises, however, the formation of single product, single market units would require an enormous and expensive superstructure containing many levels of management and providing specialized staff support at each level. Multinational enterprises have attempted to find ways of avoiding the overhead without at the same time losing the benefits of specialization.

A global structure represents a departure from the traditional philosophy. A worldwide product division, for example, is responsible for a product line in many markets. The wider scope of the responsibilities of the managers reduces the number of levels of management needed in the structure. But there is the danger that managers do not pay adequate attention to all the important aspects of their task. The manager of an area division may, for instance, concentrate on one product line and ignore the potential for developing other product lines.

Some firms have established committees to cope with these problems. Divisional managers, together with staff specialists, are charged with a collective responsibility for coordinating the interdivisional transactions and for ensuring that potential benefits from new types of coordination are not ignored. Product committees in firms with area divisions, or area committees in firms with worldwide product divisions attempt to maintain an appropriate balance of management attention.

Often these committees simply formalize the informal relationships that existed previously. On the other hand, there have been cases of strong resistance to the establishment of committees; many managers of foreign subsidiaries have been concerned that the committee would become too powerful and interfere too much with their operations. Experience indicates, however, that such resistance is reduced when the managers of the subsidiaries are themselves involved in the deliberations of the committee and in the formulation of policy.

Coordinating committees have appeared in many different forms. Some are informal and random gatherings of senior executives; some are formal bodies with regularly scheduled meetings and an agenda; some, like Sperry Rand's "umbrella companies," are even legal entities. In many cases they have performed successfully. But there are situations where the conflicts of interest among the committee members are so great that committees are powerless to foster cooperative action.

In such situations, a few firms have made changes in the structure of the divisions and in the systems for controlling and evaluating the divisional managers. These firms are among the largest and most widely diversified of all multinational enterprises. They have broken down the clear lines of responsibility and authority previously maintained in the global structure, and have developed a new form of structure. In this new structure, the foreign subsidiaries report simultaneously to more than one divisional headquarters; worldwide product divisions share with area divisions responsibility for the profits of the foreign subsidiaries.

These innovating firms have taken different approaches in designing and experimenting with their new structures. Nevertheless, all the approaches have in common the characteristics of responsibility being shared among divisions, and of managers having multiple reporting relationships.[2] In these new structures, top management responsibilities are assigned on the basis of two of the variables discussed in Chapter 5: differences in products and in areas. A subsidiary manager may, for example, report to a product manager as well as to an area manager. Both have some degree of line responsibility for the subsidiary. Because the lines of responsibility intersect, the structure is labeled "grid."

In nongrid structures, managers adhere to the traditional principle of unity of command. In order to maintain this principle at all levels in the organization, relationships among the managers are ordered by concentrating attention on one variable and by according that variable priority over the others. Differences among products are of primary concern and functional differences of secondary concern in most domestic Stage 3 structures and in worldwide product divisions. Differences among areas dominate functional differences in structures of area divisions. In a Stage 3 structure that includes an international division, or in a mixed structure, the predominant focus is on products in some of the divisions and on areas in others. However, because there is little attempt to integrate the activities of each division, these two structures are basically collections of divisions, each dominated by one variable.

To be sure, multinational, multiproduct operations require management attention on all three variables. But one of the three variables is largely ignored in the design of the familiar global structures. For instance, differences between areas affect the design of a structure of worldwide product division only at relatively low levels within each division and have little or no influence on the relationships among the divisions.

Firms that have developed a grid structure have abandoned the notion that concentration on one variable should dominate in the organization. They have designed structures in which two variables—differences in products and in areas—are of roughly equal importance; both are considered relatively more important than functional differences. Managers of products share responsibility with managers of areas. By assigning shared responsibilities, these firms are attempting to integrate their diverse activities more effectively than is possible when responsibility is assigned by traditional means.

Figure 6-1 sketches part of a grid structure to indicate how some of the separate units are related and responsibility shared. In this chart, the product and area divisions have equal status. In practice, however, the relative strength of these divisions may vary, and affect how the processes of management are carried out. Any chart of a grid structure is bound to be somewhat misleading, because there is no effective way of representing the full extent of the important informal relationships and communication patterns. Of course, these problems apply to charts of every type of structure, but for the grid they are particularly acute as a result of the multiple lines of responsibility.

An example illustrates one variant of the grid structure. In Dow Chemi-

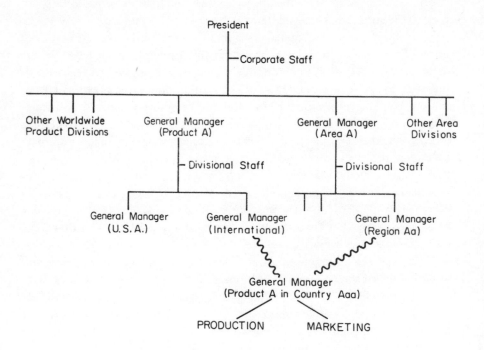

Figure 6–1   *A Grid Structure*
(partial organizational chart)

NOTE: _____ indicates reporting relationships where responsibility is not shared.

∼∼∼ indicates reporting relationships where responsibility is shared.

See text for a discussion of the reporting relationships and responsibilities for profits.

cal in the late 1960's, area divisions had prime responsibility for all the products in their territories, whereas the corporate product departments took a long-term view of product planning, capital investment, and the meeting of production schedules for the worldwide markets for each product line. These product departments, despite their apparent lack of direct involvement in the global operations of each product line, had full responsibility for product competitiveness and success in world markets. Two major functional groups in the central office provided coordination of interdivisional transactions: one group coordinated prices, schedules of investment plans for production, and made forecasts; the other group coordinated economic planning and evaluation. In addition, there were strong central financial, control, and research groups. Dow was attempting by means of this structure to develop a flexible system that could provide a pooling of product expertise to respond rapidly to changes in its global environment without muddling the clear lines of responsibility for profits in the area divisions.[3]

Links among the various divisions and departments have been strengthened by creating a series of "business teams" at many levels in the organization. These "business teams," manned by representatives from the units concerned, are committees that provide a forum where managers meet to negotiate and to commit themselves to market-oriented plans of action.

The change from a formal structure in Dow to the more informal and fluid structure just described caused many problems of adjustment. One observer commented:

The shift from stable, vertical relationships to this multiplicity of vertical and horizontal relationships was not always easy. Men worried about how the new organization would affect their departments and their jobs, about how many bosses a man could satisfy. Some of the new relationships are still being ironed out, but today it is hard to find a Dow man who is not sold on the system.[4]

In spite of the initial difficulties, the changes appeared to have resulted in great benefits for the firm as managers became familiar with their new tasks.

As is often the case, one part of Dow was not involved in these changes. The Life Sciences Department (pharmaceutical products) remained a separate worldwide product division and had no contact with the area divisions. Top management considered that the division was best separated from the rest of the organization, because of the highly research-intensive nature of the products, and because it used marketing channels completely different from those used for other products.[5]

The International Telephone and Telegraph Corporation has taken a different route in moving toward a grid structure. Historically, ITT was a loose confederation of subsidiaries scattered throughout the world. Area divisions were developed in the early 1960's. By 1966, an array of product divisions and area divisions had been established in conjunction with a series of management committees and reporting relationships cutting across the formal divisional boundaries.

That the system of sharing responsibility among the members of the committees worked effectively was largely due to the dominant personality of the president, who had drastically changed the firm since the late 1950's. The president depended on a series of regular committee meetings to communicate policies and develop plans. These meetings were informal and obviated the need for much of the elaborate formal communication system that would otherwise be necessary. But they imposed a heavy burden on the president and his key officers. For example, each year there were ten three-day meetings in Brussels at the headquarters of the European division. The president, the European group executive, staff members from the New York and Brussels offices, and managers of the most important European subsidiaries met to discuss and make decisions on policy questions and critical problems.[6] As a result of this committee system, the Brussels office in 1966 had a total payroll, including clerical staff, of approximately 200.[7] Many U.S. firms with European headquarters had larger regional staff groups to support a much smaller base of operations.

The use of staff in ITT departs from normal practice. In the European headquarters, for example, there were twenty staff officers. Seven of them had product responsibilities (components, relays, consumer products, and so on), and the others had functional responsibilities (finance, planning, marketing services, manufacturing, and industrial engineering, etc.). These men reported to the European group executive and also coordinated and monitored the responsibilities of their counterparts in the thirty-five European subsidiaries. The general managers of the subsidiaries also reported to the European group executive. In theory, over fifty executives reported to this man, an impossibly wide span of control. In practice, however, most of the day-to-day problems were handled by the staff officers and their departments, and the European group executive was directly involved only in policy matters, crisis situations, and divergences from the firm's short-term and long-term plans.

Other firms have been introducing elements of a grid structure for parts of their operations. Monsanto, for instance, has established groups with shared responsibilities for some of its foreign subsidiaries.[8] In general, however, firms have been introducing such changes only slowly. Abandoning the principle of unity of command in favor of shared responsibility requires considerable adjustment in management thinking. Because no clear methods of making the new system work effectively have been developed, managers are reluctant to abandon the old system.

Yet there are pressures forcing managers to change. And these pressures are not encountered solely in the largest multinational enterprises. Managing a set of small-scale diversified operations in foreign markets can sometimes be more difficult than managing larger operations. Particularly when different product lines share common production facilities, there are pressures to introduce some form of shared responsibility. One medium-sized firm was forced to share responsibilities between product divisions and an international division early in its expansion into Europe. In an interview, the chairman of this firm described the situation as follows:

Some of our plants in Europe produce for the local market the products of three of our domestic divisions. The economics of the businesses are such that, with small operations, we are forced to use production facilities in this way. Most of the products require very close technical links with the divisions here. At the same time, many of our best customers in Europe are our best customers here. They buy a wide range of our products and need to be treated differently from our other European customers. We are constantly improving the way we manage these European businesses, but we know that we have a long way to go before we find good answers to the problems. One of our major problems is that of control. Each division here has its own set of control procedures. But we cannot use these procedures when production is shared. How to make the right adaptations to meet our European needs is a constant headache.

Sharing responsibilities among different groups of managers is not a phenomenon restricted to multinational enterprises. Many domestic enterprises have been developing what has been called "program management teams." [9] These teams are, sometimes only temporarily, responsible for activities that cut across the boundaries of the divisions in a Stage 3 structure. In addition, the use of project management teams in high-technology industries, such as aerospace, creates many of the problems encountered in a grid structure, at least for the duration of the project. [10] Domestic firms engaged in these developments often combine parts of the normal line and staff duties in "semioperating" assignments. They have found that, although areas of responsibility become hard to define, such assignments work reasonably well. The problems they face are similar to those in multinational firms, although they appear to be more severe for the multinational firms.

Management Development

As firms move toward the full implementation of a grid structure, the demands on the managers increase. In order to make the grid structure work effectively, the managers must be capable of responding to the conflicting demands of their product and area supervisors. They must also be capable of managing all the different reporting relationships that are essential for the maintenance of adequate communication. Furthermore, they must be prepared to accept wide responsibilities without having as much specialized staff support as is provided in more formal structures. Men with special managerial qualities are needed for these broad-gauge assignments. They need to have extensive training and experience before they can become effective. As always in such pioneer situations, much of the training is inevitably of the "training by experience" variety.

One trend in training appears, however, to be emerging in many multinational firms. Personal experience of international operations is becoming increasingly important for the senior managers in the central office. Many presidents of multinational enterprises, including Colgate-Palmolive and Sterling Drug, were in charge of international divisions earlier in their careers.[11] The experience of senior executives in international business can help greatly to reduce the communication problems that exist between domestic and foreign units.[12]

The extensive management development programs that some multinational enterprises maintain appear designed to create an élite cadre of men who all know one another and who share operàting experience in different types of managerial activity. The purpose of creating these élites is to foster an environment in which men who are physically distant at any one time can communicate easily and informally. If men share common experience and perceive themselves as having similar status in the hierarchy, they generally cooperate more readily than they would in other circumstances.[13] Informal links among the members of the élite help to compensate for the absence of many formal reporting relationships and reduce the demand for specialized staff.

The existence of an élite cadre in a multinational enterprise does not necessarily mean that all decisions and actions are taken on a collective basis. Rather the élite is composed of a group of men who personify the spirit or style of management judged to be most effective for the type of complex activities the enterprise has undertaken. This spirit is based on an acceptance among managers at all levels in the hierarchy of common goals, and permeates far beyond the confines of the élite. Unilever, for example, places a high premium on the ability of men to maintain this spirit of co-operation. One director of Unilever stated that "we try to instill in our managers a spirit of mutual trust and esteem, an attitude that is compatible with discipline, but not with senior formality or junior secretiveness." [14]

As the boundaries between divisions in a global structure become in-creasingly blurred, the emphasis shifts from hierarchical to contractual management. Greater reliance is placed on the capabilities and adaptabil-ity of the managers at each link in the organization. How well these men will perform under the pressures of a grid structure remains to be seen. Ensuring that managers do not lose their effectiveness as their jobs broaden in scope and complexity remains a challenge for multinational enterprises.

Planning and Control

Planning and control activities provide the thread of cohesion that binds together the scattered units of any diversified firm. But among multina-tional enterprises, the formal parts of these activities have an especially crucial role, as they substitute for many of the informal processes by which information is transferred within a domestic firm.

There are severe difficulties in formulating adequate plans for interna-tional activities. The complexities of the task are so great that few firms plan for foreign markets in as detailed a form as they typically do for the domestic market.[15] Part of the reason for this apparent inconsistency is that most of the planners are in the central office. They tend to devote most of their energies to the United States because that is the area they know best. Some planning activity, of course, goes on in each foreign sub-sidiary. But these plans have to be evaluated centrally, and modified if necessary to meet the needs of the firm's overall international strategy. Many firms have found it difficult to determine how much planning is needed at the local level and how much is needed centrally. The location of the planner, no matter how broad his knowledge and perspective, can greatly influence the plans he generates.

Some of the problems of finding an appropriate balance between central and local planning are reduced as a firm gains experience with an annual planning cycle. Nevertheless, many of the inevitable problems remain. Par-ticularly troublesome are the problems of estimating the effect of changes that involve several separate units of the firm; each unit is likely to hold its own individual views of the matter.

Similar problems exist in the development of appropriate control procedures. It is often enormously difficult to establish procedures that meet the needs of both the central office and the subsidiaries. Men in the central office very often request too much information simply because they are unsure of precisely what it is they are attempting to control.[16] Men in the subsidiaries often withhold information because they consider the requests to be an infringement of their autonomy.[17]

As with planning, experience helps to ease but does not eliminate the problem of control. A firm may judge that control by exception is appropriate for a seasoned international manager with an outstanding track record, whereas close control is required for less experienced managers. In the Armstrong Cork Company, for example, well established subsidiaries are allowed considerably more autonomy in short-term financial management than are new subsidiaries.[18] In such cases, however, the autonomy is likely to be much more apparent than real, and to be possible only because the manager is known to be conditioned to predictable patterns of behavior that are in line with the policies of the firm.

Moves toward a system of shared responsibilities require changes that add further difficulties in both the planning and control systems. To be effective, a control system must take into account those aspects of a man's job over which he does not have sole responsibility. In the planning process, a similar and equally difficult problem exists. If the cooperative behavior of the managers becomes too great, the agreed plans can turn out to be the lowest common denominator among the alternatives. On the other hand, provided that managers share common goals, competition and conflict among them can spur the search for better alternatives and improve the quality of the eventual decisions.[19] Yet too much conflict prevents the desired cooperation.

An example of how one multinational firm has responded to these problems is the OST (Objectives, Strategies, and Tactics) system that Texas Instruments has developed. The system uses a matrix of corporate objectives and plans to bind together all the seventy-seven profit centers, which are organized in four worldwide product divisions. Planning is carried out at all levels in the firm. The plans are coordinated centrally to ensure that potential opportunities requiring cooperative action among the profit centers are not overlooked, and to identify the expected contribution of each profit center to the overall effort.[20]

In the normal fashion, the short-term action plans are the basis for the control system. But the OST system has an important difference. Expenditures on long-range projects are carefully segregated from short-term, operating expenses. Managers are evaluated both on their short-term performance, and on the progress they have made toward completing their long-range projects. This distinction is needed to "counter the drainage of strategic resources into short-term problems." [21]

In effect, managers in Texas Instruments share responsibilities for planning, but they do not share responsibilities for action. After six years of development, many problems remain to be solved before the system works as smoothly in practice as it should. Even so, senior executives in the firm consider that the system has become successful, and attribute much of that success to the organizational "culture" that has emerged as managers have learned how to use the system.

Shared responsibilities for actions as well as for planning have become an integral part of the management system used by Caterpillar. This firm seems to have been highly successful in integrating all the units in its structure of area divisions. A *Business International* report in 1967 described the reasons for this apparent success:

This is partly because the top management of the company has successfully communicated overall policies to all the top officers (and low echelon managers as well). It is partly because the top officers have all worked for the company for many years, know each other well, and respect each other. It is partly because Caterpillar, despite its size and rapid growth, is a specialized company, manufacturing a comparatively narrow range of products—earth-moving equipment. . . . It is partly because the company has succeeded in fully rationalizing the components in its products. . . . And it is partly because the buyers of the company's earth-moving equipment are similar throughout the world, and marketing, sales financing, and after-sales servicing policies are similar everywhere.[22]

Maintaining the delicate balance between the conflicting needs for cooperation and autonomy is generally easier under stable conditions of operation than when there is considerable change. Under conditions less stable and less specialized than those in Caterpillar, there are likely to be many cracks in the organizational architecture of shared responsibilities. Managers become notably reticent when asked about how they paper over the cracks. Statements such as "we maintain a system of creative conflict" or "it works simply because we are all determined that it should" are common. These typical responses suggest that managers cannot fully explain how the system functions, though they feel that it does work. The challenge for the future is the development of more clearly understood and better solutions to the problems of maintaining a growing and efficient organization.

Part II
STRATEGY AND OWNERSHIP POLICIES

SEVEN / Choosing Ownership Policies for Foreign Subsidiaries

The Businessman's Point of View

In the first part of this study, the problem of control over the foreign subsidiary has been viewed primarily as one internal to the organization. The task has been viewed as that of deciding on a structure that generates the required area or product coordination. However, when a manager decides to set up some kind of facility outside the enterprise's home country, he faces other decisions that have a significant influence on the amount of control that the multinational enterprise will be able to exercise over the new entity. Among the most important is whether the enterprise should undertake the operations alone or whether a partner should be included.[1]

Opinions of businessmen as to whether a partner should be included in a foreign subsidiary have varied greatly. Some managers have condemned joint ventures unequivocally:

General Motors holds that unified ownership for coordinated policy control of all of its operations throughout the world is essential for its effective performance as a world-wide corporation.[2]

Others have praised them. An official of the Celanese Corporation declared:

I have a strong opinion that every company establishing a manufacturing facility in Mexico, or anywhere else for that matter, should organize it as a venture jointly owned with local capital.[3]

The actual behavior of American firms abroad has reflected these widely varying attitudes. In the group of 187 American-based multinational enterprises covered in this study, some had a high propensity for setting up partnership arrangements in their foreign operations; others were obviously avoiding such arrangements.

A few preliminary words are needed in order to clear the decks of confusing terminology. The phrase "joint venture" has been used in different contexts. Sometimes it has been used to refer to partnerships between enterprises that were sharing costs and risks for the development of a project in some remote country that was "foreign" to all the partners. Arrangements of this sort are not the focus of this study. Instead, we concentrate on arrangements under which equity is shared between a foreign firm and local owners. The local owners, as it turns out, are usually one or a small number of private partners holding large blocks of shares. There are a few cases where the partnership is between a foreign firm and a large number of local shareholders.[4] There are also a very few cases in which the local partner turns out to be a government agency.[5]

One additional point. The issue of ownership seems to be much more critical for manufacturing subsidiaries than for sales offices and other types of operations. That is one reason why this study deals primarily with overseas facilities that include manufacturing in their activities.[6]

Table 7-1 offers a picture of the extent to which U.S.-based multinational enterprises were involved in joint ventures in their overseas manufacturing operations in 1966. The table, like most of those that follow it, covers only those countries in which the enterprises were presumed to have some choice in the matter of ownership; it excludes subsidiaries located in Japan, Spain, Ceylon, India, Mexico, and Pakistan.

TABLE 7-1 *Multinational Enterprises, Classified by Percentage of Their Foreign Manufacturing Subsidiaries That Were Joint Ventures in 1966*[a]

Percentage of enterprise's foreign manufacturing subsidiaries that were joint ventures	Number of enterprises
None	33
1-10	17
11-20	27
21-40	43
41-60	38
61-80	17
81-99	10
100	2
Total	187

[a]Excludes subsidiaries in Japan, Spain, Ceylon, India, Mexico, and Pakistan.

As the table shows, only thirty-three of the 187 firms had no foreign joint ventures at all; and only two had partners in all their overseas manufacturing subsidiaries. More than a third of the enterprises had partners in at least 40 percent of their foreign manufacturing operations in countries where the enterprise has some freedom of choice.

The propensity for joint ventures can, of course, be measured by the output of joint venture plants rather than by the number of subsidiaries that have partners. That approach, however, produces the same disparate results. In response to a questionnaire that we sent the firms, the ninety-nine enterprises that responded exhibited the patterns that are shown in Table 7-2. In nearly a third of the enterprises, more than 40 percent of foreign manufacturing was done in joint ventures. At the same time, in one sixth of the firms no manufacturing at all was done through partnership arrangements.

TABLE 7-2 *Multinational Enterprises, Classified by Percentage of Their Foreign Manufacturing Accounted for by Joint Ventures*

Percentage of enterprise's foreign manufacturing that was accounted for by joint ventures	Number of enterprises
None	16
Less than 20	48
20-40	6
40-60	6
60-80	9
More than 80	14
Total	99

The literature on joint ventures has done little thus far to explain the wide ranges in attitudes and actions of businessmen toward the inclusion of partners in foreign operations. What this study suggests is that much of the variation can be understood as a rational response of different kinds of enterprises to the costs and benefits that are associated with such arrangements. Both joint ventures and wholly owned subsidiaries offer their special advantages and their special disadvantages. Local partners can bring to the multinational enterprise benefits such as management, capital, and access to markets. The absence of partners, however, offers freedom from interference by outsiders in decisions that influence the multinational firm. This study shows that for some kinds of enterprises the contributions that a partner could make outweighed the dilution of control that accompanied joint ventures. In other firms, the importance to the multinational enterprise of retaining control over certain decisions has been much greater than the contributions that a partner could make. The manager must consider some very specific characteristics of his firm when he is deciding on an ownership policy. Since these characteristics change as the enterprise develops, he will have to review the appropriateness of his policies from time to time.

The value to the multinational enterprise of the contributions from a partner might well depend on the strategy of the firm and on the availability of the contributed factor within the firm or from other sources. One might guess, for example, that a potential partner's contribution of capital would be highly valued by the firms that had little excess cash, but not by firms that were highly liquid. The firms that were short of cash might be more often willing to sacrifice some control to gain needed capital than were the firms that had excess cash. In other cases, the needed resource would not be cash but something else—knowledge of the local market, for example. Firms that had developed standard marketing programs which they used throughout the world, though, would, presumably, have less use for a partner's contribution in the marketing area than firms that had not. For the firms with standard marketing programs, the benefits of control might generally outweigh the contribution of a partner.

Could the particular strategy of a firm be related systematically, then, to the value of the benefits and costs of having local partners? The first step in an effort to find out was to determine how businessmen perceived the contributions of local partners. We asked the principal international executives of 155 multinational enterprises that had agreed to cooperate in the study to tell us how important various contributions of local partners had been to overseas manufacturing operations. Those with joint ventures were asked to answer:

Of what importance have your foreign joint venture partners' contributions of the following been to your overseas operations at the time of your entry into your foreign joint ventures?

  (a) general managers?
  (b) capital?
  (c) marketing personnel?
  (d) better access to the foreign local market for goods produced outside of it?
  (e) better access to the local market for goods produced by your joint venture(s) than would have been possible with a wholly owned subsidiary?
  (f) experienced production personnel, R&D, or other technical skills?
  (g) general knowledge of the local economy, local politics and customs?
  (h) access to local raw materials or components?
  (i) speed of entry into the local market?
  (j) other (specify)?

Answering on a descending scale from "6" ("very important") to "0" ("no importance whatsoever"), the ninety-nine managers who responded ranked the contribution of the local partner as follows:

CONTRIBUTION	MEAN OF ANSWERS FOR IMPORTANCE
1. General knowledge of local economy, politics, customs (g)	4.830
2. Speed of entry (i)	4.019
3. General managers (a)	3.434
4. Access to market for local goods (e)	3.340
5. Marketing personnel (c)	3.283
6. Capital (b)	2.660
7. Access to local raw materials (h)	2.596
8. Production, personnel, R&D skills (f)	2.453
9. Access to market for foreign goods (d)	2.451

Thirteen firms elected to mention contributions not on the list. Seven of these said that partners enabled them to meet government requirements for local ownership or they provided political advantages. Two enterprises mentioned that the partners had brought complementary product lines to the venture.

To determine what costs were associated with having partners, we asked the managers of firms with joint ventures to answer the following question:

Of what importance have the following policy decisions been as a source of problems between your firm and its foreign joint venture partners?

    (a)   pricing of products produced by joint ventures?
    (b)   product quality standards?
    (c)   brand names to be used?
    (d)   distribution channels, customer financing, after-sales service policy, or other marketing policies?
    (e)   amounts to be budgeted for marketing and promotion?
    (f)   markets to which the joint venture might export?
    (g)   prices at which you sell components or raw materials to joint venture subsidiaries?
    (h)   rationalization of production among your subsidiaries in a given area overseas?
    (i)   retention of earnings vs. the payment of dividends by the joint venture?
    (j)   new product introductions?
    (k)   other (specify)?

The overall results indicated the following importance of problems:

PROBLEM	MEAN OF ANSWERS FOR IMPORTANCE
1. Retention of earnings vs. dividends (i)	3.058
2. Export market allocation (f)	2.712
3. Prices at which components or raw materials are sold to joint venture subsidiaries (g)	2.250

PROBLEM	MEAN OF ANSWERS FOR IMPORTANCE
4. Distribution channels, customer financing, after-sales service policy, or other marketing policies (d)	2.250
5. Amounts to be budgeted for marketing and promotion (e)	1.942
6. Rationalization of production within a given area (h)	1.827
7. New product introduction (j)	1.808
8. Pricing of products of joint venture (a)	1.682
9. Product quality standards (b)	1.673
10. Brand names to be used (c)	1.314

Four firms added other problems. These were conflicts over royalty payments and over expansion of plant, problems with local tax concessions, and differences between the partners in attitudes toward management philosophy and labor relations.

The variation in responses among the enterprises was especially evident. For contributions from local partners, only "general knowledge" was ranked consistently high by the respondents. Most firms have found local partners to be useful in providing knowledge of the local economic and political situation. The evaluation of the partners' contributions of three "factors of production," general management, capital, and marketing inputs (access to markets and marketing personnel), turned out, along with speed of entry, to be useful in linking the attitudes of the enterprise toward local partners to the strategy of the enterprise.

There were other patterns that seemed to be related to strategy. For example, certain kinds of problems, as perceived by the managers, tended to appear together. Managers that expressed a high degree of concern over problems of "production rationalization" also tended to show concern with problems of transfer pricing and problems associated with export marketing.[7]

In order to move from general impressions such as these to a classification of each firm according to its perception of the relative importance of the different benefits and problems, we had to make some adjustments to the responses. In effect, each firm had to be classified on the basis of the sequences in which it ordered the various contributions or problems, not on the basis of the actual number that it assigned to the importance. For example, consider the case of a firm that evaluated all the contributions as "2," except for "capital" which it evaluated as "4," and compare it with the case of another firm that evaluated everything except capital as "6," but evaluated capital as "4." If one were to compare the two firms based on an average of their answers for capital, both would evaluate it as "4." However, relative to the other contributions, the first firm clearly ranks capital higher than does the second one.

To adjust for different interpretations of the scales, we related a firm's scoring of each factor to its average rating for all factors. The "normalized" value for any factor would be the difference between its value as assigned by the firm and the average for all the factors rated by the firm. For the first hypothetical firm above, the "normalized" rating for capital would be

$$4 - \frac{4 + (8 \times 2)}{9} = 1.78.$$

For the second firm, the normalized rating would be

$$4 - \frac{4 + (8 \times 6)}{9} = -1.77.$$

This "normalized" evaluation played an important role in the analysis of how firms that were following different strategies differed in their evaluation of the costs and benefits of joint ventures. It is used each time we compare the answers for different groups of firms.

The Government Point of View

Government policy makers seem to be only a little more united than businessmen in their view of the advantages of joint ventures. Japan, Spain, Ceylon, India, Mexico, and Pakistan are often cited as countries that have insisted that foreign-owned enterprises which want to manufacture locally must find local partners. The behavior of these countries seems, on the surface, to have been rather erratic. For example, in the least developed countries on this list—Ceylon, India, Mexico, and Pakistan—31 percent of the manufacturing subsidiaries formed between 1960 and 1967 by the 187 firms that we examined were wholly owned by the multinational enterprise. But the numbers varied from 3 percent for India to 66 percent for Ceylon. Even Japan allowed 11 percent of the foreign operations established in this period to be wholly owned by the multinational firm.

Many less developed countries not on this list have paid frequent lip service to the idea of joint ventures. However, Table 7-3 shows that the less developed countries have ended up with about the same percentage of majority and minority joint ventures as the advanced countries, even though the latter have placed less stress on the issue of local ownership.[8] These data seem to reveal no pattern in the outcome of the encounters between government and foreign firm over ownership.

E*

TABLE 7-3 *Multinational Enterprises' Foreign Manufacturing Subsidiaries in Existence in 1966: Subsidiaries Classified by Ownership and by Country of Incorporation*

Multinational enterprise's ownership at time of entry	Country of incorporation			
	Advanced countries except Japan and Spain		Less developed countries except Ceylon, India, Mexico, and Pakistan	
	No. of subs.	%	No. of subs.	%
Wholly owned (95-100%)	944	62.9	789	60.5
Majority owned (51-94%)	215	14.3	210	16.1
Minority owned (5-50%)	341	22.7	305	23.4
Total	1,500	100%	1,304	100%

Nonetheless, this study suggests that there have been systematic patterns in the results of the negotiations between the multinational enterprises and the host governments that prefer joint ventures. The ability of the host government to induce the foreign investor to include more local ownership in his facilities has varied with certain characteristics of the country and with the strategy of the particular multinational enterprise.

Whether the net benefits that the host government receives from joint ventures outweigh those that come with wholly foreign subsidiaries is, however, not clear. This study suggests that any simple conclusion in this complicated field is dangerous. The behavior of the multinational enterprise toward its joint ventures and its treatment of wholly owned subsidiaries differ in very complex ways. There are cases in which joint ventures may bring benefits to the host country, such as relieving pressure on the balance of payments by reducing payments abroad. But wholly owned subsidiaries may also bring benefits not offered by joint ventures. Wholly foreign operations have, for example, supplied export markets that were not available to joint ventures. The relationship of the costs to the benefits for the host country depends on the country's objectives. But before the government policy maker can proceed with this analysis, he must understand a great deal about the motivations of the multinational enterprise.

EIGHT / The Drive for Unambiguous Control

Multinational enterprises that prefer wholly owned subsidiaries to joint ventures clearly have their reasons. In some cases, the resources that a local partner could bring to the venture were resources that the firm had in rather abundant supply. Accepting some dilution of control in order to secure a contribution of dubious value hardly made sense. In most cases in which firms showed a strong preference for wholly owned subsidiaries, the issue of control appeared to be paramount. Although some of the contributions of local partners could have been of value to the multinational enterprise, retention of unambiguous control of foreign operations was critical to the success of the firm's strategy. A local joint venture partner is rarely a completely passive shareholder.[1] When the policies of the foreign parent appear to harm his interests, there is a strong possibility that the local partner will make himself heard. When the conflicts are likely to occur over decisions that affect policies which are of great importance to the multinational enterprise, the local partner is difficult to tolerate.

In earlier chapters, a case was made that the structure of a multinational enterprise could be associated with its strategy. Certain strategies demanded tight central controls; others did not. It turned out that the same strategies that are generally effected through a tightly controlled organization are also usually associated with a strong preference for wholly owned subsidiaries.

What are these strategies? They include: (1) use of marketing techniques to differentiate products, (2) rationalization of production facilities to reduce manufacturing costs, (3) control of raw materials, and (4) development of new products ahead of competitors. For each of these groups of firms, the need for control over subsidiaries has been the critical factor that has led to a preference for wholly owned operations. The choice was, in most cases, bolstered by the low value that the firms placed on the contributions that local partners could make to the enterprise.

Of course, many enterprises have followed complex strategies that have changed over time. The ownership patterns for some of the subsidiaries will reflect preferences that result from decisions made under older strategies within the same firm. In part of the analysis that follows, we will attempt to place some firms into boxes that correspond neatly to particular strategies. We will, for example, examine the ownership of foreign manufacturing subsidiaries of firms that are marketing oriented as if all the ownership decisions were the result of this single strategy. For some firms, this crude approach seems appropriate. At other times, the occasion will call for the multinational enterprise to be broken down into smaller pieces. For example, the ownership patterns for subsidiaries that manufacture old product lines are different from those that make new products. For firms that are diversifying rapidly, this distinction is very important. These types of subsidiaries are examined separately. An effort to evaluate the effects of strategies that change over time will be left for a later chapter.

Strategies that Concentrate on Marketing Techniques

Firms that rely heavily on a strategy of product differentiation through advertising have a strong preference for subsidiaries that are wholly owned (95 percent or more) by the multinational firm. Figure 8-1 relates the level of expenditures on advertising to the form of ownership of foreign manufacturing subsidiaries.[2] The data demonstrate clearly that the firms that turned heavily to advertising to create a barrier to entry have been very reluctant to have joint ventures. The aversion to minority-held interests is particularly strong, a relationship that will appear repeatedly in the tables that follow. As a matter of fact, though the chart does not show it, half the firms with expenditures of over 10 percent of sales on advertising entered no joint ventures at all between 1961 and 1967. There were two firms with large expenditures on advertising that appeared on first impression to be "misfits," since joint ventures accounted for more than 30 percent of their new subsidiaries. But one of these firms had converted all its joint ventures to wholly owned subsidiaries by 1966. Apparently this enterprise found that it could not live with the problems that were caused by the conflicts or potential conflicts with partners. In the other firm, all the joint ventures lay in products that were outside the main industry of the parent, that is, products that were probably not accounting for the large advertising expenditures.

Which were the firms that had large expenditures on advertising? Most were manufacturers of food, beverages, and detergent products, such as Kellogg, and Procter and Gamble. There were a few other firms that seemed to be marketing oriented but which did not get picked up by the

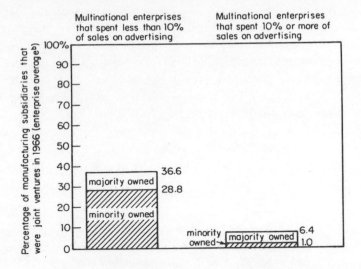

Figure 8–1   *Relative Importance of Joint Ventures*
among Multinational Enterprises:
Enterprises Classified by Level
of Reported Advertising Expenditures
in 1966 [a]

[a] Excludes extractive enterprises and subsidiaries in Japan, Spain, Ceylon, India, Mexico, and Pakistan.
[b] The percentage was first calculated for each enterprise. Then the percentages for all the enterprises in the category were averaged.
SOURCE: Advertising expenditures from *News Front,* March 1966.

advertising measure, since they did relatively little direct advertising to the consumer. A check of such firms, such as the ethical drug firms, indicated that they also had a strong preference for wholly owned manufacturing facilities abroad.[3]

The general preference of marketing-oriented firms for wholly owned facilities has been a result of two factors: the availability of marketing skills within the firms and the commitment to a given marketing strategy. These factors have led such enterprises to place a low value on the contributions of local partners in the marketing area. In addition, control over marketing policies in the subsidiaries has been critical to the strategy of the firm. This centralized control would lead to conflict if a partner were present at the subsidiary level.

Some evidence for this conclusion came from the responses of the international managers to the questionnaire. Although the previous chapter indicated that multinational enterprises generally perceive marketing knowl-

edge as an important contribution of the joint venture partner, the firms
with a marketing orientation did not value this contribution as highly as
did other firms. Table 8-1 distinguishes the responses of the four firms
with large expenditures on advertising that answered the questionnaire
from those of the rest, when asked to rate the importance of the local partner's contribution of marketing personnel and of access to the market for
foreign-produced goods. The firms with large advertising expenditures
failed to value these contributions as highly as did the other firms. The relationships held for the unadjusted data. But they also held when the answers were "normalized" according to the procedure described in Chapter
7, that is, by rating each firm's evaluation in relation to its evaluation of
other contributions of the local partner.

TABLE 8-1   *Local Partners' Contribution of Marketing Skills as Perceived by
Multinational Enterprises: Enterprises Classified by Level of
Reported Advertising Expenditures in 1966*[a]

Local partners' contribution of	Multinational enterprises that spent less than 10% of sales on advertising		Multinational enterprises that spent 10% or more of sales on advertising[b]	
	Average rating, scale of 0 (low) to 6 (high)	Normalized rating[c]	Average rating, scale of 0 (low) to 6 (high)	Normalized rating
Marketing personnel	3.172	−0.035	1.250	−1.444
Access to market for foreign goods	2.679	−0.492	2.000	−0.694

[a]Excludes extractive enterprises.
[b]Only four firms in this category answered the questionnaire.
[c]For definition, see Chapter 7.
Source: Advertising expenditures from *News Front*, March 1966.

Note how this conclusion relates to the product life cycle concepts that
proved so helpful in earlier chapters. Many of the firms with high advertising expenditures have standardized elements of their marketing techniques
around the world. As a rule, very large expenditures on marketing were
also associated with mature products. Since such products were likely to be
at the same stages of the product life cycle in different countries, the firm
has been able to standardize elements of the marketing mix around the
world. By contrast, the firm with a newer line was likely to face markets at
different stages of development in various countries. A particular marketing technique in the American market, in which the product was close to

being a "necessity," would be different from one for Spain, for example, where the product was still regarded as a luxury item. However, a very old product would be much closer to being a necessity in all markets.

The strategies of firms that have used standardized marketing techniques in different national markets are well illustrated by the examples of soft drink firms. In an earlier chapter, we briefly mentioned the standard marketing programming in Pepsi-Cola's strategy. Coca-Cola, in addition to having standard marketing programs, has been described as sending "to all its local managers a suitcase packed with materials including a bible which gives all the ads to be printed in color, those to appear in black and white, the number of times it can be full page or half page, and so on. The suitcase specifies each photo, every line of copy to be used, and the tapes of music to be played over radio. The local managers can do nothing on their own without first clearing it with headquarters in Atlanta." [4] The policies of Heinz, as described by another author, sound slightly less universal, but the importance of transferring marketing programs from one country to another is emphasized.[5] And as most international travellers noticed, a few years ago a large number of the world's automobile owners, though located in many different countries, were simultaneously considering putting tigers in their tanks. It is not surprising that these firms are not eager for local marketing inputs.

In addition, firms that rely heavily on a marketing strategy generally recognize that they would most likely have serious conflicts with joint venture partners.[6] Decisions in this important area, as earlier chapters have indicated, are usually made at a level in the organization that is above the individual subsidiary. The literature on joint ventures is full of the history of conflicts between multinational enterprises and local partners over marketing policies. Interviews with executives of enterprises that were included in this study brought out evidence of such conflicts. A manager of one of the firms with large expenditures in advertising said that it would "be difficult to get minority holders to accept a policy [of large expenditures on advertising] which would mean no dividends for five or six years." Managers described conflicts over channels of distribution, marketing messages, and pricing strategies. Two studies of American investment in Japan described in some detail cases of joint ventures where conflicts over marketing and distribution were important.[7] According to one of these studies, marketing problems provided the greatest source of conflict between the foreign and Japanese partners.

Despite the generalization that marketing-oriented firms are likely to avoid joint ventures, some of them have found that local partners can make useful contributions in certain cases. If the market is sufficiently large, a special marketing program is sometimes worth developing. In that case, the objection to a local partner is reduced because he may prove useful in providing local knowledge for the development of this program. The data provide some evidence to support this hypothesis. The joint ventures of the firms that had large expenditure on advertising seemed to be larger than the average subsidiary of these firms, suggesting that where the market is sufficiently important, the firm may value a local partner.

Whatever attractions a local partner may have in connection with the operation of manufacturing facilities, the attraction seems weaker where sales subsidiaries are concerned. Almost 90 percent of the sales subsidiaries of the multinational enterprises were wholly owned in 1966. When sales operations are involved, the tolerable choices facing the multinational enterprise seem to be a wholly owned subsidiary or the use of an independent importer and distributor. Either the multinational enterprise or the local distributor has the marketing skills. Neither potential partner needs to turn to someone else for the relatively little management and capital required, while the effects of dilution of control can be considerable. Since most of the purchases of the sales operations are from an affiliate, the primary determinant of profits in the sales operation is the transfer price. But the interests of the parties in any given price are very different. And an objective price for the transfer is often exceedingly difficult to determine. When the multinational enterprise has the marketing skills, the choice is generally a sales subsidiary—wholly owned, of course.

Though the decisions of marketing-oriented firms to choose wholly owned subsidiaries mean that they can exercise more control over their foreign operations, it also means that some of the benefits local partners can bring to an operation are sacrificed. A number of multinational enterprises have, however, found ways to obtain some of the advantages of overseas joint ventures, notably the contribution of management and capital by local partners, without yielding control over critical marketing decisions. We encountered many cases of a licensing arrangement whereby a local firm did only the manufacturing, contributing capital and management, while a wholly foreign-owned entity controlled the marketing. Such arrangements have been particularly common in the highly marketing-oriented food industry, especially for the bottling and marketing operations of soft drink firms. And they were not infrequent in other industries.[8]

Where local government has insisted on joint ventures for manufacturing, multinational enterprises have sometimes linked wholly owned sales operations with joint manufacturing operations. An example was Colgate's arrangement in Ceylon, where the government wanted joint ventures in manufacturing, but allowed wholly foreign operations in sales.[9] A Colgate sales subsidiary handled the output of its local jointly owned manufacturing subsidiary. Such arrangements have also been common in Japan.

Similar arrangements appeared where the multinational enterprise found itself under pressure to control distribution channels. When firms price identical products at different levels in various markets, that practice opens up the possibility of cross-shipments which would endanger the firms' pricing policies. In these situations, some of the multinational enterprises have maintained complete ownership of distribution channels. There is some evidence, for example, that control of distribution channels has been critical in the farm equipment industry to prevent shipment of tractors from one market to another.[10] At the same time, some of the enterprises feel content to use joint ventures or licensing arrangements for the manufacturing operations where control is less important.

Strategies Involving Rationalization of Production

As products mature, some enterprises rely principally on marketing techniques for survival. Another response to the threats that go with maturity, however, is an attempt to lower manufacturing costs. As a rule, such a strategy leads to the concentration of production in large plants and to the specialization of plants in different countries, as we described in Chapter 4. This specialization is especially likely to be found in industries where returns to scale are large. Some enterprises, such as the automobile firms, have responded to competitive pressures by using a number of common parts to assemble somewhat different final product models in various countries. Others, such as Singer, have filled in their product lines in each country by importing models manufactured in other countries.[11]

The result of a strategy of production rationalization is to vest production decisions in a level of the multinational enterprise that is higher than the subsidiary. As one writer said: "When there is an international dispersion and specialisation in the production-processes for products sold in various local markets ensuing intra-company deliveries, a need arises for central planning and coordination, which in most cases leads to a more or less centralised structure." [12] When a higher level of the organization has been required to decide which subsidiary can best manufacture each product, to determine the transfer prices that are to govern shipments among subsidiaries of parts, components, and assembled products, and to allocate markets to each operation, the possibility of conflicts of interest at the subsidiary level has been great. These conflicts have involved the very heart of the strategy of the enterprises concerned.

The issue is nicely illustrated by the case of Massey-Ferguson. The problem that Massey-Ferguson was facing at a critical point in its history, according to one account, was that competition was arising among the Massey-Ferguson units for export markets. The need, therefore, was "to coordinate manufacturing, marketing, engineering and inter-company movement of finished and component parts. . . ." [13] The potential conflicts with local partners in individual subsidiaries are easy to visualize.

The questionnaire responses summarized in Chapter 7 suggested that conflicts with partners over transfer prices, allocation of markets, and production rationalization were very much in the minds of the managers of multinational enterprises. The literature on foreign investment has frequently mentioned similar conflicts. In a description of the automobile industry's policies toward joint ventures, "the desire to integrate worldwide operations" was said to be an important factor pushing enterprises toward the elimination of locally held stock.[14] Conflicts with a partner interested in maximizing profits in one country were seen as likely to upset the implementation of the strategy of the multinational enterprise.[15] Ford Motor Company's purchase of the minority interests in its British subsidiary in 1960 has been frequently cited as an example of the need for avoiding local participation in a subsidiary when production rationalization is becoming an important part of strategy.

Unfortunately, it is almost impossible to devise a direct measure of the degree of production rationalization in a multinational enterprise. An indirect measure that incorporates production rationalization and marketing orientation was, however, available in the form of the organizational structure of the multinational system. A firm that is following a strategy with heavy marketing orientation, or one with emphasis on the rationalization of production, or both, according to evidence presented in earlier chapters, is likely to be structured by geographical area, with either area organizations within the international division or an area breakdown at the divisional level. That relationship is reflected in the responses of area-organized firms to certain items of the questionnaire about joint ventures. Managers were asked:

How important to your firm (or division) is it to have the same policies worldwide or areawide (e.g., in Europe) with respect to subsidiaries:

    (a)   pricing of finished products?
    (b)   quality standards?
    (c)   product names?
    (d)   product design, models, or styles?

(e)   customer financing or after-sales service?
(f)   product mix?
(g)   dividend policy?
(h)   budgeting and control procedures?

On the "6" to "0" scale described earlier, the firms that were organized on an area basis attached significantly greater importance than the other firms to standardization of quality, name, design, and product mix. Table 8-2 presents the average evaluations of the importance of each policy for the two groups of firms.[16] Standardization of pricing and service policies seems to have been more a function of the transportability of the product across borders and whether service was important to performance.

TABLE 8-2 *Importance of Worldwide or Areawide Standardization of Various Policies as Perceived by Multinational Enterprises: Enterprises Classified by Their Organizational Structure*

Standardized policy	For multinational enterprises organized by area, average rating, scale of 0 (low) to 6 (high)	For multinational enterprises not organized by area, average rating, scale of 0 (low) to 6 (high)
Pricing of finished products	3.370	3.383
Quality standards	5.607	4.681
Product names	4.667	4.255
Product design, models, or styles	4.037	3.644
Financing and after-sales service	2.357	2.511
Product mix	2.077	1.872

With organizational structure as a surrogate measure for strategy, the data on the relationship between ownership and strategy proved striking. In 1966, the fifty-five firms with area organizations had only 16 percent of their manufacturing subsidiaries jointly owned; the ninety-one firms organized on other lines had 39 percent in joint ventures.[17] For subsidiaries in which the multinational parent had only a minority interest, the differences between the two groups of firms are even more impressive. While 25 percent of the manufacturing operations of the enterprises organized on a basis other than geography were minority-held joint ventures, only 7 percent of the manufacturing subsidiaries of the area-organized firms were mi-

116   STRATEGY AND OWNERSHIP POLICIES

nority owned. An examination of subsidiaries that were set up more recently, between 1960 and 1967, revealed the same pattern.

The use of organizational structure as a surrogate for policy seems to be justifiable, based on the findings of earlier chapters. However, that kind of classification has its risks. As a further check on the link between strategy and ownership, a comparison was made directly between the firm's indication of the importance of standardizing certain policies and the ownership of manufacturing subsidiaries. The assumption was that firms which placed a value on the importance of standardization of policies concerning product design or product mix tended to pursue centralized marketing strategies or production rationalization. Accordingly, the multinational enterprises were classified by their answers to the questions on these policies. Firms that scored the importance of both kinds of policies as "5" or "6" were considered to evaluate this kind of standardization as "very important." If one or the other policy was scored as "5" or "6", the firm was classified as putting "important" emphasis on standardization. Table 8-3

TABLE 8-3 *Relative Importance of Joint Ventures among Foreign Manufacturing Subsidiaries of Multinational Enterprises: Enterprises Classified by Their Perceived Need for Standardization of Product Design and Product Mix*[a]

	Firms for which standardized product design and product mix was reported as:		
	Unimportant[b]	Important[b]	Very important[b]
Joint ventures as a percentage of all manufacturing subsidiaries existing in 1966			
All joint ventures	*39.7%*	*30.6%*	*26.4%*
Majority joint ventures	15.2	12.1	3.5
Minority joint ventures	24.5	18.5	22.9
Joint ventures as a percentage of all manufacturing subsidiaries entered between 1960 and 1967			
All joint ventures	*47.2%*	*40.1%*	*39.8%*
Majority joint ventures	20.4	15.3	18.8
Minority joint ventures	26.8	24.8	21.0

[a]Excludes extractive enterprises and subsidiaries in Japan, Spain, Ceylon, India, Mexico, and Pakistan.
[b]Enterprises that reported the importance of both product design and product mix standardization at values lower than 5 were placed in the "unimportant" category; those that scored one or the other at 5 or more, in "important"; those that scored both at values of 5 or more in "very important."

shows that firms which rated standardization of product design and product mix as being "important" or "very important," according to this classification, had a greater propensity to have wholly owned subsidiaries than did the firms that rated standardization lower.

Strategies Based on Control of Raw Materials

Although most of the analysis so far has centered on the manufacturing subsidiaries of multinational enterprises, some of the underlying principles bear just as much on the ownership patterns associated with subsidiaries devoted to the extraction of raw materials. As in the case of firms that have a strong marketing orientation and firms that rationalize their production facilities, the desire for control has usually led multinational enterprises to require wholly owned subsidiaries for extractive activities. Supporting this tendency has been the fact that local private entrepreneurs were rarely available with sufficient capital to participate in mining, oil, and plantation operations, which have tended to be very large in scale.

In the group of 187 multinational enterprises, 72 percent of the extractive operations that were organized as subsidiaries were wholly owned by one of the multinational firms. The great majority of the remaining extractive subsidiaries were joint ventures between two or more international competitors. In the advanced countries, one of the partners has often been from the country in which the extraction takes place; joint ventures between local and foreign firms for extraction in Australia and Canada have been common. For example, Broken Hill Proprietary Co. joined with American and Japanese firms for the development of iron ore resources in Australia.[18] However, in the less developed countries, the joint ventures have almost always been among foreign enterprises alone. U.S., Dutch, and Canadian firms have agreed to exploit nickel jointly in Indonesia;[19] Swedish, Italian, Belgian, and American steel companies have been involved together in a Liberian iron ore operation;[20] American, Canadian, French, German, and Italian firms negotiated together for rights jointly to extract bauxite from Guinea; and crude oil consortia have been common for the operation of concessions in the Middle East.

Arrangements of this sort between major international firms have not presented the same problems as the joint ventures that are the focus of this study. Issues concerning control could be negotiated in advance. The partners have had a common interest in the most critical element of control, namely keeping the raw material out of the hands of potential new entrants into the oligopoly. Each partner has been interested in obtaining raw materials of the proper quality and on a reliable schedule. Where common interests did not exist, that fact usually became clear at the very outset, before joint negotiations with the government had been completed. The objective in these joint ventures, apart from the development of common control, has generally been that of resource mobilization or risk reduction.

Extensive mobilization of resources has been called for because many extractive operations can be developed only on a large scale. The Mt. Newman project in Australia, for example, has involved an investment on the order of $250 million. In some cases, especially in the period before World War II, concessions for extractive activities covered large geographical areas.[21] To exploit even a significant proportion of the potential of such grants has meant a huge investment in development.[22]

Risk reduction has been important because of the size of the unknowns, at least at the outset. As a rule, little is known about the quality or comparative costs of extraction in advance. The oil may or may not exist. The copper ore may be known to exist, but little is known about what it will cost to bring it out to a seaport. The future political stability of the host country is often unpredictable; a change in government could lead to the source of supply being cut off at some time in the future. Enterprises facing these risks have looked for ways of spreading their investment over a large number of projects so that they would not be hurt too seriously if one operation should sour.

Closely related to the large size and substantial risks of most extractive ventures has been the need of the developers to provide assurance that customers exist for the output of the project. At the same time, users of the raw material have sought assurance of supplies for times of scarcity.

In industries in which the major suppliers of raw materials are vertically integrated, a user who does not have his own sources of raw materials may find it difficult to acquire them when they are scarce. With long lead times and large entry costs in the development of new sources of supply, mine owners are able to extract prices far above marginal costs in times of scarcity. In times of surplus, the extractive operation that has no ties to consumers finds it difficult to dispose of its output; prices on the merchant market approach marginal costs. There is, then, pressure for users to have tied sources. And there is pressure for the developer of an extractive operation to make sure that customers will take the output of the project. The result is frequently a joint venture that roughly matches the needs of the partners to the expected output of the mine. The arrangement usually calls for each partner to take a certain part of the output of the operation at prices that reflect average costs.[23]

A description of the background of one joint venture in aluminum indicates the importance that enterprises attach to linking their raw materials with the market. American Metals Climax, Sumitomo Chemical, Showa Denko, Holland Aluminium, and Vereinigte Aluminium-Werke pooled their interests in a bauxite and aluminum operation in the Kimberley region of Western Australia. The reason, according to *Business International,* was that "the inclusion of at least three international aluminum companies in the consortium provides a ready-made market for the aluminum produced and a source of financing for the project." [24]

Arrangements for extraction that include long-term sales contracts with international firms are sometimes difficult to distinguish from joint ventures. Some firms have provided debt financing for mining ventures in return for long-term contracts for a portion of the output. The low prices at which they take ore provides a return for the financing in a form that begins to resemble equity arrangements.

There have, of course, been numerous cases of equity sharing with host governments for extractive operations. When the joint ventures have been between foreign enterprises and local government partners, they were usually the result of a strong bargaining position on the part of the host government. [25] When the needed markets were not under the control of a small group of firms, governments have pushed hard and successfully for joint ventures. As the bargaining position of the foreign firm decreases, the local government generally has attempted to obtain a voice in management, or at least to acquire the appearance of having some control over the use of local resources. PERTAMINA in Indonesia and NIOC in Iran provide examples of government enterprises that participate actively in petroleum operations, reserving the right to review and to approve plans for expansion and plans for marketing the output.

Remember that we have been arguing only that the *extractive* operations of multinational enterprises generally avoid the use of local private partners. Firms that have mining and other resource-based activities do commonly seek local partners in their *manufacturing* operations. But that is a story to be covered when we turn again to some of these firms in the next chapter.

Strategies that Emphasize Innovation of Products

When firms follow a strategy based on the continuous generation of new products, the problem of controlling foreign subsidiaries takes on special importance. New product development is usually associated with heavy expenditures on research and development. As a rule, if U.S.-based multinational enterprises are involved, the expenditure occurs in the United States, close to the largest market for many new products.[26] Expenditure on R&D in the United States provides one measure of the firm's orientation toward product innovation. Figure 8-2 shows that high R&D expenditures as a percentage of sales have clearly been associated with a high preference for wholly owned subsidiaries. IBM is the case par excellence in this category.

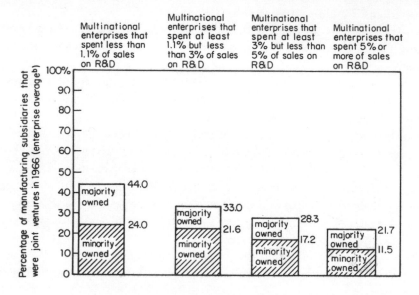

Figure 8–2   *Relative Importance of Joint Ventures*
among Multinational Enterprises:
Enterprises Classified by Their Expenditures
on Research and Development in 1966 [a]

[a] Excludes extractive enterprises and subsidiaries in Japan, Spain, Ceylon, India, Mexico, and Pakistan.
[b] See Figure 8–1.
SOURCE: R&D expenditures from *News Front,* November 1965 and January and February 1966, and annual reports of the firms.

One reason why high-technology firms prefer wholly owned subsidiaries is that they cannot easily arrive at arrangements with local partners that provide what they consider to be a fair return for the technology they contribute. Published statements of managers indicate that acceptable compensation for technology has been difficult to arrange. Typical is the following: "Minority shareholders just get a free ride." [27] The same report goes on: "This viewpoint is based on the fact that the foreign partner has developed and will continue to generate new products and technology in which it has proprietary rights. The local shareholders provide nothing, in this view, but receive a proportion of the profits based on the foreign partner's technical and marketing abilities." Similar terms have been used to describe the benefits that the local shareholders in IBM's single joint venture —in the United Kingdom—received from IBM's research.[28] Another interpretation of the same point is that these enterprises have a monopoly advantage gained from a technological lead. In a typical joint venture, a local partner shares in the monopoly rents without having contributed to the costs of developing the technology that gave rise to the rents. And it is next to impossible to require that a local partner's share be bought at the fully capitalized value of the research, if indeed this value can be determined.

A similar problem exists in any enterprise that transfers to a foreign subsidiary any valuable resource that has been developed in the United States, whether technology or something else. Payment by a joint venture partner is, in most cases, difficult to negotiate. The problem is probably less difficult for the firm that transfers marketing techniques than for the firm that transfers technology. The partner shares automatically in the local costs. Where marketing techniques are transferred, the local costs of utilizing the asset represent a much higher portion of the total costs of the asset than when transfers of technology are involved. In the case of the R&D-oriented firms, however, the major costs associated with the technology are sunk, remote, and intangible.

Some firms that are R&D oriented have, of course, found ways to recover a return on technology. In some cases, the foreign firm put up little or no cash for its equity. The enterprise can thus obtain a share of the profits greater than its direct cash investment in the subsidiary. For example, Rheem Manufacturing Company frequently obtained equity shares for know-how alone.[29] Interviews with eight chemical firms indicated that the managers were interested in joint ventures primarily when they could obtain equity without contributing anything other than know-how.[30]

A study of foreign investment in Japan showed the relative importance of capitalization of know-how in minority joint ventures.[31] According to the study, where the non-Japanese partner held 25–30 percent of the equity, about 50 percent of the contribution was capitalized as know-how. In 50/50 arrangements, know-how accounted for 25 percent of the non-Japanese contribution. Where the non-Japanese partner held over 50 percent of the equity, no know-how was capitalized.[32] Although many firms have traded technology for equity in joint ventures, the technique does not seem to provide all firms with what they consider to be fair compensation for their technology.

Royalty payments have served as another way for the multinational enterprise to capture some of the monopoly rents from a technological lead. In subsidiaries in which the enterprise holds all the equity, royalty payments are not needed to provide a return on technology. All the profits accrue to the multinational enterprise in any case—though even in this case royalties may play a role in reducing taxes or in moving profits through foreign exchange controls. However, in a joint venture, royalties play the additional role of distributing to one of the partners a share of the profits over and above the profits associated with his share of equity. There is some evidence that joint ventures pay larger royalties and fees for know-how and management than do wholly owned subsidiaries. For example, the interviews with chemical firms, referred to above, revealed that they more frequently required fees for technical service from their joint ventures than from wholly owned subsidiaries. By placing limits on the amount of royalty payments that can go abroad, many host governments do, however, restrict the ability of the multinational enterprise to use this means of recovering a return on technology.[33] But governments, as a rule, are more willing to allow payments for technology in the case of joint ventures than in cases where all the equity of the subsidiary is owned by foreigners.[34]

Even in cases where royalty fees or capitalization of know-how would allow the high-technology enterprise to receive an adequate return on its contribution of know-how, the firm still faces the problem of maintaining control over its technology. Critical know-how can slip out of the control of the parent through local partners. Interviews conducted in Indonesia suggested that there were cases in which the foreign partner was attempting to avoid revealing to the local partners how certain steps of the manufacturing process were carried out.[35] In these cases, the joint ventures had been formed under government pressure. A careful study of foreign investment in New Zealand mentioned the desire for secrecy on the part of foreign investors.[36] A confusing case involving the threat of a leak of technological know-how through a joint venture has been the Goodrich joint venture with N. V. Rubberfabriek Vredestein (RV) of Holland. According to *Business International,* Goodrich was trying to prevent the purchase of the partner's shares by Goodyear, since Goodyear would then have access to what Goodrich considered to be proprietary technical information.[37]

In some cases, the firm that is technologically oriented has been in a better position than other enterprises to resist government pressures to take in a partner. These enterprises have had a technology that was needed by the country so that manufacture of a certain product could be done locally. The government could turn to few other firms for the technology. For an advanced computer technology, for example, a country can turn only to IBM or a few other firms. In such situations the high-technology enterprise is in a strong bargaining position vis-à-vis host governments for its new products. The unsuccessful efforts of India and Japan to induce IBM to depart from its policy of limiting its investments to wholly owned facilities illustrate the point.[38] A study of petrochemical manufacturers confirmed the ability of firms to insist on complete ownership of facilities for new products, that is, for products that were in the early stages of the product life cycle. The firms were less able to do so as the technology became more widely available, primarily because of the large number of producers that were willing to grant licences.[39]

Although the fear of loss of control over technology and the difficulties of arranging compensation for contributions of technology lead many R&D-oriented firms to prefer wholly owned subsidiaries, there are a number of such enterprises that are willing to dilute control in order to secure contributions from local partners. These are principally the firms that have been using their R&D efforts to generate a wide line of new products. Such enterprises find themselves short of the marketing skills that they need to carry their new lines to other countries. Accordingly, the diversified firms with large R&D expenditures have entered joint ventures more frequently than have undiversified enterprises with large R&D expenditures.

Among high-R&D firms, the difference between those with little diversification and those with a great deal of diversification is illustrated by the contrasting cases of IBM and Union Carbide. As has been repeatedly observed, IBM has concentrated its large R&D expenditures on improving products in a narrow line of products, and has exhibited a strong aversion to joint ventures. On the other hand, Union Carbide, which generates new products to serve a wide range of customer needs, has frequently used joint ventures. In this case, the contributions of local partners, which have generally been in the marketing area, have probably been perceived as more important than the accompanying dilution of control.

Conclusions

The need of the multinational enterprise for control over decisions in foreign subsidiaries is the common element that has led certain kinds of firms to prefer to conduct their overseas operations through wholly owned entities. If the strategy of the enterprise has meant that the presence of a local partner would be likely to generate conflicts over policies that were critical to the maintenance of barriers to entry, the firm has had a strong preference for wholly owned subsidiaries.

Strategies that emphasized marketing techniques, rationalization of production, or control over sources of raw materials have required that control and coordination occur at a level that was higher than the individual subsidiary. The decisions that the multinational enterprise made were likely to conflict with the interests of a local partner. To avoid these conflicts over critical decisions, the firm has turned to wholly owned operations.

For similar reasons, strategies that concentrated on product innovation have led to a preference for wholly owned subsidiaries. A local partner represented a potential leak for the technology that was critical to the firm's strategy. The return for this technology has been a monopoly rent. But it has been difficult for the enterprise to arrange payment from a partner for the technological contribution of the parent.

The low value that some firms have placed on a partner's marketing contributions has reinforced their preference for wholly owned subsidiaries. A partner in the country where extraction occurs was unlikely to be able to provide a large market; the output of the extractive operations of the raw material firms has been sold primarily in another country. The firm that has innovated products for a market with which it was familiar has no need for marketing know-how. But the enterprise that has developed a wide range of new products provides a different story, as we shall show next.

NINE / The Quest for Additional Resources

Although some firms regard control as more important than local resources, others value the resources more than control. The difference in view depends partly on the strategy that the multinational enterprise is following.

There are a number of situations in which the need for resources has led the multinational enterprise to turn to local partners. For example, in some cases multinational enterprises have accepted joint ventures with local firms to gain access to needed raw materials for local manufacture. Another example is provided by the relatively small enterprises, which have been led at times to turn to local partners for capital and management. As we have already suggested, firms that were diversifying their product lines have been willing to develop joint ventures in order to acquire marketing skills for their new lines.

Diversifying the Product Line

Product diversification is one way by which firms maintain their growth when the traditional product line begins to mature. Diversified firms have had a larger portion of joint ventures among their overseas manufacturing subsidiaries than have the firms with a narrow product line.[1] Figure 9-1 depicts the relative frequency of joint ventures for multinational enterprises, classified by the number of product lines the enterprise manufactured abroad. Joint ventures appeared less frequently in the single product firms than in the firms that manufactured several products overseas.

When a firm develops a wide range of new products, it is, as we have mentioned, usually concentrating its resources on design and production. Such an enterprise frequently does not have adequate marketing skills. Each new line requires a different formula for marketing, specific to the product. As the firms begin to take their new products abroad, the shortage of marketing skills pinches particularly hard. In many cases, foreign marketing has required additional knowledge for each line, but most lines

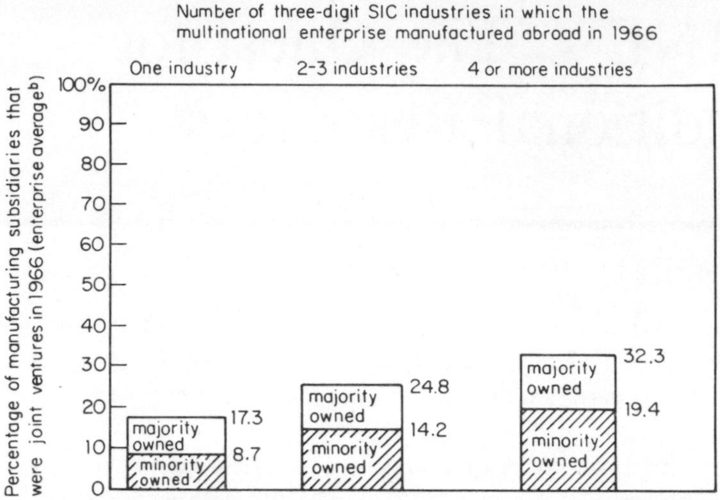

Number of three-digit SIC industries in which the
multinational enterprise manufactured abroad in 1966

Figure 9–1   *Relative Importance of Joint Ventures
among Multinational Enterprises:
Enterprises Classified by Their Foreign
Diversification in 1966* [a]

[a] Excludes extractive enterprises and subsidiaries in Japan,
Spain, Ceylon, India, Mexico, and Pakistan.
[b] See Figure 8–1.

have not promised an immediate market that was large enough to justify
the lumpy investment in the acquisition of know-how. Frequently, local
partners have been able to contribute the knowledge and skills that were
required to tap a market.

It was suggested in the previous chapter that an innovating firm was
more likely to include local partners if the firm's innovation was leading to
diversification than if the innovation was confined to a narrow product
line. Table 9-1 lends support to this proposition. The response of the
R&D-oriented firms to our questionnaire demonstrated the importance of
local partners' contributions of marketing skills for the firms with wide
product lines. Table 9-2 shows that the marketing contributions of partners were perceived as being more valuable by those firms that manufactured many products abroad than by those that had only a few lines. For
the normalized responses, that of only one undiversified firm was inconsistent with the general pattern.

The firms with little expenditure on research and development present a
somewhat more complicated picture. Like the product innovators, diversified firms with little R&D evaluated partners' contribution of access to the
market higher than did their undiversified counterparts. In addition, the di-

TABLE 9-1 *Relative Importance of Joint Ventures among Foreign Manufacturing Subsidiaries of Multinational Enterprises That Spent 3 Percent or More on R&D in 1966: Enterprises Classified by Their Foreign Diversification*[a]

| | Number of three-digit SIC industries in which the multinational enterprise manufactured abroad in 1966 | | |
	One industry[b]	2-3 industries	4 or more industries
Joint ventures as a percentage of all manufacturing subsidiaries existing in 1966			
All joint ventures	*0.0%*	*27.6%*	*35.0%*
Majority joint ventures	0.0	21.0	19.0
Minority joint ventures	0.0	6.6	16.0
Joint ventures as a percentage of all manufacturing subsidiaries entered between 1960 and 1967			
All joint ventures	*15.0%*	*19.4%*	*29.7%*
Majority joint ventures	15.0	10.4	10.5
Minority joint ventures	0.0	9.0	19.2

[a]Excludes extractive enterprises and subsidiaries in Japan, Spain, Ceylon, India, Mexico, and Pakistan.
[b]Only two firms for which data were available fell into this class.
Source: R&D expenditures from *News Front*, November 1965, January and February 1966, and annual reports of the firms.

TABLE 9-2 *Local Partners' Contribution of Marketing Skills, as Perceived by Multinational Enterprises That Spent 3 Percent or More of Sales on R&D in 1966: Enterprises Classified by Their Foreign Diversification*[a]

| | Number of three-digit SIC industries in which the multinational enterprise manufactured abroad in 1966 | | | |
| | 2-3 industries[b] | | 4 or more industries | |
Local partners' contribution of	Average rating, scale of 0 (low) to 6 (high)	Normalized rating[c]	Average rating, scale of 0 (low) to 6 (high)	Normalized rating[c]
Marketing personnel	2.750	−0.194	2.823	0.103
Marketing access for local goods	3.000	0.056	2.941	0.221

[a]Excludes extractive enterprises.
[b]Only four firms in this category answered the questionnaire. The response of the single firm with manufacturing in only one industry has been omitted.
[c]For definition, see Chapter 7.
Source: R&D expenditures from *News Front*, November 1965, January and February 1966, and annual reports of the firms.

versified firms that were not innovators put a great deal of weight on partners' contribution to the speed of entry to a market. Table 9-3 shows the effect of diversification on the evaluation of the contributions of local partners for firms with low R&D expenditures. The emphasis on this particular contribution, speed of entry, seems to be the result of the fact that firms which were not product innovators have chosen a different route to diversification than those which were innovators.

TABLE 9-3 *Local Partners' Contribution of Marketing Skills and Speed of Entry as Perceived by Multinational Enterprises That Spent Less than 1.1 Percent of Sales on R&D in 1966: Enterprises Classified by Their Foreign Diversification*[a]

| | Number of three-digit SIC industries in which the multinational enterprise manufactured abroad in 1966 | | | |
| | 2-3 industries[b] | | 4 or more industries[c] | |
Local partners' contribution of	Average rating, scale of 0 (low) to 6 (high)	Normalized rating[d]	Average rating, scale of 0 (low) to 6 (high)	Normalized rating
Marketing personnel	4.250	0.861	1.333	−1.519
Marketing access for local goods	2.500	−0.889	3.000	0.148
Speed of entry	4.250	0.861	4.667	1.815

[a]Excludes extractive enterprises.
[b]Only four firms in this category answered the questionnaire. No firms with manufacturing in only one industry answered the questionnaire.
[c]Only three firms in this category answered the questionnaire.
[d]For definition, see Chapter 7.
Source: R&D expenditures from *News Front*, November 1965, January and February 1966, and annual reports of the firms.

As was suggested in Chapter 3, the firms that spent little on R&D have tended to accomplish a significant part of their diversification by acquiring existing foreign companies. Remember, for example, the diversification strategy of Phelps Dodge, which was described earlier. As a group, the undiversified firms with low R&D expenditures obtained only about 27 percent of their manufacturing subsidiaries by purchasing existing foreign enterprises, whereas diversified firms with low R&D expenditures purchased about 69 percent of their subsidiaries as going businesses. The firms that accomplished their diversification through large R&D expenditures obtained a far smaller proportion of their foreign subsidiaries by direct purchase. Acquisitions have provided a quick route to diversification for the firm that did not have a large program of research and development.

The acquisition of existing businesses by multinational enterprises has in general led to joint ventures more often than the creation of new entities. Of the manufacturing subsidiaries that were newly formed, about 65 percent were wholly owned, as Table 9-4 indicates. For subsidiaries that were acquired, the equivalent figure was about 57 percent. Though this difference is not great, the association between acquisition and joint ownership has been noted by others.[2]

TABLE 9-4 *Multinational Enterprises' Foreign Manufacturing Subsidiaries, Classified by whether Subsidiary Was Newly Formed or Acquired as an Existing Enterprise*

Multinational enterprise's ownership at time of entry	Method of entry into multinational enterprise			
	Newly formed		Acquired	
	No. of subs.	%	No. of subs.	%
Wholly owned (95-100%)	1,032	64.7	661	57.3
Majority owned (51-94%)	210	13.2	206	17.8
Minority owned (5-50%)	352	22.1	287	24.9
Total	1,594	100.0%	1,154	100.0%

The explanation of the relationship between acquisitions and ownership probably lies partly in the area of marketing know-how. The firms with low expenditures on R&D have been as eager as the other diversifying firms to obtain marketing skills for their new lines. Allowing the original owners of the company that is acquired to retain some of the equity has, no doubt, been a way of retaining their interest. The multinational enterprise could draw on their market know-how for the newly acquired subsidiary.

The negative correlation between the product diversification of the multinational enterprises and their propensity to enter a market through sales subsidiaries provided an additional indicator of the relationship between diversification and the firm's need to acquire marketing skills. We argued earlier that a tendency to use sales subsidiaries was a sign of the existence of marketing skills internal to the firm. The infrequent use of sales subsidiaries by diversified firms is consistent with the view that they have not had the needed marketing skills inside the enterprises; they have turned to sources outside the firm for skills in marketing their wide range of products.

F

One additional set of data provides evidence of the link between diversification and the need to acquire resources from local partners. Facilities
that manufactured products that the parent did not make at all in the
United States were more likely to be joint ventures than were the parent's
other facilities. Table 9-5 shows clearly that the role of joint ventures has
been less important for products in the older, principal lines than in those
outside the major SIC industry of the parent.

TABLE 9-5   *Multinational Enterprises' Foreign Manufacturing Subsidiaries,*
Classified by Ownership and by whether Products Manufactured
Were Same as or Different from Primary Industry of
Multinational Parent[a]

Multinational enterprise's ownership at time of entry	Products manufactured			
	Same as primary line of parent		Different from primary line of parent	
	No. of subs.	%	No. of subs.	%
Wholly owned (95-100%)	767	66.3	893	57.6
Majority owned (51-94%)	166	14.3	252	16.2
Minority owned (5-50%)	224	19.3	406	26.1
Total	1,157	100.0%	1,551	100.0%

[a]Excludes subsidiaries in Japan, Spain, Ceylon, India, Mexico, and Pakistan.
Source: The primary industry of U.S. firms is identified on a three-digit basis by the U.S.
Department of Commerce.

The choices of strategy, of organization at the division level, and of
ownership of subsidiaries have been interrelated in intricate ways. A strategy of diversification has pushed firms toward organizing along product
lines. At the same time, the strategy has led the firm to attempt to acquire
resources that a joint venture partner could contribute. In addition, the
choice of product divisions as a form of organization has meant that
the firm has sacrificed certain abilities to control and coordinate foreign
subsidiaries. The lack of ability to control and coordinate has meant that
the main benefit of wholly owned subsidiaries was not very important to
the enterprise. The result is that joint ventures have been attractive to the
diversifiers, because they could use the partners' contributions; their disadvantage in loss of control was less important for the diversifiers, who failed
to adopt product structures, than for the other firms. In 1966, joint ventures accounted for 33 percent of the manufacturing subsidiaries of the
thirty firms with worldwide product divisions. The figure for the other en-

terprises was 21 percent. Similar results were found for the new ventures established between 1960 and 1967.

Tables 9-1 and 9-6 combine diversification and R&D measures to illustrate the effect of one variable at a time. The tables confirm the points that have been made. As has been the case with other variables, the relationship is particularly strong for minority-held interests in joint ventures. Firms with low R&D expenditures tended to enter more joint ventures than did firms with large expenditures on R&D. However, as they became more diversified, firms with heavy emphasis on R&D have behaved much more like firms with little expenditure on R&D. Both have turned frequently to local partners for marketing resources. For the firms that have concentrated on product innovation, the needs for marketing skills of local partners for product lines with which the firms have had little experience were more important than the problems associated with joint ventures.

TABLE 9-6 *Relative Importance of Joint Ventures among Foreign Manufacturing Subsidiaries of Multinational Enterprises That Spent Less than 1.1 Percent of Sales on R&D in 1966: Enterprises Classified by Their Foreign Diversification*[a]

	Number of three-digit SIC Industries in which the multinational enterprise manufactured abroad in 1966	
	2-3 industries	4 or more industries[b]
Joint ventures as a percentage of all manufacturing subsidiaries existing in 1966		
All joint ventures	*44.7%*	*43.2%*
Majority joint ventures	23.5	15.8
Minority joint ventures	21.2	27.4
Joint ventures as a percentage of all manufacturing subsidiaries entered between 1960 and 1967		
All joint ventures	*47.8%*	*61.9%*
Majority joint ventures	23.3	19.4
Minority joint ventures	24.5	42.5

[a]Excludes extractive enterprises and subsidiaries in Japan, Spain, Ceylon, India, Mexico, and Pakistan.

[b]Only four firms for which data were available fall into this class. No firms that had R&D expenditures less than 1.1% of sales and which manufactured in only one industry answered the questionnaire.

Source: R&D expenditures from *News Front*, November 1965, January and February 1966, and annual reports of the firms.

Developing a Vertical Structure

In the previous chapter we pointed out that firms attempting to control their sources of raw materials have shown a preference for wholly owned subsidiaries; but that has been the preference for control in *extractive* operations. These same firms have often turned to local partners in their *manufacturing* operations so that they could ensure the existence of markets for the raw materials.

Figure 9-2 shows the frequency of joint ventures for manufacturing by firms that had few extractive operations, as compared with those that had three or more extractive subsidiaries outside the United States. The data show the markedly higher propensity of the extractive firms to join with local partners in their manufacturing operations.

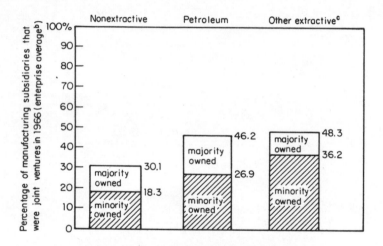

Figure 9–2   *Relative Importance of Manufacturing*
Joint Ventures among Multinational Enterprises:
Enterprises Classified by whether Their
Principal Activity Was Nonextractive,
Petroleum, or Other Extractive, in 1966 [a]

[a] Excludes subsidiaries in Japan, Spain, Ceylon, India, Mexico, and Pakistan.
[b] See Figure 8–1.
[c] An enterprise was classified as extractive if it had three or more overseas subsidiaries engaged primarily in extractive activities in 1966.

The development of a mine or an oil well has generally required large and risky expenditures for exploration, as well as major investments in roads, railroads, and other infrastructure. Once the well or mine was in operation, the incremental costs of extracting another barrel of oil or ton of ore have been small, compared to the average costs. A joint disposition among the oligopolists not to compete on prices has led each firm in the leadership to concentrate on assuring outlets for its raw materials.

To obtain markets, the multinational enterprises have been willing to enter joint ventures with local firms that had access to the market. The multinational enterprises could capture their oligopoly rents by charging a sufficiently high transfer price for the raw material; the local partner was assured access to a needed input in time of shortage. As a National Industrial Conference Board study reported, "if the primary consideration is expansion or maintenance of the market for raw materials or components, the foreign investor only needs control (not necessarily 51%) to insure that materials from other sources are not used." [3]

The response of the multinational enterprises to our questionnaire provided evidence of the importance to extractive firms of the access that local partners could provide to markets for goods produced outside the partner's country. The average normalized evaluation of this contribution by the petroleum firms was 2.094; for the other extractive firms, it was 0.221. These measures compare with an average evaluation of 0.014 by the other firms that responded to the questionnaire. More evidence of the relationship between extractive activities and the value of market access in the downstream stages is provided by the fact that only one extractive firm assigned "no importance"—that is, "0"—to this contribution, while 31 percent of the other firms declared it to be of "no importance."

Of course, not all extractive operations have been characterized by large exploration and development costs and low marginal costs of production. Typically, these characteristics have been associated with mining and petroleum operations, less so with food, rubber, and timber firms.

An examination of the manufacturing operations of only mining and petroleum firms gave even stronger support to the relationship between control over raw materials and use of joint ventures in downstream operations.[4] Table 9-7 shows that the mining and petroleum firms have a very large portion of their manufacturing operations in joint venture form. Over 70 percent of the entries into manufacturing by the mining firms between 1960 and 1967 were joint ventures.[5] Not shown on the table is the fact that every mining firm responding to the questionnaire indicated that joint ventures accounted for 80 to 100 percent of overseas manufacturing.

Further evidence of the willingness of the mining and petroleum firms to take in local partners when they can assure access to a market is provided by the ownership of sales subsidiaries. In all cases, most of the sales oper-

TABLE 9-7   *Relative Importance of Joint Ventures among Foreign Manu-*
facturing Subsidiaries of Multinational Enterprises: Enterprises
Classified by whether their Principal Activity was Nonextractive,
Petroleum, or Mining[a]

	Principal activity of enterprise		
	Nonextractive	Petroleum	Mining[b]
Joint ventures as a percentage of all manufacturing subsidiaries existing in 1966			
All joint ventures	*30.1%*	*46.2%*	*65.0%*
Majority joint ventures	11.8	19.3	15.0
Minority joint ventures	18.3	26.9	50.0
Joint ventures as a percentage of all manufacturing subsidiaries entered between 1960 and 1967			
All joint ventures	*35.7%*	*53.2%*	*70.9%*
Majority joint ventures	16.4	27.2	14.5
Minority joint ventures	19.3	26.0	56.4

[a]Excludes subsidiaries in Japan, Spain, Ceylon, India, Mexico, and Pakistan.
[b]An enterprise was classified as mining if its primary SIC industry was 326 or 333 and if it had three or more extractive operations outside the United States.

ations of the multinational enterprise were wholly owned. But the extractive firms had a considerably larger proportion of minority joint ventures
among their sales operations than did the other firms. Table 9-8 shows the
ownership pattern for sales subsidiaries in all countries for the mining and
petroleum enterprises that we examined. Again, the differences are great-

TABLE 9-8   *Multinational Enterprises' Foreign Sales Subsidiaries, Classified*
by Ownership and by Principal Activity of Multinational Parent[a]

	All activities		Petroleum		Mining[b]	
Multinational enterprise's ownership in 1966	No. of subs.	%	No. of subs.	%	No. of subs.	%
Wholly owned (95-100%)	1,697	89.2	334	83.9	23	85.2
Majority owned (51-94%)	99	5.2	27	6.8	0	0.0
Minority owned (5-50%)	106	5.6	37	9.3	4	14.8
Total	1,902	100.0%	398	100.0%	27	100.0%

[a]Excludes subsidiaries in Japan, Spain, Ceylon, India, Mexico, and Pakistan.
[b]An enterprise was classified as mining if its primary SIC industry was 326 or 333 and if it had three or more extractive operations outside the United States.

est in the minority interests. Many examples of joint ventures for petroleum distribution are well known. No doubt, the extractive firms have entered joint ventures in sales for the same reasons that they have entered them in manufacturing: to tie a user to a particular source.

A clear description of the role of downstream joint ventures in extractive firms is provided in a restricted Harvard Business School case. The case quotes in some detail the statements by the president of a large petroleum enterprise concerning the firm's willingness to enter joint ventures. In the case of refineries, he described a European joint venture: "Perhaps, however, it is worth pointing out that our relationship [with a European company] will save us from having to create our own European marketing setup for the gasoline we shall be obtaining from the [source area] crude. . . ." The president described in similar terms joint ventures for liquified petroleum gas, petrochemicals, and carbon black.

A study of European investment in the United States describes the motivation for some European firms.[6] According to the study, a number of the European enterprises needed an immediate market for raw materials. They turned to acquisitions or joint ventures in the United States to gain quickly the required brand names, marketing channels, and fund-raising capability.

The petroleum and copper firms illustrate the general proposition that enterprises which obtained their oligopoly positions primarily by controlling raw materials turn frequently to local partners for markets in the downstream stages.[7] The aluminum industry provides an example where control is exercised at an intermediate stage. Bauxite has been a relatively plentiful raw material. Oligopoly positions in the aluminum industry have been based on control of the smelting operation, where the required investment is very large and technological barriers are higher than at other stages in the vertical chain.[8] Joint ventures with local partners have been rare in smelting; where joint arrangements have existed at this stage, they were generally with other international aluminum firms. Like the petroleum and copper firms, local partners have been included by the aluminum firms at a stage downstream from the point where control was critical. But in this case, downstream has meant the fabrication stage where barriers to entry are low.

The use of joint ventures to achieve downstream integration has not been limited to firms in extractive industries. A study of the chemical industry's joint ventures in Europe describes arrangements whereby one partner was the major purchaser of an important by-product in the manufacture of a chemical.[9] Because no open market existed for that by-product, the purchaser was in a strong position to insist on participation. In situations of this sort, joint ventures are common.

A similar finding was made in a study of foreign investment in New

Zealand. The foreign firms had a "genuine desire" for participation with
local interests "where the shareholders represented a significant potential
market." [10] Some firms "which had only a few major New Zealand customers for their output felt it sensible for the latter to have a financial interest
in the supplier, thereby guaranteeing the firm's market." Another study describes a specific example. Bristol de Mexico, a joint venture for the over-
haul and maintenance of aircraft, included as local partners Cia. Mexicana
de Aviación and Aeronaves de Mexico, the principal customers for the enterprise. [11] The investment by Reichold Chemical, Inc., in Costa Rica, was
another case of a venture between a supplier and a customer, Kativo Chemical. [12] Kativo had operations in a number of Central American markets.
The chemical plant was planned to supply the Costa Rican market, of
which Kativo represented a major element. In addition, the output would
be sold in other Central American Common Market countries, where
Kativo had operations that would use the Costa Rican output. The literature on foreign investment includes many more examples of joint ventures
with customers that control access to the market.

Another rather special case for local vertical integration has existed
when the outputs of the manufacturing process were not easily stored (perishable intermediates, for example). When the user did not buy regularly,
the suppliers of the product have tended to integrate forward in an attempt
to provide a steady market for the product. An interesting example of this
situation came to light in an interview with an American investor in the
Middle East. He was producing a highly perishable intermediate product
that required a long period in process. The local users provided a highly
variable demand; they were unreliable in taking delivery of orders and erratic in their relationship to suppliers. The American firm found itself frequently with spoiled products on its hands. Although the firm had had no
desire to be in the downstream business, nevertheless, it began to form
joint arrangements with the buyers. The purpose was to tie them to purchasing from the American firm and to assist the management in the
downstream stage in organizing production processes that would smooth
out the buying patterns.

Joint ventures have arisen from the need to integrate upstream as well
as from pressure to integrate downstream. When a local company is able
to exercise considerable control over the inputs needed by the foreigner, it
sometimes can insist that it be a partner in the foreigner's local manufacturing operations. A study of joint ventures in the chemical industry, to
which we referred earlier, reported as follows:

The difficulty to obtain ample and low-cost supplies may be a powerful reason
in establishing a joint venture. Such a decision will be even more likely when

no merchant markets exist. In many instances, the production strength of the established participation will be immense, to the extent that it may preclude entry. Thus, a foreign entrant may be quite lucky if he finds a willing partner.

Joint ventures influenced by the supply problem are common. Often, they are merely glorified supplier-customer relationships, and it is often difficult to distinguish between a joint venture and a simple long-term contract.[13]

That conclusion is quite consistent with the results of our questionnaire in which thirteen firms noted access to raw materials as an important contribution of local partners. It is worth observing that many of these firms were in the chemical industry.[14] The findings are also consistent with those reported by the International Chamber of Commerce: "On the purchasing side, the local partner is in a better position to procure local materials and parts. During periods of scarcity or inflation this is a valuable aspect of a joint venture."[15]

Still, the need to form joint ventures with local suppliers has not been universal. Partly, the need has depended on the nature of the manufacturing process. In cases where the fixed costs of the American's manufacturing operations have been high, the threat of irregular inputs has been more serious. The need has also varied from country to country. Where imports have not provided a reasonable alternative source, the bargaining power of a local supplier has been great. Import quotas, high tariffs, or local content requirements on the part of the government have forced the foreign firm to rely on local suppliers in many cases. And where a small market or weak antitrust regulation has led to a great deal of concentration among suppliers, the increased risks of being cut off have probably led the multinational enterprise to give a stake in the success of the operations to a local firm that could supply the needed inputs.

Many of the manufacturing joint ventures with government partners can be best understood in the framework of vertical integration. Although the government was, in some cases, the only local source for large amounts of capital,[16] the major contribution of the government partner in the manufacturing joint ventures seems to have been access to markets or to materials. Frequently, the government has been the major customer. All the sixteen cases of joint ventures with governments that were identified in this study involved petroleum, chemical, pharmaceutical, or farm equipment firms.[17] For the petroleum firms, the distribution system that would sell the output was a government monopoly. Government participation in the refineries assured that the distribution system would buy from the joint venture. The chemical firms entered the joint ventures for the manufacture of explosives, fertilizers, and nylon. For the joint ventures in explosives, fertilizers, farm equipment, and pharmaceuticals, the government was again the

F*

major customer. For the nylon producers, the only source of the chemicals needed for manufacture was controlled by the government. Where the government had a monopoly on markets or materials, the multinational enterprise has sometimes been willing to sacrifice some control over the subsidiary to gain access to the resources that it needed.

Of course, there have been other reasons for the arrangements with governments. In some countries, designated sectors of the economy have been reserved for government participation. If a foreign firm was to manufacture in these sectors, it had to include a government partner. Mexico, Brazil, India, Egypt, Algeria, Italy, and France are among the countries that have required such government participation in certain parts of the economy. But in the vast majority of cases, the role of the government as the principal customer or the main supplier seems to have been the driving force behind the joint venture.

The Smaller Firms' Special Needs

One more factor seems to have played a role in pushing some firms to take in local partners: the type of need associated with firms that are relatively small. Figure 9-3 shows that joint ventures have played a larger role in the foreign manufacturing operations of enterprises that were small in their industry than in those of their larger competitors. "Small" is a relative term. The smallest firms covered in the chart had sales of $115 million and assets of $93 million in 1966. The "small firms" include enterprises such as Chrysler. However, there is some evidence that a similar relationship between size and use of joint ventures would have been found if the study had included still smaller firms. One author noted that for joint ventures in India and Pakistan there was a strong correlation between size of the subsidiary and size of the parent.[18] Several studies that have included a wider range of investors in a single country have found that smaller subsidiaries were more likely to be joint ventures than larger ones.[19] Since the size of the subsidiary probably is correlated to some extent with the size of the parent, these studies provide some additional support for the basic proposition.

The higher incidence of joint ventures among the manufacturing subsidiaries of relatively small firms stems partly from the distinct characteristics of their strategies. In industries that are highly concentrated in structure, consisting of a few large firms, the sardines that exist among the sharks are obliged to play an especially careful game.[20]

One strategy for survival has been called "the preparation against the

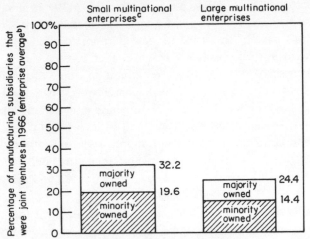

Figure 9–3   *Relative Importance of Joint Ventures
among Multinational Enterprises:
Enterprises Classified by Their Relative Size
in Their Industry in 1966*[a]

[a] Excludes extractive enterprises and subsidiaries in Japan,
Spain, Ceylon, India, Mexico, and Pakistan.
[b] See Figure 8–1.
[c] A firm was considered to be "small" if its sales were less
than one half of those of the largest firm in the same primary industry.

worst contingency," [21] or "the minimax strategy." [22] When a leading firm
in the industry takes an action that is potentially upsetting to the equilibrium of the industry, other firms in the industry view the action as a threat
to be countered. If the step consists of setting up a subsidiary in a foreign
country, and if that step is viewed as potentially giving the investing firm
the power to produce at lower costs or to preempt a future market, the
other firms in the industry respond by making similar investments.[23]

   Smaller firms that pursue this strategy, however, are likely to find that
their internal capital and management resources are insufficient to counter
each move of the larger competitors. If resources were available in proportion to size, the smaller firm could theoretically respond by setting up an
operation that is of a size in proportion to its relationship to the larger
competitors. But smaller firms appear not to have free resources in proportion to their size.[24] Besides, the needed resources often cannot be tailored
to the size of the parent. Plants, distribution systems, and other parts of
the required organization come in lumpy units, requiring minimum
amounts of capital and management.[25] The firm that is a quarter the size
of its competitor cannot usually get by with providing one fourth the capital and management supplied by the larger firm to set up a plant to pro-

duce a quarter of the output. As a result, the smaller firm pursuing this strategy has found itself strapped for cash and management. To gain capital, such firms have often turned to local partners. A study of petrochemical investment abroad concluded that "smaller companies, either U.S. or foreign, because of lack of resources, prefer a joint venture or licensing agreement rather than a wholly owned subsidiary." [26] In a similar vein, another writer has claimed that because Japanese and Italian firms are small relative to American firms, they have had to turn to joint ventures for financial resources.[27] On the human resource side, an author said: "Small firms are rarely in a position to assign or recruit personnel required to effect successful transplants of technology to less developed countries." [28]

The results of the questionnaire in this study affirmed the general tendency. The contributions of capital by a local partner were given somewhat larger importance by smaller firms than by larger enterprises. For example, the average normalized value for the importance of capital contribution was -0.448 for the small firms; for the large ones it was -0.779. By eliminating firms from the "large" category in those cases where there were no small firms in the same industry, the results were made considerably stronger.

The questionnaire responses concerning the value of partners' contribution of management were less revealing. Only when we eliminated the large firms which were the only firms in the industry, as we did above, did the evaluation of partners' contribution of management come out higher for the small firms than for the large ones. But this adjustment brought out a significant difference between the two groups of firms. Assigning equal weights to each industry gave the larger firms an average normalized evaluation of 0.046 for the management resource from local partners; the measure for smaller firms was 0.162.

Instead of following a minimax strategy, some small firms have pursued a strategy of high risk, that of generating new products.[29] As small firms develop new products, they often find themselves comparatively short of the capital and management that they need to set up production.[30] To enter markets quickly, before the large firms could copy their innovation and put facilities in place, small firms have turned to joint ventures. The responses of the firms to the questionnaire indicated the importance that joint ventures had in speeding up entries. The average normalized answers for the importance of this contribution from joint ventures were 1.08 for the small firms and 0.747 for the larger ones.

Another factor that may have contributed to the greater use of joint ventures by small firms is that they feel less inhibited by the fear of antitrust action. The U.S. Justice Department has sometimes challenged market allocation agreements among joint ventures and among the partners in a licensing arrangement.[31] But such agreements are more likely to be challenged if the partner is a past, present, or prospective competitor of the U.S. firm and if American trade is likely to be materially affected by the agreement. These conditions probably affect large U.S. enterprises more often than the small ones. Accordingly, large U.S. enterprises may see some advantages in avoiding joint ventures and using the less contentious wholly owned subsidiary as a vehicle for foreign expansion.

One popular hypothesis that would be consistent with the findings just summarized is that joint ventures have been used by the foreign investor as one of the steps in a sequence for learning about foreign markets. According to the proponents of this idea, firms have first licensed independent producers abroad, then gone into joint ventures; later, after they had acquired experience, they have turned to wholly owned subsidiaries. Since large size and long foreign experience are found together among U.S. multinational enterprises, this hypothesis might have explained why small firms had relatively more joint ventures than the larger ones.[32]

Despite the plausibility of the learning hypothesis, a simple check did not support it. Table 9-9 compares the use of joint ventures by each enterprise in its first five manufacturing investments outside the United States and Canada with the firm's overall propensity to enter joint ventures. There is no indication that the firms have actually entered joint ventures more frequently in their very early ventures than they did in their later ones.

TABLE 9-9 *Multinational Enterprises' Foreign Manufacturing Subsidiaries, Classified by Ownership and by whether They Were among the Enterprise's First Five Foreign Ventures*[a]

Multinational enterprise's ownership at time of entry	First five ventures[b] (percentage)	All ventures (percentage)
Wholly owned (95-100%)	73.4	62.4
Majority owned (51-94%)	10.0	14.0
Minority owned (5-50%)	16.1	23.4

[a]Excludes Japan, Spain, India, Mexico, and Pakistan.
[b]The calculation was made for the number of subsidiaries that was greater than three but closest to five which could be identified from a table showing the subsidiaries by the decade within which they were founded. If, for example, a firm entered six subsidiaries in the first decade it went abroad, the ownership figures were counted for six, not five, operations.

Conclusions

The propensity of a multinational enterprise to enter joint ventures has been increased by at least three factors. One has been the need for local marketing know-how, a need that has been especially strong among firms that were constantly enlarging their product lines. A second has been a need on the part of some firms to forge or to extend a vertically integrated structure. The contributions of partners have been especially important where the firm had already gained oligopoly control over some link in the production chain and needed to ensure that it could be supplied with the necessary materials or gain access to needed markets at another stage. Finally, there have been the special needs of smaller firms, whether they were pursuing a strategy of risk avoidance by emulating their larger competitors or a strategy of high adventure by concentrating on innovation. In both situations, small firms have been up against the need to acquire lumpy inputs of resources in order to execute their strategies.

TEN / The Influence of Complex and Changing Strategies

To treat strategies at one point in time is to study a racing style with one still photo. And to handle multinational enterprises as if each could be classified neatly according to a particular kind of strategy is to ignore much of the complexity of international business. A firm's strategy evolves over time. For example, a number of the enterprises included in this study began their foreign expansion with a single product line and only much later turned to a strategy of diversification. Viewed currently, the firm may show in its ownership patterns the leftovers of its past strategies along with the results of decisions that have been made recently. In addition, an accurate description of the strategy of a multinational enterprise at a single point in time may require mention of more than one of the strategies that we have discussed. For example, a firm may be pursuing both a marketing-oriented strategy and a strategy associated with relatively small firms. To be able to say, for such a firm, that its size or its marketing orientation was the critical factor predisposing it to joint ventures requires more subtle measuring sticks than the simple tables so far presented. Although the tables have the virtue of simplicity, they cannot handle the very complex interrelationships. Various efforts were made to capture some of the complex relationships in order to be sure that the simple tabular analyses were not generating misleading signals.

One approach was the use of multiple regression techniques. The results, which are presented in Appendix C, tended to indicate that the relationships between strategy and ownership of subsidiaries continue to appear even when account is taken of complex strategies. When a firm's strategies were measured on several dimensions at one time, the direction of influence of each strategy on the ownership patterns was generally consistent with what has been described in the previous chapters. The regressions also suggested that the relationship between strategy and ownership has been strongest for the minority-held ventures. In many instances, of majority ownership, the multinational enterprises seem to have been able to retain sufficient control over the subsidiaries that partners could be tolerated, even with a strategy that required the exercise of control from the center. The findings will all be evident to the reader who returns to the charts of Chapters 7 and 8.

Historical Patterns

Tests of hypotheses concerning complex business decisions are rarely very powerful. The decisions with regard to the joint venture are as complex and elusive as any. By exploring questionnaire responses and statistical analyses, one begins to see a certain plausibility in a given set of propositions. The historical development of ownership policies of the multinational enterprises provides an added source for verifying some of the basic impressions.

What have been the overall trends in ownership policies? That joint ventures have accounted for an increasing portion of American investment in manufacturing overseas is very well known. Table 10-1 shows the dramatic increase in the proportion of joint ventures among the subsidiaries formed or acquired in the 1950's and 1960's by the multinational enterprises covered in this study. A very similar pattern is evident in data that cover larger numbers of enterprises.

TABLE 10-1 *Foreign Manufacturing Subsidiaries, Classified by Multinational Enterprise's Ownership and Period of Entry*[a]

| | Multinational enterprise's ownership at time of entry | | | | | |
| | Wholly owned | | Majority owned | | Minority owned | |
Period of entry	No. of subs.	% of total in period	No. of subs.	% of total in period	No. of subs.	% of total in period
1900-1909	48	73.8	16	24.6	1	1.6
1910-1919	52	91.2	5	8.8	0	0
1920-1929	131	78.4	13	7.8	23	13.8
1930-1939	158	75.2	18	8.6	34	16.2
1940-1949	115	62.5	18	9.8	51	27.7
1950-1954	136	64.8	28	13.3	46	21.9
1955-1959	300	62.0	67	13.8	117	24.2
1960-1967	780	55.3	260	18.4	371	26.3

[a]Excludes subsidiaries in Japan, Spain, Ceylon, India, Mexico, and Pakistan.

Some analysts have attributed the increase in joint ownership to nothing more than the businessman's propensity for following the current fashion.

But there are other explanations that go a long way toward explaining the increased importance of joint ventures in foreign investment, explanations much more consistent with the propositions of earlier chapters.

During the 1950's and 1960's the make-up of the firms that were undertaking new investments abroad was changing. More and more of the investments were accounted for by relatively small firms, precisely those that could be expected to seek resources by turning to local partners. At the same time, an increased proportion of the investments resulted from changes in strategy of the sort associated with the use of joint ventures. And there is some evidence that there were changes occurring in some host countries that made joint venture partners easier to find.

The increase in overseas manufacturing activities by relatively small firms during the postwar period is demonstrated by the figures in Table 10-2. According to the table, firms classified as "small" in 1966 accounted for less than 40 percent of the manufacturing subsidiaries formed or acquired before World War II; from 1960 to 1967, however, they accounted for 56 percent.

TABLE 10-2   *Foreign Manufacturing Subsidiaries of Multinational Enterprises: Subsidiaries Classified by Period of Entry and by the Relative Size of the Multinational Parent in Its Industry in 1966[a]*

| Period of entry | Relative size of multinational parent in 1966[b] | | | |
| | Large | | Small | |
	No. of subs.	% of total in period	No. of subs.	% of total in period
1900-1909	55	85.9	9	14.1
1910-1919	48	87.3	7	12.7
1920-1929	113	69.3	50	30.7
1930-1939	122	60.1	81	39.9
1940-1949	88	49.7	89	50.3
1950-1954	93	47.0	105	53.3
1955-1959	199	43.4	259	56.6
1960-1967	585	44.0	743	56.0

[a]Excludes subsidiaries in Japan, Spain, Ceylon, India, Mexico, and Pakistan.

[b]A firm was considered to be "small" if its sales were less than one half of those of the largest firm in the same primary industry. For consistency with other calculations, where only a single firm in an industry was covered in this study, its subsidiaries were dropped from this table. The exclusion of these subsidiaries made no significant change in the patterns.

At the same time, there was a dramatic increase in diversification by the firms in our group. Table 10-3 shows the ownership of manufacturing subsidiaries classified by the kind of products that they produced. Up until the

1950's, never more than half of the subsidiaries of the multinational enterprises were manufacturing products that were outside the principal product line of the parent.[1] However, by the 1960's, two-thirds of the new subsidiaries were created for the manufacture of products outside the main industry of the parent. The diversification process was not, of course, limited to overseas activities of U.S. firms. The process had begun much earlier in the United States.[2] As the diversification was extended abroad, the multinational firms found themselves more receptive to local partners for the marketing resources such partners could bring to a joint venture.

TABLE 10-3 *Foreign Manufacturing Subsidiaries of Multinational Enterprises: Subsidiaries Classified by Period of Entry and whether Products Manufactured were Same as or Different from Primary Line of Multinational Parent*[a]

| | Products manufactured | | | |
| | Same as the primary product line of parent | | Different from primary product line of parent | |
Period of entry	No. of subs.	% of total in period	No. of subs.	% of total in period
1900-1909	53	58.2	38	41.8
1910-1919	64	59.3	44	40.7
1920-1929	149	54.4	125	45.6
1930-1939	175	57.8	128	42.2
1940-1949	156	52.0	144	48.0
1950-1954	148	43.8	190	56.2
1955-1959	320	43.8	411	56.2
1960-1967	703	33.2	1,417	66.8

[a]Excludes subsidiaries in Japan, Ceylon, India, Mexico, and Pakistan.

Source: Primary industry of parent determined on three-digit SIC basis from U.S. Department of Commerce classifications.

Along with the process of diversification, multinational enterprises were beginning to place more stress on acquiring overseas enterprises as going businesses, rather than building up such subsidiaries from scratch. We have suggested that acquisition was a means of diversification for the firms that had little research and development skill. Table 10-4 shows that although acquistions accounted for less than a third of the new manufacturing subsidiaries in 1954, they accounted for 46 percent of the new entries in the period 1960 to 1967. Acquisitions of going enterprises, it will be recalled, have led to joint ventures more frequently than have formations of new subsidiaries.

TABLE 10-4 *Foreign Manufacturing Subsidiaries of Multinational Enterprises: Subsidiaries Classified by Period of Entry and whether Subsidiary was Newly Formed or Acquired as an Existing Enterprise*[a]

| Period of entry | Method of entry | | | |
| | Newly formed | | Acquired as existing enterprise | |
	No. of subs.	% of total in period	No. of subs.	% of total in period
1900-1909	59	78.7	16	21.4
1910-1919	71	81.6	16	18.4
1920-1929	151	67.7	72	32.3
1930-1939	186	72.7	70	27.3
1940-1949	184	70.2	78	29.8
1950-1954	205	69.0	92	31.0
1955-1959	395	65.1	212	34.9
1960-1967	1,005	54.0	855	46.0

[a]Excludes subsidiaries in Japan, Spain, Ceylon, India, Mexico, and Pakistan.

The Effects of Changes in Strategy

How surely can it be said that the observed changes in ownership patterns were due to changes in strategy? The data provide a certain amount of evidence that firms do indeed change their attitude toward local partners when certain changes are made in their strategies. Although the figures, such as R&D expenditures, advertising expenses, and diversification, do not exist to provide a direct history of the changes in strategy that individual firms have adopted over the years, the changes in organizational structures through which they have passed provided a useful measure. Organizational changes, according to our argument, closely mirror changes in the strategy of the firm.

The relationship between organizational structure and ownership patterns—hence, presumptively between strategy and ownership patterns—has already been pointed out. The firms that had organizational structures which delegated a great deal of autonomy to overseas subsidiaries had local partners in a large portion of their overseas manufacturing subsidiaries; [3] in 1966, the figure was 45 percent. The multinational enterprises that were organized on a product basis worldwide had somewhat fewer joint ventures overseas, 35 percent in 1966. The firms that were organized on an area basis had few joint ventures among their foreign manufacturing operations, 16 percent in 1966. The area-based organizations were presumably the firms that were following strategies requiring considerable centralized control.[4]

The relationship between strategy and ownership of subsidiaries appears also to hold when multinational enterprises change their strategies and their organizational structure. One of the most striking demonstrations of the direct relation between strategy changes and changes in ownership patterns was provided by a recent study which was aimed at answering the following question: "What makes for instability in overseas subsidiaries involving U.S.-based multinational enterprises and local partners?" [5] A systematic analysis of the joint ventures, covering the same sample of firms as is covered here, produced solid results. Some 315 of the 1,100 joint ventures that were examined experienced major ownership changes at some point. Joint ventures were especially prone to instability when certain explicit kinds of organizational changes occurred. When enterprises reorganized their structures primarily along geographical area lines—a clear sign of a desire to tighten central controls—they tended to change minority holdings to majority control, or to buy out the joint venture partners altogether. When one of these alternatives was not possible, they sold their interests in the venture or liquidated the operation. In fact, for many of the enterprises, there was a clear "peaking" of instability in the relationships with partners within a couple of years of the change in organizational structure. On the other hand, when the organizational structure was changed to worldwide product divisions or mixed forms, nothing like this response occurred; in such cases there was no observable tendency toward change in the ownership of existing subsidiaries.

Changes in strategy have not only been associated with a shift in the firm's relations with existing joint ventures; such changes have also altered the propensity of the firm to enter new joint ventures. Our data show that once an enterprise has shifted over to an area organization, its propensity to enter joint ventures in the decade following the change has typically registered a significant drop.[6] For changes to product divisions, on the other hand, the entry ratios for the decade following the change showed no characteristic shift in either direction. Changes in strategy that lead to the need for more control appear to lead the firm to reevaluate the costs and benefits of existing joint ventures, and to adjust its policies for new subsidiaries in order to reflect its new strategies.

Availability of Partners

What all these bits and pieces add up to is the prospect that changes in the mix of multinational enterprises and changes in strategies of such enterprises have accounted for much of the increase in the relative importance of joint ventures in recent years. But one more factor, mentioned earlier, has probably played a role as well. While changes were occurring in the characteristics and strategies of the enterprises involved in setting up overseas subsidiaries, rapid industrialization in the less developed countries was making it easier for the enterprises to find a suitable local partner.[7] A multinational enterprise that went to West Africa before 1950, for example, would have had trouble finding a potential partner who could provide him with significant resources. By the 1960's the situation had changed. In most developing countries an industrial élite had arisen that was eager to join with foreign firms. Local businessmen could provide access to and knowledge about the local market; in many cases they could obtain capital from government sources.

The fact that potential local partners began to appear in the less developed countries created options for some foreign enterprises that did not exist before. But few foreign enterprises were so greatly attracted by the options as to convert wholly owned subsidiaries already in existence to joint ventures.[8] Instead, the options were generally exercised, if they were exercised at all, at the stage when new subsidiaries were being set up. This was the stage at which the foreigner's sense of uncertainty and ignorance, as well as his perception of the need for local resources, was at its peak.[9]

On the other hand, as the possibility of finding local partners for foreign investment grew, governments of many of the developing countries began to change what had been an option for the foreign firm to a requirement. The pressures of local governments upon the foreign investor have greatly complicated the patterns of ownership and the factors generating them.

ELEVEN / Host Government Policies as Constraints

The choice between creating a subsidiary that is wholly owned or taking a local partner is not one that is left entirely up to the management of the multinational enterprise. A number of countries have instituted systematic programs aimed at influencing the foreign firm to share ownership of its subsidiary with a local partner. In the late 1960's, U.S.-based multinational enterprises generally mentioned Japan, Spain, Ceylon, India, Mexico, and Pakistan as leading countries in this respect. In many other countries, however, some steps have been taken in the same direction. In Canada, for example, the tax on dividends was lower for subsidiaries with 25 percent Canadian ownership than for operations with a lesser amount of local ownership.[1] Liberia has been known to include provisions such as the following in contracts with foreign investors:

[The Concessionaire agrees] to make available for purchase by Liberian citizens at par value fifteen (15%) percent of the shares of stock of Liberia Cement Corporation. Subscription to these shares of stock shall be kept open for a period of one hundred twenty (120) days. Should these shares remain unsubscribed to, after 120 days period, [sic] they will be offered to other investors at par value.[2]

Indonesia requires, in some cases, that the foreign investor finance the sales of shares to Indonesians. Provisions from one typical contract included the following:

Indonesian participation in the ownership of the DOMESTIC COMPANY will be provided by offering for sale to Indonesians shares of stock representing thirty percent (30%) of the capital stock outstanding of the DOMESTIC COMPANY. The offer will be made in the eighth year from the commencement of export operations. . . .

. . . The [Foreign] COMPANY will provide a special arrangement whereby Indonesians desiring to purchase shares hereunder will be allowed to pay therefor as follows: Forty percent (40%) of the selling price to be paid upon execution of an agreement to purchase by the buyer, and the balance in six equal consecutive quarterly installments at such rate of interest as may be in line with current business practice then. . . .[3]

The idea of encouraging joint ventures has received support from the governments of capital-exporting countries.[4] International organizations have usually been enthusiastic about them, although there has been an occasional demurrer from some agencies.[5] However, no government pursues a policy of this sort without some eye to the consequences. And if the consequences are to lose a foreign-owned project altogether, that fact is likely to be taken into account. Moreover, some countries, bargaining from certain elements of strength, are in a far better position than others to impose their desires. The policies, therefore, are one thing; the outcome of the policies quite another.

The Ownership Patterns

Though the outcome of an official policy favoring joint ventures depends in part on the bargaining strength of the government concerned, it is nevertheless true that the countries with the most explicit policies on this score ended up with local participation in a larger portion of the subsidiaries of multinational enterprises than did the other countries.

In Japan, for example, about 89 percent of the manufacturing subsidiaries set up by the multinational enterprises between 1960 and 1967 were joint ventures. In the other industrialized countries, joint ventures accounted for only about 37 percent of the manufacturing investments. In the less developed countries, the data are also striking. In Ceylon, India, Mexico, and Pakistan, subsidiaries in which the multinational enterprises held only a minority share represented more than 30 percent of the manufacturing investments of our multinational firms between 1960 and 1967. In other less developed nations during that period, minority joint ventures made up only 17 percent of the manufacturing subsidiaries. Table 11-1 shows the data on ownership of manufacturing subsidiaries in Ceylon, India, Mexico, Pakistan, other less developed countries, Spain, and Japan.

The developing countries that were less insistent or less explicit regarding joint ventures have not ended up with a great deal more local ownership than has been found in the advanced countries, where most governments have been much less involved in ownership policies. Table 7-3, it will be recalled, compares the pattern of foreign ownership in the less developed countries with that in the advanced nations.

Though the policies of some less developed countries seem to have been somewhat successful in pushing certain foreign-owned enterprises toward

TABLE 11-1   *Multinational Enterprises' Foreign Manufacturing Subsidiaries Entered between 1960 and 1967: Subsidiaries Classified by Ownership and by Country of Incorporation*

Country of incorporation	Multinational enterprise's ownership at time of entry							
	Wholly owned		Majority owned		Minority owned		Total	
	No. of subs.	%	No. of subs.	%	No. of subs.	%	No. of subs.	%
Japan	10	11.2	4	4.5	75	84.3	89	100
Four less developed countries	54	31.5	35	20.5	82	48.0	171	100
Ceylon	2	66.7	0	0.0	1	33.3	3	100
India	1	3.1	4	12.5	27	84.4	32	100
Mexico	50	39.7	25	19.8	51	40.5	126	100
Pakistan	1	10.0	6	60.0	3	30.0	10	100
Other less developed countries	334	52.4	124	19.5	179	28.1	637	100

the joint venture pattern, there is evidence that the countries have not managed to persuade some foreign enterprises to deviate very much from the ownership patterns they were accustomed to apply elsewhere. That conclusion is suggested by the data in Table 11-2. This table breaks down the multinational enterprises into groups by their propensity to have joint ventures in the countries that do not insist on them. For each group, it shows the proportion of the firms' foreign subsidiaries accounted for by the countries that push for joint ventures. What appears is a tendency for the "insistent" countries to account for a somewhat smaller proportion of the investments for those firms that strongly prefer wholly owned subsidiaries elsewhere.

Some additional evidence can be gleaned from the behavior of the thirty-three multinational enterprises that had no joint ventures at all in 1966 in countries that offered relatively free choice. Of these enterprises, 24 percent had no investments in Spain, Ceylon, India, Mexico, and Pakistan, whereas less than 7 percent of the other multinational enterprises had no such investments. The observed differences in behavior, according to various tests performed on the data, could not be explained by differences in industry mix or other variables of this sort.

The data in Table 11-3 indicate that some firms are willing to enter more joint ventures in the face of government pressure to do so. This table

TABLE 11-2   *Number of Manufacturing Subsidiaries of Multinational Enterprises in Spain, Ceylon, India, Mexico, and Pakistan, and Other Less Developed Countries: Subsidiaries Classified by the Propensity of the Multinational Parent to Have Joint Ventures in Countries That Did Not Have Strong Policies Favoring Joint Ventures, 1966*

Propensity of parent enterprise to have joint ventures outside JSCIMP[a]	Area of incorporation of subsidiary			
	Spain, Ceylon, India, Mexico, and Pakistan		Other less developed countries	
	No. of subs.	%	No. of subs.	%
None	29	23.9	92	76.1
Low[b]	109	23.7	352	76.3
Low-Med.[b]	98	28.9	241	71.1
High-Med.[b]	89	32.1	188	67.9
High[b]	67	25.7	193	74.3

[a]JSCIMP: Japan, Spain, Ceylon, India, Mexico, and Pakistan.
[b]Low: enterprises with 20% or less of manufacturing subsidiaries as joint ventures in 1966; Low-Med.: 40% or less, but more than 20%; High-Med.: 60% or less, but more than 40%; High: more than 60%.

groups the firms by the percentage of their subsidiaries that are wholly owned in countries that put little pressure on the enterprises to have local partners. In most cases, the firms have a smaller proportion of wholly owned subsidiaries in the countries that encourage joint ventures than in the ones that are more relaxed on the ownership issue.

The data, then, suggest that the larger proportion of joint ventures among the foreign subsidiaries in the "insistent" countries than in those with less explicit policies arises from two factors. First, the multinational enterprises that are likely to use joint ventures frequently elsewhere are even more likely to do so when faced with host government pressure. Second, some of the firms that stick with wholly owned subsidiaries in countries where they are free to do so simply do not invest in the countries that have strong policies to encourage joint ventures.

Retreating from the Policy

Though multinational enterprises that prefer not to use joint ventures have tended to avoid the "insistent" countries, they also have set up subsidiaries in those countries from time to time despite the local policies. Although the enterprises have yielded to pressure on occasion, it is clear,

TABLE 11-3   *Percentage of Manufacturing Subsidiaries of Multinational Enterprises in Spain, Ceylon, India, Mexico, and Pakistan That Were Wholly Owned: Subsidiaries Classified by Multinational Parent's Ownership of Subsidiaries in Countries That Did Not Have Strong Policies Favoring Joint Ventures, 1966*

Percentage of multinational parent's manufacturing subsidiaries in countries other than JSCIMP[a] which were wholly owned in 1966	Percentage of parent's manufacturing subsidiaries in SCIMP[b] that were wholly owned in 1966 (average for enterprises)
0	0
1-19	26.6
20-39	27.5
40-59	30.9
60-79	45.3
80-89	68.1
90-100	84.0

[a]JSCIMP: Japan, Spain, Ceylon, India, Mexico, and Pakistan.
[b]SCIMP: Spain, Ceylon, India, Mexico, and Pakistan.

in many cases, that the host governments have backed down from their requirements of local participation for these firms in order to secure the advantages of their local presence. For example, IBM, according to Business International, "convinced both the Indian and Japanese governments that it is better to have IBM invest on its own terms than not at all." [6] There is some evidence, in fact, that this response was not uncommon.

There were thirty-nine multinational enterprises in our group that seemed to have a very strong policy favoring wholly owned subsidiaries. These could be identified by the fact that 90 percent or more of their foreign subsidiaries were wholly owned in countries without strong joint venture policies. Table 11-3 indicates that the manufacturing subsidiaries of these enterprises in Spain, Ceylon, India, Mexico, and Pakistan were much less likely to be joint ventures than those of other firms. For these enterprises the "insistent" governments have allowed complete ownership in 84 percent of the cases. Not shown in the table is the fact that only five of the thirty-six enterprises had any manufacturing joint ventures in these countries; just two had joint ventures in which they held only a minority of the stock.

Table 11-1 also hints at some more complex patterns underlying the insistence of the host countries on joint ventures. As we have already stated, the data show that even the "strict" countries have, to varying extents, retreated from their policies and allowed virtually complete foreign ownership of some subsidiaries, even during recent years. We suspect that there has been a consistent pattern in the behavior of the countries, a pattern resulting from two factors. The more a country has industrialized, the more it has needed the local presence of firms of the sort that resist joint ventures. That need has grown as a result of the growth of the countries themselves. As growth occurred, the easy opportunities for import substitution were filled; the need shifted from products that required only widely available technology to more advanced products. But the technology for advanced products tends to be held by only a few firms. Some of these have been enterprises that have resisted pressures to form joint ventures. Large expenditures on research and development, for example, have been associated with a preference for complete ownership. Similarly, efforts on the part of the government to increase manufactured exports have required marketing or technological inputs that only certain foreign firms could supply. To be sure, an offsetting factor may have been at work at the same time. As the local economy's need for certain types of foreign resources has increased, the attractiveness of the country, from the viewpoint of the multinational enterprise, may also have been increasing. The growth of the internal market provided to the foreign investor, for instance, has been an offsetting appeal.

The net effect of these two trends on the relative bargaining powers of the firm and the government has probably produced the patterns that are indicated by the sketchy data in Figure 11-1. The countries that have very low per capita incomes—such as India and Pakistan—have been able to stick by their insistence on joint ventures since their requirements were generally of a sort that a large number of investors could fill. The more advanced countries, such as Mexico, have needed investors in a stronger bargaining position, and may not have had a sufficiently attractive internal market to make the potential investor retreat from his insistence on sole ownership. These countries have probably had to back down and allow wholly owned subsidiaries. However, as the attraction of the local market has increased, the foreign investor has been more willing to yield to government measures. Japan may well illustrate this case in the period that we examined. In 1970, even General Motors, a classical example of a firm that has resisted pressures to form joint ventures, was considering a minority joint venture in order to gain access to the Japanese market.[7]

Among the developing countries, more countries seem to be applying pressure on the multinational enterprise to take in local partners. Since the evidence suggests that some multinational enterprises will avoid the countries that insist on joint ventures, a policy that is inflexible may not be wise from the point of view of some host countries. The fact that multina-

156

STRATEGY AND OWNERSHIP POLICIES

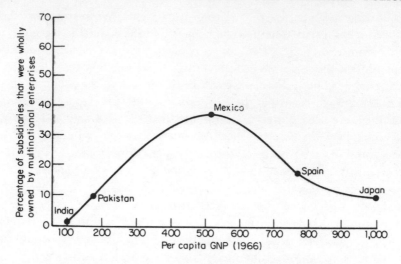

Figure 11–1   *Percentage of Subsidiaries That Were Wholly*
Owned by Multinational Enterprises in Countries
That Had Strong Policies Favoring
Joint Ventures: Countries Classified
by Per Capita GNP [a]

[a] Ceylon has been omitted, since there were only seven investments in Ceylon by the firms in this study.

tional enterprises treat their wholly owned subsidiaries differently from
their joint ventures also suggests that a simple policy of requiring all foreign investment to be in the form of joint ventures may not be in the best
interest of the host country.

TWELVE / The Host Country Interests

The motives that drive host countries to insist on joint ventures are not simple. Some are political, some economic. Both sets of motives raise an important question of fact: How do multinational enterprises treat their various types of subsidiaries?

In some instances, one can be sure, multinational enterprises do not distinguish their wholly owned subsidiaries from their joint ventures in treatment; in other cases, they clearly do. Unfortunately, the data on the differences in behavior of the multinational enterprises toward their wholly and jointly owned affiliates are scanty. Some interviews conducted under our supervision gave an indication of policies. And studies done by others have provided some additional clues. The data that are available are primarily for joint ventures that were established without pressure from the host government, whereas the critical question is primarily with respect to those that would have been wholly owned if the government had not intervened. But the existing data can be used with reasonable confidence to draw some conclusions about the direction of policies toward joint ventures that were established in response to government pressures.

The Economic Effect

Many of the multinational enterprises follow different policies for their joint ventures and their wholly owned subsidiaries. Policies that may differ include those involving capitalization of the subsidiary, transfer pricing to and from affiliates, and payments for technical services and management fees. The details of the variations in behavior are important. But they boil down to two basic differences. First, the multinational enterprise has a great deal more flexibility in dealing with its wholly owned subsidiaries than with its joint ventures. To meet the objectives of the multinational system, the parent varies its contributions to the subsidiary and its demands. Sometimes the flexibility benefits the host country; sometimes not. At any rate, a similar degree of flexibility does not exist in the treatment of joint ventures. Second—a somewhat less certain point—the transactions between parents and joint ventures generally seem to produce a poorer balance-of-payments effect in the early years than transactions with wholly owned subsidiaries. In later years, joint ventures have a more favorable balance-of-payments effect than wholly owned subsidiaries. Whether this is important depends, of course, on the comparative value to the country of foreign exchange today and foreign exchange at some future date.

THE INVESTMENT

Joint ventures and wholly owned subsidiaries generally begin their lives with rather different capital structures. To the casual analyst, the balance-of-payments issues associated with the initial investment of the foreign enterprise and its subsequent flow of dividends may appear identical, whether the subsidiary is wholly or jointly owned. In each case, the foreigner's entitlement to dividends is proportional to his investment; in the case of the wholly owned subsidiaries, the foreigner simply invests more capital at first and is entitled to more dividends later. But the benefits and costs, seen in balance-of-payments terms, appear proportionate.

In practice, however, the foreign parent's contribution in a joint venture tends to be rather different from his contribution in a wholly owned subsidiary. There are a number of indications, for instance, that foreigners have been more likely to capitalize their contribution of know-how in a joint venture than in a wholly owned subsidiary. As was said earlier, the chemical firms that were interviewed in the course of this study indicated an interest in joint ventures primarily when they could obtain equity for a contribution of know-how. The patterns for the other multinational enterprises seemed to be similar; joint ventures showed capitalized know-how more often than did wholly owned subsidiaries.[1] A study of U.S. investment in Australia also reported a larger proportion of know-how in the capitalization of joint ventures than in wholly owned operations.[2] Similarly a study of U.S. investment in Japan, mentioned earlier, discovered that capitalization of know-how was important for joint ventures but not for wholly owned subsidiaries.[3]

It is tempting to conclude from these findings that the foreign firm has acquired a claim on the profits of joint ventures that was disproportionate to its contribution. The findings, however, do not mean that foreign enterprises necessarily received an unjustifiably large claim on future earnings of joint ventures. When a multinational enterprise has complete ownership of a subsidiary, it has no need to capitalize valuable know-how and apparently has not bothered to do so in many cases. On the other hand, if it goes into a joint arrangement, it must capitalize this portion of its contribution in order to receive a return on it. That fact may explain why wholly owned subsidiaries have generally reported a higher return on book equity than joint ventures.[4] If the wholly owned subsidiaries did not capitalize know-how, the equity would be understated, relative to that of the joint venture, leading as a result to a larger apparent rate of return.

Joint ventures and wholly owned subsidiaries also differ in the role that debt plays. For the multinational enterprises in this study, the joint ventures in less developed countries borrowed more than did the wholly owned subsidiaries. And borrowing by a joint venture was, in all countries, more likely to be from local sources than was the borrowing by the wholly owned subsidiaries.[5] Other studies for Canada and Australia have also demonstrated that joint ventures were more likely to borrow locally than were wholly foreign operations.[6] If this has been the general pattern, then joint ventures have placed a double burden on local capital: first, by using the capital of a local partner that might have been used elsewhere; second, by tapping the local supply of credit. The joint ventures' more frequent use of local debt—in fact of debt in general—may be due, at least partly, to a need on the part of the joint venture to turn to debt for expansion because the local partner had been unable or unwilling to contribute his own funds when increases in capital were required.

Whether the contribution of capital by a local partner and the higher level of local borrowing have decreased capital available for other investment in the country depends, of course, on what would have happened to the funds had they not been employed in the joint venture. The foreigner's project, as seen through the eyes of local investors, may have had any of several effects. It could have provided potential local investors with (1) a more easily visible opportunity for direct investment, (2) complementary resources that raised the local return sufficiently that domestic investment took place which otherwise would not have occurred, or (3) a more active financial market that increased the opportunity for other uses of potential savings. Conceivably, therefore, the result might have been a diversion of some funds from consumption or from export to use in local investment. It is, however, unlikely that all the funds would have gone into consumption or would have been exported if the joint venture had not taken them. Official policies favoring joint ventures, therefore, have probably led to some reduction in the amount of capital available for local investment.

PAYMENTS TO AFFILIATES

In addition to differing in their capital structures, joint ventures and wholly owned subsidiaries differ in their choice of methods for transferring funds to and from affiliates.

The dividend payments of joint ventures are generally higher in the early stages and more uniform in the later stages than those of wholly owned subsidiaries. Conflicts over dividends were one of the most important sources of problems with joint ventures reported in the questionnaire. To reduce these conflicts, a formula for dividend payments has sometimes been spelled out as a part of the joint venture agreement. In the initial negotiations, the local partner may even have insisted on guarantees of regular payments. By contrast, a Canadian study highlighted the variability of dividends from wholly owned subsidiaries.[7] An Australian study found that wholly owned subsidiaries were more likely than joint ventures to suspend their dividend payments from time to time.[8] A study of foreign-owned subsidiaries in New Zealand suggested that the presence of a local partner seemed to make dividend payments more regular and perhaps larger in relation to earnings.[9]

In interpreting findings such as these, one has to note that part of the explanation for what sometimes appears to have been lower dividends from the wholly owned subsidiary may lie in the ability of the parent to find other means to withdraw profits. Pricing of goods and services sold by the parent to the subsidiary provides an example. The multinational enterprise, if acting as an "economic man," has a large incentive to remove profits from the joint venture in ways that will eliminate the need to share them with the local partner. Large payments by affiliates for services and higher prices on purchases of materials and components from related enterprises can reduce the profits that have to be shared, transferring them to another part of the multinational firm. On the other hand, it has been argued that the local partner acts as a constraint on the foreign partner's ability to use such techniques for removing profits from the local economy, even though they are commonly used to transfer funds to and from wholly owned subsidiaries.[10]

What evidence exists comes out slightly on the side of those who claim that the local partner is effective in defending his interests. The questionnaire responses indicated that transfer pricing was one of the major sources of conflict with local partners. Data for Colombia indicate that joint ventures have been charged a slightly lower price for purchases abroad than were wholly owned subsidiaries. Table 12-1 shows the extent to which prices differed for various types of purchasers. Of course, the relevance of the data can be questioned. The results could come from the fact that joint ventures have been more frequent when a foreign firm has little oligopoly power. In these cases, the foreign enterprise has been less able to overcharge on its sales to affiliates. However, other data also support the claim that there are consistent differences in the patterns of pricing to joint ventures and wholly owned subsidiaries. Interviews that we conducted with chemical firms indicated that a firm was less likely to use elevated transfer prices to take profits out of joint ventures than it was in the case of wholly owned subsidiaries.

The interviews also demonstrated the influence of local partners in another way. The multinational enterprises that had many joint ventures tended to standardize their transfer prices so that all subsidiaries were charged the same price.[11] With standardization, the flexibility to use transfer pricing as a means of shifting funds between affiliates of the multinational enterprise was greatly contracted.

TABLE 12-1 *Relative Prices Charged Manufacturing Enterprises in Colombia by Foreign Sellers for Selected Intermediate Products: Colombian Enterprises Classified by Ownership Relation to Foreign Seller*

Relation of Colombian firm to foreign seller	Ratio of prices charged in Colombia to prices on "world market"			
	Pharmaceutical materials	Chemical materials	Rubber materials	Electronic materials
Wholly owned	2.55	1.26	1.44	1.16-1.66
Joint venture	—	1.20	—	—
Local	1.19	1.22	1.00	1.06-1.50

Source: Constantine Vaitsos, *Transfer of Resources and Preservation of Monopoly Rents*, mimeographed, presented at the Dubrovnik Conference of the Harvard Development Advisory Service, June 20-26, 1970.

Findings for New Zealand also support the contention that the presence of a local partner has tended to lower the cost of purchases. Joint ventures were more frequently free to purchase from nonaffiliated suppliers than were wholly owned subsidiaries.[12] This freedom can be presumed to have served the joint venture's interests.

Although bits of evidence support the claim that transfer prices for purchases by joint ventures have generally been lower than those applied to wholly owned subsidiaries, there is some indication that the pattern has been more complex. The New Zealand study cited earlier suggests that foreign investors have charged lower prices to their wholly owned subsidiaries initially than they charged later.[13] The purpose of the low charges was probably to generate local cash for expansion in the early years. Multinational enterprises appeared reluctant to follow this practice in their transactions with joint ventures, apparently being unwilling to provide a

G

windfall for local partners. The windfall might, of course, be difficult to recoup later, because of the difficulty in adjusting the transfer prices in the presence of a partner.

There is considerable evidence that the multinational enterprise has turned to methods other than transfer pricing for withdrawing funds from subsidiaries more often for joint ventures than for wholly owned operations. Charges for the provision of know-how, trade names, and management services appear to have been higher for joint ventures than for wholly owned subsidiaries.

The interviews that we conducted with chemical firms revealed that joint ventures were much more likely to be charged for technology than were wholly owned subsidiaries. The Colombian study also provided indications that royalty payments were higher as a percentage of sales where local equity existed. The New Zealand study, in a similar vein, cites a managing director:

[The foreign parent] wouldn't quarrel with making a local issue but at present we do not have to worry enormously about prices of articles as to whether we have a fair profit here or overseas. . . .[This is] really more important insofar as ancillary services are concerned. For example, at present there are no technical services or royalty payments for know-how. This would have to be revised if a local issue was made.[14]

Reinforcing this tendency to rely on royalty payments more frequently for joint ventures then for wholly owned subsidiaries have been the policies adopted by host governments. They have been more willing to allow payments for technology in the case of joint ventures than in cases where all the equity was owned by foreigners.[15] In India and Brazil, for example, royalty payments to foreign parents have generally not been allowed for wholly foreign subsidiaries, but have been permitted for joint ventures.[16]

The net effects of these differences in methods of payments are difficult to determine. The heavier charges for services to the joint venture do not, of course, imply that the joint venture is being discriminated against, as compared with the wholly owned subsidiary. The charges may simply represent alternatives to payments of dividends or the manipulation of transfer prices as ways of shifting funds.[17] As a proportion of the foreigner's contribution, the total payments to the foreign enterprise may be no more than the payments would have been for a wholly owned subsidiary. The form is simply different.

Besides, the local partner should not be presumed to be entirely passive. He too may have found ways to protect his claim on profits. Although funds are drawn off by the foreigner through charges for services, the local partner may have a claim on dividends that gives him a proportionate return on his contribution. And there are plenty of examples in which the local partner uses appropriate transfer pricing and charges for salaries and services to shift earnings to parties that are affiliated with him.

The important point is that in the case of the wholly owned subsidiary the multinational enterprise is free to use any vehicle for transferring funds that is convenient at the moment. There is little reason for the enterprise to tie itself to overtly binding arrangements that call for regular annual payment, such as royalty fees. On the other hand, such arrangements are very attractive when a local partner is present in the subsidiary. From the viewpoint of the multinational enterprise, the sacrifice of flexibility may well be worth the gains that are made in avoiding frequent disputes over how and when the partners are to receive payments.

From the host government point of view, the relative benefits of the flows that are important in the wholly owned subsidiaries and joint ventures depend on the weights that are assigned to regularity of payment and the value of postponing payments into the future. The joint venture wins on the degree-of-predictability scale. The wholly owned subsidiary usually wins on the scale for the present value of the level of resources, because of its larger initial contribution of foreign exchange and its probable tendency to delay payments abroad in its early years.

EXPORTS AND IMPORTS

There are also differences, potential and actual, between joint ventures and wholly owned subsidiaries in their effects on the host country's trade account.

If joint ventures, for instance, had a propensity to import parts and components that were not the same as that of wholly owned subsidiaries, the two kinds of subsidiaries could generate very different effects on the foreign-exchange position of the host country. However, the data do not show clear evidence of such differences. In Canada, Australia, and New Zealand, according to the studies mentioned earlier, joint ventures did have a tendency to buy more from local sources than did other foreign subsidiaries. But the author of the Australian study cautions that the results could have arisen from the fact that a larger percentage of the joint ventures than the wholly foreign subsidiaries represented firms that had been acquired as going concerns and had established their purchasing patterns before they became associated with a foreign enterprise. In addition, as suggested earlier, some joint ventures have been set up by the foreign firm to gain access to the materials that could be supplied by the local partner. Further, the wholly owned subsidiaries, may, as we have shown, be charged more than the joint ventures for their purchases from foreign affiliates. The result of such a tendency would be that the local purchases of the wholly owned subsidiaries were understated as a percentage of all their purchases. These factors may explain the differences in the apparent propensities of joint ventures to buy more from local sources than the wholly owned subsidiaries. If they do, then there would be no reason to expect a decrease in the purchase of imported materials if the multinational enterprise is forced to form a joint venture.

On the export side, the findings are somewhat clearer. There are some indications that foreign parents in joint ventures have often been successful in maintaining some effective control over the allocation of markets in third countries. A number of techniques have been developed. For example, although many governments of less developed countries have prohibited restraints on exports in the joint venture agreements, effective control has been exercised by limiting the joint ventures in the use of know-how and trade names to specified geographical areas. About 45 percent of 1,051 joint venture and licensing agreements in effect in 1964 in India had explicit restrictions on exports.[18] Similar restrictions were found for foreign subsidiaries in Australia [19] and in Colombia and Nicaragua.[20]

Yet considerable caution must be exercised in interpreting these findings. Where control was in the hands of the foreign firm, explicit prohibition of exports was not necessary; in fact, it may have led the firm into trouble with the U.S. antitrust regulations.[21] More important, and more difficult for host governments to monitor, have been the provisions that have appeared frequently in the agreements whereby the marketing organization of the parent was responsible for all sales outside the country of operations.[22] Such an organization is able to choose wholly owned subsidiaries to supply third markets, if this choice is in the interests of the multinational enterprise.[23]

Our interviews with eight chemical firms indicated that two firms included provisions in their joint venture contracts limiting the patent rights to certain areas, while two included clauses that limited access to certain market areas more explicitly. Two other firms said that they exercised control centrally, since they had retained a great deal of decision-making power over their joint ventures. Only two firms did not attempt to restrict the exports from joint ventures.

Of course, the fact that the foreign parents have the ability to control exports from joint ventures does not mean that they actually restrict exports from these arrangements more than they do from wholly owned subsidiaries. Restrictions can be disregarded if the multinational enterprise decides to do so.

The ability to control exports does, however, prove to be useful. Frequently, the multinational enterprise has the choice of supplying an export market from a number of subsidiaries, each with some unused capacity. Some of these may be joint ventures, others, wholly owned. If the marginal costs of production in the two types of operations are identical and the transportation and tariff burdens are the same, the parent should at least theoretically choose to export from a wholly owned subsidiary. The incremental contribution from a joint venture must be shared with a local partner, even though much of it is a return on the multinational enterprise's investment in acquiring knowledge about the third market. The contribution from the wholly owned subsidiary accrues solely to the multinational enterprise.[24] The result is similar to the case of excess capacity as long as the subsidiaries are facing increasing returns to scale. There would, in most cases, have to be a fairly wide margin of production cost, transportation, and tariff differences to cause sourcing from joint ventures. The comments of the managers of the multinational enterprises that we visited indicate that businessmen explicitly think in these terms and accordingly prefer to export from wholly owned facilities.

Other factors have also pushed the parent toward exporting from a wholly owned subsidiary. The foreign parent in joint ventures sometimes is concerned, on the basis of painful experience, that if expansion of the venture is required in the future, the partner will not be able to supply his share of new investment. Expansion could be delayed. Moreover, foreign parents have sometimes felt that they would have more flexibility in the future if they exported from a wholly owned subsidiary. For example, suppose that the parent were to find it cheaper to export from another operation at some later date. In that case, the multinational enterprise that was exporting from the wholly owned subsidiary could shift its sourcing patterns without generating conflicts with local partners who had become used to exporting.

Although multinational enterprises have generally given preference to wholly owned subsidiaries in allocating third-country markets, exports from joint ventures are far from rare. Multinational enterprises have sometimes used access to export markets as a bargaining point in negotiations about ownership. International Computers and Tabulators, for example, agreed to export 30 percent of its production from its Indian venture.[25] In return, it insisted on and received a majority of the equity, in spite of India's position that foreigners should hold a minority share. India also agreed that the local equity could be sold to the public at large rather than to a clearly identifiable partner. International Harvester has begun to make its Mexican plant sole manufacturer for certain products, even though it has agreed to sell 51 percent of the equity in the subsidiary to Mexicans.[26]

The hardest bargains seem to have been driven by the multinational enterprises where assembly operations primarily for export were involved. In fact, we discovered no cases in which the multinational firms that we studied had joint ventures for this kind of subsidiary. The potential conflicts with local interests—conflicts over such issues as pricing of components for assembly and of pricing sales back to affiliates—were especially great. Apparently recognizing the importance of these investments to the country and the reluctance of the firm to conduct the operations through joint ventures, some countries, such as Mexico, have explicitly waived their joint venture requirements for export assembly plants.

Political Effects

The primary disadvantage that the multinational enterprise associates with a joint venture is a loss of control. The primary advantage that host governments associate with a joint venture is a sense of increased control.[27] Both, the evidence suggests, are correct.

This study has shown repeatedly that the multinational enterprise gives up to a local partner a certain amount of control when it enters a joint venture instead of a wholly owned subsidiary. Whether the local partner will use the control in ways that are consistent with the objectives of the host government is another matter. In some cases, there is a strong presumption that the local partner will push for policies that would be those the government would want. For example, the local partner will try to obtain as large a share of the profits as possible for himself. He will try to minimize the foreign partner's transfer of funds through means that do not benefit him, that is, through devices such as management fees, high transfer prices for imported components, and royalty fees. The interests of the partner and of the host country coincide on the advantages of increased exports. But their interests may diverge on the declaration of dividends. The local partner may insist on a steady stream of earnings to the shareholders, while the foreign firm may be willing to reinvest profits in the subsidiary. The government will generally prefer the reinvestment route.

Although there is no guarantee that the local partner will automatically push the joint venture to follow policies that are consistent with the governments objectives, .many governments seem to assume that they can more easily influence a local partner than a foreign owner. Cajoling, threatening, or applying social pressures can be effective, in the view of the government, in inducing the local partner to behave as the government wishes. But many government officials feel at a loss as to how to apply these familiar means of control to a foreign owner, who may be distant both geographically and culturally. However, whether a local businessman is really more responsive than a foreigner to the government's wishes is still an open question. Some foreign owners are extremely sensitive to their precarious position as outsiders and are perhaps even overly eager to respond to what they perceive as signals from the government. But the important thing is that host governments seem to believe that they can more effectively influence a local partner, whose future is tied up within the boundaries of the country, than they could a foreign investor.

The political advantages associated with joint ventures are not solely those that come with control to serve public ends. An increase in the appearance of control is also important, whatever the realities have been. The cries of the political opposition that the government is selling out the country to foreigners are easier to challenge if the government can claim that local businessmen exercise a great deal of control over the foreign subsidiaries. However, there are signs in some countries that the political advantages of the joint venture approach may be limited. In Chile, Mexico, India, Pakistan, and other less developed countries, there is an important strand of political opinion that includes the local partners in its condemnation of foreign investment. One such attack goes: "For the Indian big bourgeoisie, this [joint venture] gives an opportunity to strengthen their position relative to other sectors of the Indian bourgeoisie." [28]

Equally important to the government may be the support from the local business community. In some countries, requirements for joint ventures tend to make allies for the local government of local business leaders. Foreign investment can be viewed as a threat or as an advantage by local businessmen. If they view the foreign firms as competitors, local businessmen tend to withhold their support from government policies that encourage foreign investment in the country. However, if local businessmen are tied in with foreign firms as suppliers of materials and as local partners in their operations, they have a stake in the cooperative administration that attracts the capital and skills of the foreign enterprises.

It is important to note that the schemes which propose that local investors hold equity in parts of the multinational enterprise other than the local subsidiary do not deal with these important issues. Some schemes offer proposals that local investors buy shares in the parent multinational enterprises. Others suggest that local investors share ownership in a regional holding company that owns a number of subsidiaries in a particular geographical area. Neither type of scheme even seriously promises the appearance of local control. They offer little in the way of either economic or political benefits.

Conclusions

On rational grounds, the case for joint ventures as seen from the viewpoint of the host country is an uncertain one. Their economic benefits for the country are unclear, as compared with wholly owned subsidiaries. The judgment depends to a considerable extent upon the economic advantages of stability, short-run benefits, and the possibility of aborted potentials for exports. If the preference for joint ventures in foreign investment is accompanied by the loss of some foreign investment, the judgment of the effects of the policy must take that fact into account as well.

But people and their governments do not live by "economic rationality" alone; other values are important. The joint venture has come to be a major symbol, a symbol of sovereignty and control. Probably, governments will continue to pay an economic price to acquire the feelings of increased influence over their own destiny that come with some local ownership of foreign subsidiaries. But there will, no doubt, still be a limit to the price that they are willing to pay.

In many cases the economic case is so confused that the choice is thrown almost entirely into the political arena. But in the cases where the economic costs are clearly high, economics will probably win. In these cases, the choice of ownership will probably continue to depend on the relative bargaining powers of the parties concerned.

Part III
PROSPECTS FOR
THE FUTURE

THIRTEEN / Some Emerging Issues

The strategies of expansion followed by multinational enterprises seem to have played an important role in influencing choices of organizational structure and ownership policies. Management, of course, has rarely gone through the steps of stating its strategy explicitly and of weighting the contributions and costs associated with alternative organizational structures and ownership policies. Our analysis has imposed an elaborate rational framework on what is largely an intuitive decision process of the businessman. Typically, the manager has experimented, copied the examples of other firms, drawn back from his mistakes, and slowly developed sensible policies for organization and ownership that reflected the needs of his particular enterprise.

Evolutionary adaptation may be rapid enough to ensure survival when the environment is changing slowly, but it is costly and dangerous when it changes rapidly. Most evidence indicates that changes in the international business environment have been accelerating; they will probably continue to do so. In these circumstances, the multinational enterprise that can clearly anticipate the effect of external changes on the design and implementation of its strategy has a much greater chance for survival than the firm that continues to depend on trial and error.

Learning about the past does not assure the manager that he will always be able to account for all the factors that will be important in the future. But it is a useful first step in planning for what will come. There is a good chance that many of the same factors that have influenced the multinational enterprises which were the focus of this study will be important in the future as well.

Some threads of prediction began to emerge in earlier chapters from the analysis of past actions. Drawing out some of these threads may provide the businessman, as well as the government official, with some basis for projecting future problems and prospects.

Future Organizational Structures and Ownership Patterns

The pattern of organization development that has characterized the expansion of multinational enterprises in the past is likely to be repeated in the future. Firms that currently have international divisions will most probably continue to expand overseas and many of them will also add new product lines in foreign markets. Their international divisions will, no doubt, experience the same problems and conflicts that have led others to reorganize; the forms of global structure they develop will be determined, as before, by the particular strategy of each enterprise. Many other firms that have previously been oriented primarily to the U.S. market will begin to invest abroad. These firms will probably establish international divisions after an initial phase in which their first few foreign subsidiaries are allowed a great deal of autonomy.

This pattern of development reflects the responses that firms have made to the problems of learning how to manage foreign operations and of handling increasing size. By pushing more and more responsibilities down to the divisions, they have prevented diseconomies of scale from overwhelming their special competences. At the same time, they have made large investments in high-level personnel and systems that facilitate communication and control of their numerous units.

Multinational enterprises that have already developed global structures are likely to experiment with new forms of organization. If they continue to grow and to diversify their operations, they will face conflicts and choices that cannot easily be resolved by traditional means. The overhead costs associated with the staff and information systems required for adequate coordination of all the firm's activities become overwhelming; diseconomies of scale and complexity threaten to outweigh the benefits of large size. The grid structures, which we have already discussed, are the beginnings of such experimentation. But their success is far from certain.

By instituting multiple reporting relationships in a grid structure, the firm is attempting to reduce the barriers to communication among divisions, and also to reduce overhead costs by eliminating many of the middle layers of management. The enormous practical difficulties of making this structure work suggest that its adoption by large numbers of firms will be slow in coming. The shortage of adequate numbers of broad-gauge managers with the necessary capabilities is acute. Indeed, it is by no means certain that anyone is capable of sustaining the effort demanded by the structure. Not only must the key managers be able to cope with today's complexities, they must be able to recognize and adapt to future changes on all fronts of their extensive environments. Furthermore, there are unsolved problems of developing a control system that is appropriate when responsibility is widely diffused among many managers.

The creation among the managers of a sense of cooperation and shared values is one way of combating the control problem. But it is a never ending task and one that requires heavy expenditures for communications. Frequent meetings and retraining sessions are needed to indoctrinate the managers with the current values of the firm. And, as firms promote to senior positions more foreign nationals who may not share the attitudes and objectives of their U.S. colleagues, the need for meetings becomes even greater.

Advances in data processing and in techniques for transmitting information will help to ease some of the problems of communication and control in all multinational enterprises. For those firms that are moving toward a grid structure, such advances may be of crucial importance. Without some form of help, managers may be submerged beneath a rising flood of data. Machines, however, can take over only a part of the managerial task. No matter how they are processed, much of the critical data, especially those on strategic issues, can convey meaning to the decision maker only if he has personal experience of the situations and a clear sense of the people who will be implementing the decisions.

There are, of course, other ways of responding to the problems of managing multinational and multiproduct operations. Some firms may decide to maintain clear lines of accountability and responsibility in one of the traditional global structures and to use the planning process as a means of ensuring the necessary cooperation and communication among divisions. But it will not be easy to make a system of planning for global operations effective in this new role; firms will have to improve enormously upon the systems that multinational enterprises use today. Such improvements will require large investments in managerial time over many years. In spite of the difficulties, there are already signs in a few firms that such investments can eventually become profitable.

Some firms may decide to form divisions on the basis of factors other than products or areas. They may, for instance, group their businesses by similarity of customers, technology, or stage of development of the product. The products that are lumped together may look rather different from those that fall into today's product divisions. An example of such innovation is provided by a few firms that have formed "new enterprise" divisions, in which new products are nurtured. Once the new products have passed through the development stage, they are transferred to one of the major divisions.

Other variations in structure are likely to be tried as firms begin to follow new strategies of expansion. Supplementing the normal strategy of developing products and skills in the United States and then transferring them abroad at some later date, some firms will begin to use expertise developed in foreign subsidiaries. Major technological developments, for instance, may occur in the European laboratories of some firms. Some firms may allow their foreign subsidiaries a degree of independence in searching for profitable new avenues of growth in their local environments. If the products developed or acquired overseas are successful and capable of transfer to other units of the enterprise, some parts of the organization will have to adapt to the new communication and control needs. In the event that units located abroad become a major source of new products and skills for the whole enterprise, it is likely that new forms of structure, affecting all levels of management, will be needed.

Experimentation with new forms of structure will not, of course, occur in all highly diversified multinational enterprises. For some of them, the costs of developing systems for coordinating all the important interactions among the various units of the organization will seem so high that the chances of gaining some net benefit appear small. The diseconomies of scale and complexity, they may calculate, will simply outweigh the potential benefits to be gained from coordination. These firms may choose, therefore, to divide their operations into essentially independent divisions and forego the possible advantages of more interdivisional cooperation. Each division would then become its own multinational business, sharing with other divisions only ties of ownership to a common parent company.

All these possible variations in organizational response to the problems of managing multiproduct, multinational operations are likely to affect ownership policies. As firms experiment with new structures, the dominant pattern will probably be greater attempts to exercise control over their scattered subsidiaries. Many of the firms will find joint ventures harder to live with. Where new subsidiaries are being established, many enterprises will try to own the facilities outright. Where joint ventures already exist, disputes are likely to set in, leading to changes in the ownership.

Those firms that move toward gridlike structures will, we have suggested, depend a great deal on the development of feelings of shared values and responsibilities among the managers. The presence of local partners, outsiders to the multinational system, will probably be very difficult to tolerate in this kind of organization. It is hard for the partner to identify with the objectives and values of the system, especially when the interests of the system are likely to conflict with those that arise from his ownership in a single subsidiary. Because of the potential problems, enterprises that attempt to develop grid structures will most probably have a low tolerance for joint ventures.

Although many firms will develop increasingly complex operations, some may prefer not to accept the gamble of both product and area diversification. They may judge that, by remaining specialized, they will be able to concentrate their attention on developing such a high level of expertise in a narrow field that they will be able to outcompete their more diversified competitors. For them, the traditional organizational structures will suffice. As their products mature, however, these firms will be under pressure to increase the coordination of their overseas activities. To bring to bear the special competence of the multinational enterprise, levels of management above the subsidiary will issue more and more directives aimed at improving the performance of the multinational system as a whole. The managers of these firms will probably find themselves in conflict with the many joint venture partners that they picked up as they first expanded abroad. As they move toward centralizing control, the emphasis will be on shifting more ownership into the hands of the multinational enterprise. For many enterprises that are already multinational, this is likely to be the pattern.

The vertically integrated multinational enterprises may present a more complex shift in ownership patterns. These firms tend to have wholly owned facilities in the controlled stages, usually the raw material stage or an early processing operation. At the same time, they have joint ventures in the downstream facilities where control is less critical than access to markets. But these enterprises are undergoing change. Many of them are beginning to lose their oligopoly positions in the stage that they have traditionally controlled. New sources of raw materials are coming into the hands of firms that are outside the traditional oligopoly. In the oil industry, the number of "independents" with their own sources of crude oil has multiplied rapidly. A similar phenomenon is taking place in a number of mining industries. Where control is maintained at a processing stage, technology is no longer the exclusive property of a few firms, and capital sources are becoming available to the country that wishes to set up its own processing operations.

In order to reestablish some barriers to competition, some of these multinational enterprises may try to develop a greater degree of protection and control at downstream stages. Petroleum firms, for example, have been moving into petrochemicals. In the banana industry, where the major firms have lost control of the banana plantations, at least one enterprise has turned to advertising in an attempt to establish a brand preference that would reduce competition downstream. As multinational enterprises move in this direction, joint ventures downstream will be increasingly difficult to accept.

At the same time, however, these firms may be more willing to accept local partners at the upstream stages than they were in the past; in fact, a number of them will probably move slowly out of the stages that they can no longer control. They will begin to view themselves as buyers of raw materials. Where joint ventures can help in assuring a regular flow of quality inputs, they will be acceptable to multinational enterprises. In other cases, multinational enterprises will be willing to buy their raw materials from independent suppliers.

For the future, it appears that the majority of the existing multinational enterprises will try to move toward more complete ownership of their overseas facilities. There will be plenty of exceptions, to be sure. Some multinational enterprises are really just beginning their process of diversification. These firms will probably continue for quite a while to value highly the contributions that local partners can make to this strategy. In addition, there will be domestic firms that start to invest outside the United States. Many of these firms will be smaller than those already established in multinational operations in the same industry. The small firms will probably begin their foreign expansion on the basis of some innovation that seems to have overseas potential. Eager to spread their facilities while they still have a technological advantage over their larger, established competitors, these new entrants will probably continue the historical pattern of turning to local partners for the resources that they find scarce. Further exceptions will be the subsidiaries in the least developed countries. These subsidiaries will remain as joint ventures for some time, and they will probably be the last to be fully integrated into the multinational system. Although all these exceptions are important, the dominant direction of change will probably be toward a decreasing popularity of joint venture arrangements among the major multinational enterprises.

Changing Host Government Relations

With the continued growth of multinational enterprise, the challenge to the sovereignty of nations will be viewed as more serious. As governments search for ways to maintain their sovereignty, they are likely to experiment with a number of policies. One policy that will be frequently and vigorously pursued will be the attempt to enforce requirements for local participation in the ownership of subsidiaries belonging to foreign firms. Although the economic case for joint ventures from the host country's point of view is a rather qualified one, political pressures will probably lead more and more governments, particularly those in developing countries, toward insisting that much of the foreign investment that the country accepts include a local partner. With most of the firms moving toward centralization of control through complete ownership, and with governments demanding more joint ventures, what will be the result? Obviously, we do not know, but there is some basis for projection.

The ability of a foreign firm to resist the pressures of a host government depends, to a great extent, on how much the country needs what the firm has to offer and how many alternative sources for the foreigner's contribution exist.

Technology has been the trump card for most U.S. investors as they went overseas. If the technology was new, and if few firms had it, those firms were loath to bid against each other to meet the demands of a host country. But technology slips out of the hands of the innovating firms. Unless the foreign enterprise can offer something new, its bargaining position with a host government declines. Some firms have responded by coming up with a newer technology that has enabled them to regain their bargaining strength. Others have simply lost their bargaining position and been compelled to give ground to government pressures, including pressures for joint ventures.

Some firms have followed a different path. As they lost control of the technology that had provided their original bargaining strength, they began to offer access to foreign markets as a substitute. The signal for that shift was the use of foreign subsidiaries as sources to ship parts, components, and final products to other countries in which the multinational parent had plants and subsidiaries.

Of course, the original bargaining power of some enterprises was never based on an advanced technology. Some of the marketing-oriented firms came with a trade name so well known and so attractive to users that no alternative was available. This kind of situation was especially common for countries that felt the need to respond to internal consumer pressures, including the needs of their foreign tourist trade.

Multinational enterprises that can continue to offer new technology, access to foreign markets, or particularly strong trade names will probably remain in a strong position to resist the mounting pressures of host governments for joint ventures. Even the most insistent countries make exceptions in their requirements for joint ventures for the firms that they really need. The most common exception is for the firm that will provide access to foreign markets for manufactured exports.

Although some firms will end up with wholly owned facilities even in the most insistent developing countries, there will probably be a certain amount of improvisation or novelty in some of the new ownership arrangements. Increasingly one will probably encounter arrangements that allow the foreign firm to exercise unambiguous control only for so long as it continues to make a critical contribution. The arrangements will call for increasing local control when these contributions diminish.

Where the extent of the contribution is clear at the outset, such arrangements can be rather straightforward. A foreign firm can be allowed to control the enterprise for a fixed number of years, a period that appears to be long enough for the contribution to be absorbed. At the end of that period, the control can go to the local government or to a local enterprise.

An example is provided by an agreement for a refinery in Africa. It grants complete ownership to the foreign firm for eleven years; at the end of this period, the host government can buy the shares, counting as part of its payment the income taxes that were excused under the tax holiday scheme. There are several arrangements that have the effect of turning shares over to local investors after a specified period in exchange for a down payment; the balance of the payment is to be made, not completely logically, from the dividends that accrue to the shares. Although the details vary widely, there are now quite a few arrangements that provide for an orderly shift of control from the foreign firm to local investors.

In fact, requirements for arrangements of this kind are beginning to appear in the legislation of developing countries. The most sweeping demands at the moment are those that have appeared in the draft rules for the treatment of foreign capital in the Andean Subregional Group.[1] The suggested regulations stipulate that those foreign firms that are either already in the region or desiring to enter and that wish to take advantage of the tariff liberalization must make a commitment to offer 51 percent of their equity within not more than fifteen years of the approval of the investment. Practically the only exception in manufacturing is the firm that exports 80 percent of its production outside the Andean bloc. This type of exporting firm is exempt altogether from the regulations on ownership, but does not enjoy the privileges of the liberalization of tariffs within the region.

It is doubtful that the Andean Group will be able to live with such sweeping regulations. The pressure on member countries to relax the terms for multinational enterprises with advanced technology, an important trade name, or access to export markets will probably prove too great. Nevertheless, the draft agreement is almost certainly an indication of the direction that the policies of host governments will move, at least in the developing countries.

What happens when the value and duration of the contributions offered by the multinational enterprise are less obvious? There are many cases where host countries are not eager to risk a premature departure on the part of foreign investors. There are some proposals that try to deal with just this contingency.[2]

These proposals provide a series of options which are designed to keep the foreign firm only so long as it makes itself indispensable. The foreign firm is offered a relatively free rein for a number of years, say seven to ten. After this point, local partners have an option to purchase a certain proportion of the equity on the basis of a pricing formula that has been agreed upon initially. The innovation is that the foreign firm has a "put" option if local ownership increases beyond a certain point, say 49 percent. At this point, the foreign firm has the option of insisting that all the remaining shares be bought by the local partner, if the foreign owner does not want to live with this much local control.

The assumption is, of course, that the local partner will not exercise his option beyond the point that allows the foreigner to force the sale of all his shares if the consequences of the foreigner's withdrawal would be very unfavorable. The foreign firm therefore has some assurances of control as long as his presence appears indispensable. Once the foreigner is seen as dispensable, the host country is assured of a way to reduce the foreign presence in an orderly and, one hopes, equitable way.

Determining a satisfactory pricing formula has been a major stumbling block in past negotiations for fade-out arrangements. But some recent agreements have shown that price need not be a problem, provided that both parties are willing to agree on the principle of the fade-out arrangement; for the firm, the importance of the discounted present value of the price ten years in the future is small, compared to the value of the expected stream of earnings.

The commitment to an eventual shift of control will prove easy for some multinational enterprises, difficult for others. One category for which it should prove relatively easy involves the subsidiary that is set up as a downstream outlet for the output of another affiliate. This is the kind of situation in which long-term sales contracts may do just as well as actual control. Once the downstream facility has been successfully set up and is functioning, the parent may have few reservations about turning over the actual day-to-day control to local partners. An example is provided by a joint venture for reconstituted milk, sold under a local brand name, in a

Southeast Asian country. The foreign partner is an exporter of dry milk. The arrangement calls for the gradual purchase of shares by the local partner and for the foreign partner to continue to be the supplier of dry milk. Currently, the foreign partner is active in ensuring that the local product is of high quality and that the joint venture obtains a large share of the market. But the local partner will soon be able to take over the relatively simple plant and marketing system.

In situations where the shift in control affects other subsidiaries, multinational enterprises will be extremely unwilling to make any commitments. If, for example, an international brand name is involved, the foreign firm will not wish to run the risk of changes in price or quality that are out of line with changes in other markets. Where the subsidiary is an integral part of a rationalized production system spread over many countries, the foreign firm will attempt to prevent the local partner from doing anything that will upset the system.

Many of these more novel arrangements to cover ownership and control promise to blunt the edge of conflicts between multinational enterprises and host governments. They do not, however, remove the basic source of the conflict. The arrangements allow governments to exercise their bargaining power only at the periphery of each multinational enterprise. Many of the crucial decisions about the allocation of resources and the transfer of technology will remain in the hands of the multinational enterprises.

There will almost certainly be many more attempts by individual governments to regulate the activities of these firms. But such attempts at the national or regional level are likely to be frustrated by the ability of multinational enterprises to organize themselves in ways that enable them to ignore local government policies.

Individual governments may attempt to increase their bargaining power by banding together to create an international body that deals with the problem of the multinational enterprise. Indeed, a number of proposals for international regulation have already appeared.[3] The challenges to national sovereignty posed by the multinational enterprise are probably not yet sufficiently serious to induce governments to devote enough of their resources to create a workable international agreement. But as the enterprises grow even more sophisticated, and as the frustrations of trying to deal with the problems at the national level become apparent, government interest and effort in negotiating international controls will almost certainly increase.

Managers of the enterprises themselves have not been very concerned about past proposals for international regulation. Although vague codes of conduct have received their enthusiastic support, proposals that have sufficient teeth to impose constraints on the activities of the enterprises have, at best, been ignored. However, as attempts to introduce international regulation continue to be thwarted, government action at the national level will probably become more disruptive to the activities of multinational enterprises, even though such action may not be in the economic interests of the country itself. At that point, managers of the enterprises will begin to find that their interests lie in cooperating with governments in the development of policies for international regulation.

Appendices

APPENDIX A /
Classifications
of Product Diversity

A highly diversified product line is defined in this study by the condition that:

ns is greater than 1, where n = number of two-digit industries represented in the product line

and s = proportion of total sales generated by products outside the major industry

For example, a firm with sales divided in the percentages of 40, 30, 30, among three industries satisfies the condition of ns greater than 1, since $n = 3$ and $s = 0.60$. Such a firm is, therefore, in the category of high product diversity.

Similarly, low product diversity is defined by the condition that ns lies between 0 and 1. Thus, a firm operating in two two-digit industries is necessarily classified in the low category even if there is an equal share of the total sales in the two industries. Firms that have all their operations entirely within a single two-digit industry are classified as having no product diversity.

Values of n for each firm were available and apply to the 1965 product lines.[1] The sales data to calculate the relative industry importance measure, s, were collected from published sources and interviews.[2] Measures of s were not available for the domestic activities of twenty-two firms and estimates had to be made. For a known value of n, the maximum value of s to satisfy the low category may be calculated. For example, if $n = 6$, then s must be less than or equal to 0.17. The estimates were based on qualitative evidence that suggested which side of the appropriate boundary value of s each of the twenty-two firms lay.

Separate classifications of the diversity of the product lines in the United States and abroad were made for each firm by this procedure. Values of n for the foreign product lines of each firm were adjusted, as in the domestic case, to allow for the effects of vertical integration across industry boundaries.[3] Estimates of the value of s were made for the foreign activities of thirty firms.

Classification at the two-digit level of aggregation sacrifices some degree of detail and raises the possibility of biasing the results. For example, a candy manufacturer (SIC 207) with a small specialty chemical business (SIC 28) is considered to be more diversified by product than a food company with a wide range of products, from sausages to soft drinks, all within SIC 20. An examination of this possible bias suggested, however, that it is small. Firms diversified at the three-digit level tend also to be diversified at the two-digit level. Values of s at the three-digit level were not available, so that direct comparisons of the two-digit categories and similar three-digit categories could not be made. An indirect comparison was possible by ranking the firms in ascending order of values of n at the three-digit level and assigning cut-off points to produce three groups with the same numerical population as those produced by the procedure using the ns values. The two sets of groups contained lists of firms that were in reasonably close agreement. The ns index at the two-digit level was used because it is conceptually more appropriate than the alternative groupings for examining the relationship between product diversity and structure.

There are, of course, many other possible measures of product diversity based on more detailed industry classifications, and the use of variables such as earnings, employment, or payroll instead of sales. Gort [4] used seven measures of diversity, weighted by payroll and employees outside the primary two-digit and four-digit industries, and a measure similar to the one used in this study. The high correlations that were found to exist among all the measures suggest that the relative rankings of diversity remain approximately constant whatever weighting variable is used to rank the firms in order of increasing product diversity. Support for the methodology used in this study is provided by the correlation between Gort's index based on employment [5] and the ns index. There are eleven industries, represented in the sample by five or more firms, for which comparisons with Gort's index may be made. The mean values of the two indices in each industry were ranked in order of increasing diversity. The Spearman coefficient of rank correlation between the two indices is 0.86.

The choice of the boundaries between the three categories was influenced more by a desire to provide groups that divided the sample into three roughly equal parts than by a need to provide a logical mathematical formula for identifying categories. No great significance is claimed for the boundary between the low and high categories; certainly no executive would notice when his firm crossed the divide between low and high although he would probably be aware of increasing needs for communication and coordination between the separate parts of the enterprise. All that is claimed for the method of dividing the sample into three numerically equivalent categories is that the pressures on management from product diversity have rough equivalence within each group.

Notes

1. The source of these data was Fortune, *Plant and Product Directory 1965* (New York: Fortune, 1966). The data apply to products manufactured during 1965, and exclude products outside the manufacturing sector.

2. For example, annual reports of the firms and their 10-k reports to the Securities and Exchange Commission.

3. The source of the necessary product-line information was the data bank compiled by James W. Vaupel and Joan P. Curhan for their sourcebook, *The Making of Multinational Enterprise* (Boston: Harvard Graduate School of Business Administration, Division of Research, 1969).

4. Michael Gort, *Diversification and Integration in American Industry* (Princeton: Princeton University Press, 1962), pp. 6, 7.

5. *Ibid.*, Table 8, p. 33. The index is based on data in U.S. Bureau of Census, *Company Statistics: 1954 Census of Business, Manufacturing, Mineral Industries* (Washington, D.C.: U.S. Government Printing Office, 1958), Table 2. This index remains relatively stable over time, so that it should retain some relevance for the present problem.

APPENDIX B /
Classifications
of Structure

The structures identified in this study indicate the different ways in which the formal responsibilities of senior general managers reporting directly to the president of each firm were defined at the end of both 1966 and 1968. The taxonomy of organizational structure used here consists of a small number of categories, although, in reality, there are a number of alternatives. Structures were classified according to their dominant tendency, a practice that tended to overlook some significant aberrations. Various rules were developed to control the amount of aberration that was allowable for each classification. These rules were as follows:

First, specialist functions, such as exporting, importing, licensing, patent or trademark protection, are not considered separately in the classifications. Staff groups may coordinate functions without any close ties to the general managers. For example, the National Distillers and Chemical Corporation has a strong import-marketing organization operating independently from the other foreign activities managed by an international division.

Second, extractive activities such as mining or agriculture are not considered as part of the manufacturing activities. They are ignored for the purposes of structural classification just as they are in the measures of product diversity. Generally, these extractive activities are managed quite separately from manufacturing. The Firestone rubber plantation managers in Liberia, for example, report directly to a special department in the corporate headquarters and have nothing to do with the international division. Service activities abroad, such as geophysical surveying or automobile rentals, are also ignored in the classifications for the same reasons.

Third, Canadian subsidiaries are treated as a part of the U.S. operations, reflecting the fact that most firms either ignore the 49th parallel for organization purposes at senior levels or treat Canada separately from the rest of their foreign business.

Fourth, where one or two foreign joint ventures accounting for an insignificant proportion of the foreign business are attached to a subsidiary in a different product division, their presence is ignored. Similar minor exceptions to the general rule of classification by the reporting relationships among general managers are made for the other structural forms.

The structures used in most of the analysis are those of 1968, even though the measures of strategy apply to 1966. The later date for structure was used because changes in structure normally (as Chapter 5 shows) lag behind changes in strategy. Many of the firms had changed their strategies of expansion abroad within a few years prior to 1966. By making allowance for these lags, it is thought that the results are a reasonably accurate representation of the relationship between strategy and structure under relatively stable conditions of operation.

Exceptions to this procedure were made for four firms. These were the only firms included in the study that changed their strategies during the period 1966–1968 sufficiently to warrant changes in the categories of measurement. In two cases, firms sold a worldwide product division, leaving the foreign business in a single industry to be administered by the remaining worldwide product division. The other two firms, both in the food industry, elected to diversify their food businesses abroad, one by investing in chemical production and one by merging with an international firm in other products. Both moved to a mixed structure. These four changes were ignored and the data on both the strategies and structures of these firms are those existing prior to the change, about 1966.

Note that the classification procedure does not explicitly take into account the informal structure of management. During periods of stability in strategy and structure, however, the formal and informal structures are generally closely related. Only during periods of change do important discrepancies between the two structures appear. These discrepancies are discussed in Chapter 4 for the few cases where they affect the interpretation of the results of the analysis.

Much of the data upon which the structural classifications are based were collected from published sources. The principal sources were (1) publications by firms, such as annual reports, reports of annual meetings, and presentations to financial analysts, (2) newspaper and journal articles, (3) company histories,[1] and (4) management surveys.[2] In addition, interviews with over thirty firms were used to check the judgments made about the structure. The results of these interviews indicated that the prior judgments based on published information were sufficiently accurate for the purposes of this study.

Notes

1. For example, Alfred D. Chandler, Jr., *Strategy and Structure* (Cambridge: M.I.T. Press, 1962), and Glenn D. Babcock, *History of the United States Rubber Company* (Bloomington: Bureau of Business Research, Indiana University, 1966).

2. A wealth of data is available in such publications as: Enid B. Lovell, *The Changing Role of the International Executive* (New York: National Industrial Conference Board, 1966); Alexander O. Stanley, *Organizing for International Operations* (New York: American Management Association, 1960), Research Study No. 41; Harold Steiglitz, *Organization Structures of International Companies* (New York: National Industrial Conference Board, 1965); Business International, *Organizing for Worldwide Operations; Structuring and Implementing the Plan* (New York: February 1965).

APPENDIX C / A Multiple Regression Approach to Ownership Policies

Stepwise and multiple regressions were used to test the propositions about the relationships between strategy and ownership patterns. Linear regressions were calculated by using measures of the propensity of the firm to have foreign manufacturing joint ventures as the dependent variable and the various indicators of strategy as the independent variables.

Three types of measures of the propensity of the multinational enterprise to employ joint ventures abroad were used. One measure, available for ninety-nine firms, was the percentage of foreign manufacturing accounted for by joint ventures, as indicated in the questionnaire responses. A second measure was the fraction of manufacturing subsidiaries that were joint ventures in 1966. The third type of measure considered only those manufacturing subsidiaries that were entered between 1960 and 1967. These latter two measures were broken down into separate ratios for only minority and only majority joint ventures.[1] They were available for 152 of the multinational enterprises.

The independent variables were indicators of the strategies that have been discussed in the previous chapters. In several cases, dummy variables were used. Table C-1 summarizes the definitions of the independent variables and Table C-2 shows the simple correlation coefficients among them.

Two types of regression runs were made. The first was a stepwise regression in which the first variables to enter were those that contributed most to reducing unexplained variance. Tables C-3 to C-7 show the sign of the coefficient of regression for each variable and the coefficient of multiple correlation by the time that the independent variable had entered the regression equation.[2]

A second type of regression calculation was made to account for the fact that some of the independent variables were actually surrogates for combinations of other measures that were included in the equations. The organizational form of the multinational enterprise reflected some of the elements of strategy that were picked up by other variables, such as the percentage of sales spent on advertising. Similarly, the fraction of subsidiaries accounted for by sales operations was another measure of marketing orientation. To capture the effects of the measures of single strategies, we constrained the entry of those two variables, organizational structure and the propensity of the firm to enter sales subsidiaries, until after the other variables had entered the stepwise regressions. The results of this round of calculations are shown in the second parts of Tables C-3 to C-7.

The regression results were consistent with the propositions that have been set forth. In all the cases in which the percentage of manufacturing accounted for by joint ventures or the ratios of minority joint ventures to all manufacturing subsidiaries were used as dependent variables and the composite independent variables were allowed to enter the equations only after the other variables, the signs of the coefficients were as hypothesized. Extractive activity, propensity to acquire rather than to form, and higher diversity were associated with a larger percentage of manufacturing by joint ventures and a larger ratio of minority joint ventures to all manufacturing subsidiaries. Higher advertising expenditures, larger R&D efforts, more centralized organizational structures, and a higher propensity to enter sales subsidiaries were associated with less importance of joint ventures and less minority joint ventures.

The regression results provide hints of other relationships. For example, the advertising variable is a better predictor of the percentage of minority joint ventures among recently established subsidiaries than of the percentage of overseas manufacturing done in joint ventures. This relationship supports the hypothesis that marketing-oriented firms have been able to tolerate a joint venture partner better in a large market, where the size was sufficient to justify a custom-marketing strategy, than in smaller markets where the firms have been more disposed to use imported strategies. Also, suggestive of the role of diversification in the recent strategy of the multinational enterprises is the greater power of this variable in explaining the ownership of recently formed or acquired subsidiaries than in explaining the ownership of the overall stock of subsidiaries. For example, diversification is a more powerful variable for the explanation of minority joint ventures between 1960 and 1967 than it is for the holdings of minority joint ventures in 1966 or for the percentage of all manufacturing accounted for by joint ventures. The traditional product line of the systems probably represented a large percentage of the manufacturing output, but the diversified lines accounted for proportionally larger numbers of subsidiaries, especially among recent entries. What we have observed may be the result of the increase in foreign diversification in recent years as firms have carried abroad their new lines from the United States.

The regression results for the proportion of majority joint ventures in any foreign manufacturing subsidiaries showed weaker relation between strategy and the choice of ownership than did those for minority ownership. The same results are evident in the charts of the two previous chapters. The choice between majority ownership and complete ownership may not be as influenced by strategy as is the choice between both of these and minority ownership. Probably, many of the multinational firms have found ways to retain control over critical decisions in joint ventures in which they hold a majority of the stock.

In spite of their many weaknesses, the regression results lend support to relationships previously described. Although variables for which measures were available explained about half the variance in the measure of minority joint ventures, the contributions of the last few variables to enter the stepwise equations were small. The results provide little evidence of the relative importance of the different elements of strategy because of the differing quality of the measures. In fact, there were no direct measures available for some elements of strategy—rationalization of production and attempts at vertical integration in manufacturing enterprises, for example. An additional weakness arises from the fact that we were often dealing with small numbers of observations in calculating the propensities of the firms to enter joint ventures in a particular period. The number of minority joint ventures entered by a particular enterprise between 1960 and 1967 might, for example, be only two or three. Although the calculations of the proportion of manufacturing subsidiaries that were joint ventures as of a particular date usually avoided the problems of small members, they probably reflected many decisions made in the past under a different strategy. If the firms were slow to change their existing operations to reflect new strategies, this problem would be serious.

Notes

1. Subsidiaries in Canada, Japan, Spain, Ceylon, India, Mexico, and Pakistan were excluded in all ratios.

2. The calculations were made on an IBM 360 computer, using the *SPSS* program. See Norman H. Nie, Dale H. Bent, and C. Hadlai Hull, *Statistical Package for the Social Sciences* (New York: McGraw-Hill Book Company, 1970). Missing observations were handled by pairwise deletion of variables.

H

TABLE C-1 *Independent Variables in Regression Equations*

Variable	Number of enterprises for which measure was available	Definition
1. Advertising	136	Advertising expenditures as a percentage of sales according to *National Advertising Investments*, 1966-1967
2. Diversification	152	The number of three-digit SIC industries in which the system manufactured outside the United States and Canada in 1966
3. R&D	98	R&D expenditures as a percentage of sales, as collected from *News Front*, November 1965, January and February 1966, and annual reports of the firms
4. Extractive	152	A dummy variable to indicate whether the system had three or more extractive operations outside the United States in 1966. 1 = nonextractive, 3 = extractive
5. Relative size	140	A dummy variable indicating whether the system was the largest to one-half the largest firm in its primary three-digit SIC industry, as measured by sales. 1 = large, 2 = small
6. Organization	147	Variable coded to indicate expected tolerance of organization for joint venture; most tolerant assigned the lowest number:
		Stage 2 in U.S., international division without intermediate area organization — 3
		Stage 3 in U.S., international division without intermediate area organizations — 4
		Worldwide product divisions, with reorganization as a result of merger with other firms — 5
		Worldwide product divisions — 6
		Grid — 7
		Mixed — 8
		Stage 3 in U.S., international division with intermediate area organizations — 9
		Area divisions — 10
		Stage 2 in U.S., international division with intermediate area organizations — 11
7. Sales subsidiary ratio	151	For each multinational enterprise, the ratio of the number of subsidiaries that were initially engaged in sales to those that were engaged in sales plus those that were initially engaged in manufacturing
8. Acquisition ratio	151	For each multinational enterprise, the ratio of the number of subsidiaries that were acquired as going concerns to those that were acquired and those that were newly formed

TABLE C-2 *Simple Correlation Matrix for "Independent" Variables*

	Adver-tising	Diversi-fication	R&D	Extrac-tive	Relative size	Organi-zation	Sales subsidiary
Advertising	1.00						
Diversification	−0.12	1.00					
R&D	0.01	0.06	1.00				
Extractive	−0.01	0.22	−0.13	1.00			
Relative size	0.06	−0.09	−0.02	−0.05	1.00		
Organization	0.12	−0.08	−0.17	−0.17	−0.08	1.00	
Sales subsidiary	−0.13	−0.27	0.27	−0.18	−0.11	0.31	1.00
Acquisition ratio	0.00	0.08	−0.15	−0.03	0.02	−0.11	−0.31

TABLE C-3 *Regression Results, Dependent Variable = Percentage of Foreign Manufacturing Accounted for by Joint Ventures*[a]

1. Stepwise regression, entry of independent variables constrained such that first variables to enter are those that contribute most to reducing explained variance.

Independent variable by order of entry	Sign of b on entry	Multiple R[b]
Organization	Neg.**	0.54
Extractive	Pos.**	0.62
Sales subsidiary ratio	Neg.**	0.67
Advertising	Neg.**	0.68
Relative size	Pos.*	0.70
R&D	Pos.	0.70
Acquisition ratio	Pos.	0.70
Diversification	Neg.	0.70

2. Stepwise regression, entry of independent variables constrained such that organization and sales subsidiary ratio must enter after other variables. Otherwise, entry by order of reduction of unexplained variance.

Independent variable by order of entry	Sign of b on entry	Multiple R[b]
Extractive	Pos.**	0.39
Acquisition ratio	Pos.**	0.43
Relative size	Pos.**	0.46
Advertising	Neg.**	0.49
Diversification	Pos.	0.49
R&D	Neg.	0.50
Organization	Neg.	0.66
Sales subsidiary ratio	Neg.	0.70

*"b" significant at 0.05 level.

**"b" significant at 0.01 level.

[a]Regression of the form $y = a + b_1 x + b_2 x_2 \ldots b_n x_n$.

[b]Coefficient of multiple correlation, with the variables that have entered the stepwise regression up to this point.

TABLE C-4 *Regression Results, Dependent Variable = Ratio of Minority Joint Ventures to All Manufacturing Subsidiaries in 1966*[a]

1. Stepwise regression, entry of independent variables constrained such that first variables to enter are those that contribute most to reducing unexplained variance.

Independent variable by order of entry	Sign of b on entry	Multiple R[b]
Organization	Neg.**	0.49
Sales subsidiary ratio	Neg.**	0.53
Advertising	Neg.**	0.58
R&D	Neg.	0.58
Extractive	Pos.	0.59
Relative size	Pos.	0.59
Diversification	Pos.	0.59
Acquisition ratio	Pos.	0.60

2. Stepwise regression, entry of independent variables constrained such that organization and sales subsidiary ratio must enter after other variables. Otherwise, entry by order of reduction of unexplained variance.

Independent variable by order of entry	Sign of b on entry	Multiple R[b]
Advertising	Neg.**	0.24
R&D	Neg.**	0.33
Diversification	Pos.**	0.37
Extractive	Pos.	0.39
Relative size	Pos.	0.41
Acquisition ratio	Pos.	0.42
Organization	Neg.**	0.57
Sales subsidiary ratio	Neg.**	0.60

**See Table C-3.
[a]See Table C-3.
[b]See Table C-3.

TABLE C-5 *Regression Results, Dependent Variable = Ratio of Majority Joint Ventures to All Manufacturing Subsidiaries in 1966[a]*

1. Stepwise regression, entry of independent variables constrained such that first variables to enter are those that contribute most to reducing unexplained variance.

Independent variable by order of entry	Sign of b on entry	Multiple R[b]
Sales subsidiary ratio	Neg.**	0.21
Advertising	Neg.**	0.28
Relative size	Pos.	0.31
Diversification	Pos.	0.34
Organization	Neg.	0.36
Extractive	Pos.	0.36
R&D	Pos.	0.36
Acquisition ratio	Neg.	0.36

2. Stepwise regression, entry of independent variables constrained such that organization and sales subsidiary ratio must enter after other variables. Otherwise, entry by order of reduction of unexplained variance.

Independent variable by order of entry	Sign of b on entry	Multiple R[b]
Diversification	Pos.**	0.21
Relative size	Pos.**	0.27
Advertising	Neg.	0.30
Extractive	Pos.	0.31
Acquisition ratio	Neg.	0.35
Sales subsidiary ratio	Neg.*	0.35
Organization	Neg.	0.36

*See Table C-3.
**See Table C-3.
[a]See Table C-3.
[b]See Table C-3.

TABLE C-6 *Regression Results, Dependent Variable = Ratio of Minority Joint Ventures to All Manufacturing Subsidiaries Entered between 1960 and 1967*[a]

1. Stepwise regression, entry of independent variables constrained such that first variables to enter are those that contribute most to reducing unexplained variance.

Independent variable by order of entry	Sign of b on entry	Multiple R[b]
Organization	Neg.**	0.48
R&D	Neg.**	0.51
Diversification	Pos.**	0.54
Advertising	Neg.**	0.56
Extractive	Pos.	0.57
Sales subsidiary ratio	Neg.	0.57

2. Stepwise regression, entry of independent variables constrained such that organization and sales subsidiary ratio must enter after other variables. Otherwise, entry by order of reduction of unexplained variance.

Independent variable by order of entry	Sign of b on entry	Multiple R[b]
R&D	Neg.**	0.26
Advertising	Neg.**	0.34
Diversification	Pos.**	0.39
Extractive	Pos.	0.41
Relative size	Pos.	0.41
Acquisition ratio	Pos.	0.41
Organization	Neg.**	0.57
Sales subsidiary ratio	Neg.	0.57

**See Table C-3.

[a]See Table C-3.

[b]See Table C-3.

TABLE C-7 *Regression Results, Dependent Variable = Ratio of Majority Joint Ventures to All Manufacturing Subsidiaries Entered between 1960 and 1967[a]*

1. Stepwise regression, entry of independent variables constrained such that first variables to enter are those that contribute most to reducing unexplained variance.

Independent variable by order of entry	Sign of b on entry	Multiple R[b]
Sales subsidiary ratio	Neg.**	0.19
Advertising	Neg.	0.24
Organization	Pos.	0.28
R&D	Pos.	0.29
Acquisition	Neg.	0.30

2. Stepwise regression, entry of independent variables constrained such that organization and sales subsidiary ratio must enter after other variables. Otherwise, entry by order of reduction of unexplained variance.

Independent variable by order of entry	Sign of b on entry	Multiple R[b]
Advertising	Neg.	0.12
Diversification	Pos.	0.13
Extractive	Pos.	0.13
R&D	Pos.	0.14
Acquisition ratio	Neg.	0.14
Sales subsidiary ratio	Neg.**	0.27
Organization	Pos.	0.30

**See Table C-3.
[a]See Table C-3.
[b]See Table C-3.

NOTES

ONE

1. This set of firms provided the basic sample for the project "The Multinational Enterprise and the Nation State," of which this study is a part. For a description of the data collection and some additional information on the enterprises, see James W. Vaupel and Joan P. Curhan, *The Making of Multinational Enterprise* (Boston: Harvard Graduate School of Business Administration, Division of Research, 1969). Where no other source is indicated, this central collection effort and the information that we collected from interviews, questionnaires (described later), annual reports of the enterprises, and other published materials was the source of data in the analysis. The tables cover all the firms for which the required data were available. The appendices at the end of the book and, in some cases, footnotes to the tables indicate the number of firms covered by each type of data.

2. An "industry," in this case, is one defined at the three-digit level of aggregation in the Standard Industrial Classification (SIC).

3. For more data on these points, see Raymond Vernon, *Sovereignty at Bay: The Multinational Spread of U.S. Enterprise* (New York: Basic Books, 1971).

4. The reasons for the foreign investments of the firms are developed in *Ibid.*, Chapters 2 and 3.

TWO

1. Alfred D. Chandler, Jr., *Strategy and Structure* (Cambridge: M.I.T. Press, 1962), p. 13.

2. For a similar definition, see *Ibid.*, p. 14.

3. Bruce R. Scott, "A Stages Model of Corporate Development," unpublished mimeograph, February 1968. This theme is elaborated and applied to French firms in John H. McArthur and Bruce R. Scott, *Industrial Planning in France* (Boston: Harvard Graduate School of Business Administration, Division of Research, 1969), Chapter 4.

4. Russell L. Ackoff, "Systems, Organizations, and Interdisciplinary Research," in D. P. Eckman, ed., *Systems: Research and Design, Proceedings of the First Systems Symposium at Case Institute of Technology* (New York: Wiley, 1961), p. 28.

5. See James C. Emery, *Organizational Planning and Control Systems* (New York: Macmillan Book Company, 1969), pp. 5–14, for a fuller discussion of the effect of hierarchies in reducing channel requirements.

6. Herbert A. Simon, *The Shape of Automation for Men and Management* (New York: Harper and Row, 1965), p. 100.

7. See, for example, Thomas J. Allen, "The Differential Performance of Information Channels in the Transfer of Technology," in William H. Gruber and Don G. Marquis, eds., *Factors in the Transfer of Technology* (Cambridge: M.I.T. Press, 1969); and Daniel Katz and Robert L. Kahn, *The Social Psychology of Organizations* (New York: Wiley, 1966).

8. Jay W. Forrester, *Industrial Dynamics* (New York: Wiley, 1961).

H*

9. James G. March and Herbert A. Simon, *Organizations* (New York: Wiley, 1958), Chapter 6.

10. Oliver E. Williamson, *Corporate Control and Business Behavior* (Englewood Cliffs: Prentice-Hall, 1970), Chapter 2.

11. M. Glanzer and R. Glazer, "Techniques for the Study of Group Structure and Behavior, II," *Psychological Bulletin*, no. 58 (1961): 1–27; and Harold J. Leavitt, *Managerial Psychology* (Chicago: University of Chicago Press, 1958), Chapter 13.

12. Chandler, *Strategy*, p. 41.

13. See Chandler, *Strategy*, for a detailed description of the problems and the processes by which changes were introduced in these firms.

14. Emery, *Organizational Planning*, Chapter 2.

15. See Joseph L. Bower, *Managing the Resource Allocation Process; A Study of Corporate Planning and Investment* (Boston: Harvard Graduate School of Business Administration, Division of Research, 1970); see also Norman Berg, "Strategic Planning in Conglomerate Companies," *Harvard Business Review*, 47, no. 3 (May–June 1965).

16. The need for intermediaries to help resolve conflicts stemming from differences in time horizon is explored at length in Paul R. Lawrence and Jay W. Lorsch, *Organization and Environment: Managing Differentiation and Integration* (Boston: Harvard Graduate School of Business Administration, Division of Research, 1967).

17. Rensis Likert, *New Patterns of Management* (New York: McGraw-Hill, 1967), pp. 104–108, develops the concept of managers playing a linch-pin function to make subsystem behavior serve rather than undermine the goals of the overall system.

18. Chandler, *Strategy*, p. 312.

19. See Louis T. Wells, Jr., "Test of a Product Cycle Model of International Trade," *Quarterly Journal of Economics*, 83, no. 2 (February 1959); and Robert B. Stobaugh, Jr., "The Product Life Cycle, U.S. Exports and International Investment," unpublished doctoral dissertation, Harvard Business School, 1968, for empirical studies that examine U.S. export performance of products that were developed in response to American market stimulation.

20. See Yair Aharoni, *The Foreign Investment Decision Process* (Boston: Harvard Graduate School of Business Administration, Division of Research, 1966), and Endel J. Kolde, *International Business Enterprise* (Englewood Cliffs: Prentice-Hall, 1968), for more complete examinations of the initial investment decisions.

21. Robert B. Stobaugh, Jr., "Financing Foreign Subsidiaries of U.S.-Controlled Multinational Enterprises," *Journal of International Business Studies*, 1 (Spring 1970).

22. The concept of the vital role a "champion" plays in the expansion of new business activities is developed by Donald A. Schon in his perceptive study, *Technology and Change* (New York: Delacorte Press, 1967), of the management changes resulting from decisions to acquire new research-based product lines.

23. Gilbert H. Clee and Wilbur M. Sachtjen, "Organizing a Worldwide Business," *Harvard Business Review*, 42, no. 6 (November–December 1964).

24. William Blackie, Chairman of Caterpillar Tractor, as reported in "The Global Company in a Changing World," *Dun's Review* (August 1967), considers that this effect gave his company an undesirable "split personality."

THREE

1. Gene W. Dalton, Louis B. Barnes, and Abraham Zaleznik, *The Distribution of Authority in Formal Organizations* (Boston: Harvard Graduate School of Business

Administration, Division of Research, 1968), pp. 162–163. The conclusion is Zalez-nik's alone and is disputed by his coauthors.

2. See Allan Nevins and Frank E. Hill, *Ford: Expansion and Challenge: 1915–1933* (New York: Charles Scribner's Sons, 1957).

3. For an excellent treatment of the product life cycle theory, a summary of empirical research, and a discussion of some of the conceptual problems remaining in the model, see Roland Polli and Victor Cook, "Validity of the Product Life Cycle," *The Journal of Business*, 42, no. 4 (October 1969): 385–400.

4. There are many problems in defining what is meant by a "new" product. For a discussion of these problems, see Polli and Cook, *Product Life Cycle*; see also Robert D. Buzzell and Robert E. M. Nourse, *Product Innovation in Food Processing 1954–1964* (Boston: Harvard Graduate School of Business Administration, Division of Research, 1967). In this study, products are considered to be new when they are in early stages of their life cycles.

5. For summaries of the literature on this theme, see Harold H. Kassarjian and Thomas S. Robertson, *Perspectives in Consumer Behavior* (Glenview: Scott Foresman and Company, 1968); James F. Engel, David T. Kollat, and Roger D. Blackwell, *Consumer Behavior* (New York: Holt, Rinehart and Winston, 1968), p. 653; and Everett M. Rogers, *Diffusion of Innovations* (New York: The Free Press of Glencoe, 1962).

6. Leonard Wrigley, "Diversification and Divisional Autonomy," unpublished doctoral dissertation, Harvard Business School, 1970.

7. Bureau of the Budget, *Standard Industrial Classification Manual, 1967* (Washington, D.C.: U.S. Government Printing Office, 1967).

8. The source of these data was Fortune, *Plant and Product Directory 1965* (New York: Fortune, 1966). The data apply to products manufactured during 1965 and exclude products outside the manufacturing sector.

9. These data required some modification so that the results would not be biased by vertical integration in production across one or more of the SIC industry boundaries. Intermediate products that were further processed by the same firm were not included in the count.

10. Michael Gort, *Diversification and Integration in American Industry* (Princeton: Princeton University Press, 1962), pp. 6, 7.

11. See, for example, Tom Burns and Graham M. Stalker, *The Management of Innovation* (London: Tavistock Publications, 1961).

12. For a detailed exploration of the factors involved in the choice of directions of diversification for any one firm, see Edmund P. Learned, C. Roland Christensen, Kenneth R. Andrews, and William D. Guth, *Business Policy: Text and Cases* (Homewood: Irwin, 1965), or Igor Ansoff, *Corporate Strategy* (New York: McGraw-Hill Book Company, 1965).

13. For a detailed treatment of the industry, see Edith Penrose, *The Large International Firm in Developing Countries: The International Petroleum Industry* (London: Allen and Unwin, 1968); see also Alfred D. Chandler, Jr., *Strategy and Structure* (Cambridge: M.I.T. Press, 1962), for a description of the organizational development of Standard Oil of New Jersey before World War II in terms that are consistent with this analysis.

14. Subsidiaries engaged in extractive activities, such as mining, are excluded from this calculation. Firms that originated abroad, such as ITT, are also excluded.

15. William H. Gruber, Dileep Mehta, and Raymond Vernon, "The R&D Factor in International Trade and International Investment of U.S. Industries," *Journal of Political Economy*, 75, no. 1 (February 1967): 20–37.

16. The measure of foreign product diversity used in this study applies only to those products manufactured abroad; it does not include exports from the United

States. The difficulty of obtaining the appropriate data prevented the inclusion of exports in the measure.

17. As quoted in "How a Global Market Strategy Pays Off in Rising Multinational Profits," *Business Abroad*, 95, no. 7 (July 1970): 19.

18. Quoted in Cedric L. Suzman, "The Changing Export Activities of U.S. Firms with Foreign Manufacturing Affiliates," unpublished doctoral dissertation, Harvard Business School, 1969, p. 529.

19. See Eugene W. Burgess and Frederick H. Harbison, *Casa Grace in Peru* (Washington, D.C.: National Planning Association, 1954), for a discussion of local government relations in Latin America.

20. The data on which this case is based were provided in interviews by managers of the firm.

FOUR

1. Lawrence G. Franko, tentatively titled *Joint Venture Survival in Multinational Corporations*, to be published by Praeger Publishing Company, New York.

2. For a discussion of some of the problems and advantages of regional centers, see F. Newton Parks, "Survival of the European Headquarters," *Harvard Business Review*, 47, no. 2 (March–April 1969): 79–84.

3. The diversity of products is the force that most often breaks up international divisions. Only in the absence of product diversity are stresses from area diversity associated with structural change. For a similar observation, see Alfred D. Chandler, Jr., *Strategy and Structure* (Cambridge: M.I.T. Press, 1962), pp. 42–44.

4. Quoted in David M. Kieffer, "Reorganization for International Operations: Part I," *Chemical & Engineering News*, 44, no. 26 (June 27, 1966): 105.

5. In cases where data for foreign sales were missing, foreign net assets, expressed as a percentage of total net assets, was used.

6. For an analysis of an interesting early treatment of product differentiation and a summary of some of the more recent literature from economics on the subject, see Robert B. Ekelund, "Price Discrimination and Product Differentiation in Economic Theory: An Early Analysis," *Quarterly Journal of Economics*, 84, no. 2 (May 1970): 268–278.

7. William S. Comanor and Thomas A. Wilson, "Advertising Market Structure and Performance," *The Review of Economics and Statistics*, 49, no. 4 (November 1967): 423–440.

8. See Joe S. Bain, *Barriers to New Competition, Their Character and Consequences in Manufacturing Industries* (Cambridge: Harvard University Press, 1956), for an analysis of the effectiveness of advertising as an entry barrier to competitors.

9. The effects of scale in advertising are examined by Corwin D. Edwards, "Advertising and Competition: An Evaluation of Exhortative Programs," *Business Horizons*, 11, no. 1 (February 1968): 74–76.

10. Advertising includes all media expenditures in television, radio, magazines, newspapers, and also direct mail. These data were available for eighty-seven firms in *News Front*, 10, no. 2 (March 1966): 40–43.

11. For a full discussion of the research and marketing practices of this industry, see Senate Subcommittee on Antitrust and Monopoly of the Committee of the Judiciary, *Hearings on the Medical Restraint of Trade Act, Part I* (Washington D.C.: U.S. Government Printing Office, 1967); see also Hearings of the U.S. Senate Subcommittee on Monopoly of the Select Committee on Small Business, *Competitive Problems in the Drug Industry* (Washington D.C.: U.S. Government Printing Office, 1968).

12. L. P. Snow, "Marketing Proprietary Drugs," *Drug and Cosmetic Industry*, 105, no. 6 (June 1968): 51, 52.

13. Business International, *Organizing for European Operations* (New York: 1967), p. 47.

14. Charles R. Williams, "Regional Management Overseas," *Harvard Business Review*, 45, no. 1 (January–February 1967): 89.

15. Warren J. Keegan, "Five Strategies for Multinational Marketing," *European Business*, no. 24 (January 1970): 35–40.

16. For an examination of these costs and benefits, see Robert D. Buzzell, "Can You Standardize Multinational Marketing?" *Harvard Business Review*, 46, no. 6 (November–December 1968): 102–113.

17. See, for example, *Special Report on Prices*, (Ottawa: Royal Commission on Farm Machinery, December 1969), Chapter 2.

18. See H. W. Wertheimer, *The International Firm and International Aspects of Policies on Mergers* (Cambridge: Cambridge Conference, 1969), International Conference on Monopolies, Mergers and Restrictive Practices, September 23–26, pp. 1–9, for a discussion of some of the effects of changes in the locus of decision making.

19. Frederic G. Donner, *The Worldwide Industrial Enterprise* (New York: McGraw-Hill Book Company, 1967), pp. 35–36.

20. Lloyd N. Cutler, *Joint Ventures with Foreign Business Associates, Investors, and Governments* (Dallas: Institute on Private Investments Abroad, 1959), pp. 261–284, provides a comprehensive lawyer's description of transfer-pricing disputes. See also James S. Shulman, "Transfer Pricing in Multinational Business," unpublished doctoral dissertation, Harvard Business School, 1967.

21. Business International, *Organizing for European Operations* (New York: 1967), p. 60.

22. For a similar assessment, see Warren J. Keegan, "Key Questions in Multinational Marketing Management," *Worldwide P & I Planning*, 4, no. 4 (July–August, 1970): 64–70.

23. Buzzell, *Marketing*, pp. 104–105, describes the Hoover effort in greater detail.

24. Quoted by E. P. Neufeld in *A Global Corporation* (Toronto: University of Toronto Press, 1969), p. 227. Neufeld provides a good description of the problems that Massey-Ferguson faced in developing its present organizational structure.

FIVE

1. Alfred D. Chandler, Jr., *Strategy and Structure* (Cambridge: M.I.T. Press, 1962), pp. 380–381.

2. For a discussion of the relationship between formal and informal structures, see, for example, Herbert A. Simon, *Administrative Behavior* (New York: Macmillan, 1959), 2nd edition, p. 149.

3. See, for example, Alfred P. Sloan, Jr., *My Years With General Motors* (Garden City: Doubleday, 1964).

4. Edmund P. Learned, C. Roland Christensen, Kenneth R. Andrews, and William D. Guth, *Business Policy: Text and Cases* (Homewood: Irwin, 1955), pp. 370–392, provides a comprehensive description of the changes introduced.

5. Leonard Wrigley, "Diversification and Divisional Autonomy," unpublished doctoral dissertation, Harvard Business School, 1970.

6. *Ibid*.

7. Robert B. Stobaugh, Jr., "Financing Foreign Subsidiaries of U.S.-Controlled Multinational Enterprises," *Journal of International Business Studies*, 1 (Spring 1970).

8. Part of this section is adapted from an unpublished paper, "The Instability of the International Division," by Lawrence E. Fouraker and John M. Stopford. We are grateful to Dean Fouraker for allowing us to borrow so freely from this work.

9. See, for example, Michel Crozier, *The Bureaucratic Phenomenon* (Chicago: University of Chicago Press, 1964).

10. See, for example, Melville Dalton, *Men Who Manage* (New York: Wiley, 1959).

11. Joseph L. Bower, *Managing the Resource Allocation Process* (Boston: Harvard Graduate School of Business Administration, Division of Research, 1970), p. 302.

12. Edward A. McCreary, "Those American Managers Don't Impress Europe," *Fortune* (December 1964); and Dimitris N. Chorafas, *Developing the International Executive,* American Management Association Research Study 83, 1967, Chapter 8.

13. See, for example, W. H. Read, "Upward Communication in Industrial Hierarchies," *Human Relations* (January 1962), for evidence that middle managers withhold from their superiors information that might limit their mobility. In the same vein, see also Michael Z. Brooke and H. Lee Remmers, *The Strategy of Multinational Enterprise* (London: Longmans, 1970), pp. 53–54.

14. There are some firms that have developed area structures dividing the U.S. market. These firms typically make products, such as bread, that have a short shelf life. For an examination of the characteristics of these firms, see George A. Smith, Jr., *Managing Geographically Decentralized Companies* (Boston: Harvard Graduate School of Business Administration, Division of Research, 1958). Such cases were not observed among the firms in this study and are ignored for purposes of this analysis.

15. Finance, being consistently administered centrally, is not included in this argument.

16. Richard M. Cyert and James G. March, *A Behavioral Theory of the Firm* (Englewood Cliffs: Prentice-Hall, 1963).

17. See, for example, Kenneth J. Arrow, *Social Choice and Individual Values* (New York: Wiley, 1951); and James M. Buchanan and Gordon Tullock, *The Calculus of Consent* (Ann Arbor: University of Michigan Press, 1962).

18. The simple correlation coefficient between total sales and foreign ROI was -0.002.

19. The simple correlation coefficient between total sales and consolidated ROI was $+0.033$.

20. The simple correlation coefficient was $+0.024$.

21. See, for example, Edith T. Penrose, *The Theory of the Growth of the Firm* (Oxford: Blackwell, 1959), pp. 212–213.

22. See Joseph L. Bower, "Planning Within the Firm," *American Economic Review,* 60, no. 2 (May 1970): 186–194.

23. Lawrence E. Fouraker and John M. Stopford, unpublished working papers.

SIX

1. For a discussion of similar dilemmas, see Enid B. Lovell, *The Changing Role of the International Executive* (New York: National Industrial Conference Board, 1966), Chapter 6.

2. Michael Z. Brooke and H. Lee Remmers, *The Strategy of Multinational Enterprise* (London: Longmans, 1970), provide an illuminating description of a similar (Type D) structure.

3. The 1968 Annual Report of Dow Chemical Company discusses some of these

arrangements; see also Business International, *Organizing the Worldwide Corporation* (New York: 1970), p. 20.

4. Bruce Bendow, "Dow Faces Up to Its New World," *Chemical World* (April 22, 1967): 95.

5. 1968 Annual Report of Dow Chemical.

6. Business International, *Organizing for European Operations* (New York: 1967), Case Study 8, pp. 77–79. Much of the discussion of ITT is based on this source.

7. *Ibid*, p. 79.

8. See E. Raymond Corey and Steven H. Star, *Organization Strategy: A Marketing Approach* (Boston: Harvard Graduate School of Business Administration, Division of Research, 1971), pp. 370–389.

9. *Ibid.*, Chapter 1.

10. See, for example, J. S. Baumgartner, *Project Management* (Homewood: Irwin, 1960).

11. No systematic analysis of promotion patterns was undertaken, but over thirty such promotions were observed during the course of this study.

12. Dimitris N. Chorafas, *The Communication Barrier in International Management* (New York: American Management Association, 1969), pp. 63–64.

13. James G. March and Herbert A. Simon, *Organizations* (New York: Wiley, 1958), p. 78.

14. Pieter Kuin, a director of Unilever, made this statement in a paper, "Meeting Economic and Social Needs in a Variety of Countries," presented to the 13th International Management Congress, New York, 1963.

15. Millard H. Pryor, Jr., "Planning in a Worldwide Business, *Harvard Business Review*, 43, no. 1 (January–February 1965).

16. Chorafas, *Management*, p. 63.

17. Brooke and Remmers, *Enterprise*, pp. 53–54, reach similar conclusions.

18. Irene W. Meister, *Managing the International Financial Function* (New York: National Industrial Conference Board, 1970), pp. 94–95.

19. Joseph L. Bower, "The Role of Conflict in Economic Decision Making Groups," *Quarterly Journal of Economics*, 79, no. 2 (May 1965): 253–277.

20. Grant A. Dove, a vice president of Texas Instruments, described the OST system in considerable detail during an address to the London Graduate School of Business Studies on May 22, 1970.

21. *Ibid*.

22. Business International, *Organizing for European Operations*, p. 70.

SEVEN

1. There are, of course, other alternatives. We have not considered the licensing option, for example.

2. "General Motors Position on United Control of Foreign Operations," General Motors Corporation (February 11, 1966): 3.

3. A public statement by a vice president of Celanese Corporation of America, quoted on page 12 of Richard D. Robinson, "Management Attitudes toward Joint and Mixed Ventures Abroad," *Western Business Review*, 6, no. 1 (February 1962).

4. Less than 1 percent of the manufacturing subsidiaries were identified as having publicly traded stock.

5. For the firms in this study, there were sixteen manufacturing joint ventures that were clearly identified as having as a partner the local government. A number of arrangements with governments probably slipped into the "unknown" category,

because the students who coded the data were told to record a government partner only if the name made it clear to them that the partner was a government entity. A few joint ventures with governments also probably made their way into the "private" classification.

6. Consistent with our practice in the analysis of organization, we excluded subsidiaries that were located in Canada. Also, eliminated, unless otherwise stated in the text, were subsidiaries that were acquired with the subsidiary's parent or by merger with another American corporation. In these cases, no separate decision was made by the current parent on the form of ownership.

7. The simple correlation coefficients between pairs for the answers to problems (f), (g), and (h) were all positive and significant for at least the 0.05 level of confidence.

8. A subsidiary was considered to be majority owned by the multinational enterprise if the parent held directly or indirectly more than half but less than 95 percent of the stock. Arrangements in which the multinational firm held at least 5 percent but not more than half the stock were called minority joint ventures. The distinction between majority and minority is, or course, rather artificial. In some cases, the multinational enterprise may have management control even though it owns less than 50 percent of the shares. Control may be exercised through a management contract, or the local shares may be divided among local parties who do not band together. It is also possible that the local partners have effective control over some ventures where the foreign investor has more than half the stock. This is especially likely to be the case in countries with strong protection for minority shareholders. But the crude classification was helpful.

EIGHT

1. Of the multinational enterprises that responded to our questionnaire 88 percent indicated that the local partners typically had at least some voice in management.

2. As in the earlier chapters, expenditures were available only for the United States. They were obtained from *News Front*, March 1966.

3. An additional check was made by examining the use of sales subsidiaries by the firm. On the assumption that manufacturing operations which began as sales subsidiaries were likely to be ones in which the multinational parent has sales skills, we compared the ownership of manufacturing subsidiaries that began their life as sales operations with those that did not. The data indicated that such a facility was much less likely to be a joint venture than was a plant where no such conversion of activities had been made. Multiple regression techniques showed the negative relationship between the general propensity of a system to enter sales subsidiaries and its propensity to use joint ventures in manufacturing operations. Both of these tests provided some additional support for the claim that firms that have their own marketing skills are more likely than other firms to prefer wholly owned subsidiaries. We also tried another measure of advertising expenditures. *National Advertising Investments*, 1966–1967, volumes 18–19, provided data that covered a larger sample of firms than was covered by the *News Front* measure that we used initially. However, the *National Advertising Investments* data covered only three media, while *News Front* covered five. Since the correlation coefficient between the two measures was 0.740, it is not surprising that the same relationship appeared between subsidiary ownership and these two measures. We also converted both figures to a percentage of value added instead of a percentage of sales. The conversion was made by using the average ratio of sales to value added for the primary industry of the parent. Again, the relationship of advertising to joint ventures was borne out.

4. Warren J. Keegan, "Five Strategies for Multinational Marketing," *European Business*, no. 24 (January 1970): 36.

5. John F. Lawrence, "How They Sell: Foreign-Tasting Food, U.S.-Style Promotion Score Abroad for Heinz," *The Wall Street Journal* (November 9, 1964): 1–10.

6. The questionnaire responses showed that conflicts over marketing decisions were some of the most important sources of friction with joint venture partners. We were somewhat surprised to find that there was not a strong relationship between the firms' advertising expenditures and their questionnaire answers as to which problems were important in *existing* joint ventures. The explanation seems to lie in the fact that the few joint ventures that were entered by these firms were for some very special situations where the firms were willing to give more autonomy than usual to the local subsidiary. In these few cases, to which we turn later, apparently sufficient agreement was reached in advance with the local partner in the critical marketing elements that serious conflicts did not arise. Our questionnaire did not ask what *potential* conflicts with partners led the firm to prefer wholly owned operations. We have to rely on other literature, on the evaluation of conflicts by firms that did not enter many joint ventures, and on interviews to support the contention that the potential for conflict over a critical element of strategy led the marketing-oriented firms to choose ownership that would give them control over subsidiaries.

7. Robert J. Ballon, *Joint Ventures and Japan* (Tokyo: Sophia University Press, 1967), and Thomas F. M. Adams and Noritake Kobayashi, *The World of Japanese Business* (Tokyo: Kodansha International, Ltd., 1969), Chapter 10.

8. For a description of such arrangements before World War II, see Dudley M. Phelps, *Migrations of Industry to South America* (New York: McGraw-Hill Book Company, 1936). Ralph A. Sorenson, "An Analysis of Competition between Local and International Companies in Two Central American Industries," unpublished doctoral dissertation, Harvard Business School, 1967, describes in some detail the marketing and production operations of an American detergent company in Central America; also, Cedric L. Suzman, "The Changing Export Activities of U.S. Firms with Foreign Manufacturing Affiliates," unpublished doctoral dissertation, Harvard Business School, 1969, treats wholly owned marketing arrangements in a chemical firm where joint ventures were used for manufacturing.

9. See Hugo E. R. Uyterhoeven, "Foreign Entry and Joint Ventures," unpublished doctoral dissertation, Harvard Business School, 1963, p. III-46.

10. *Special Report on Prices* (Ottawa: Royal Commission on Farm Machinery, December 1969).

11. For a description of rationalization in the farm equipment industry, see *Ibid*.

12. H. W. Wertheimer, *The International Firm and International Aspects of Policies on Mergers* (Cambridge: Cambridge Conference, 1969), International Conference on Monopolies, Mergers and Restrictive Practices, September 23–26, pp. 1–9.

13. E. P. Neufeld, *A Global Corporation* (Toronto: University of Toronto Press, 1969), p. 227.

14. Russell M. Moore, "The Role of Extrazonally Controlled Multinational Corporations in the Process of Establishing a Regional Latin American Automobile Industry: A Case Study of Brazil," doctoral dissertation, Fletcher School of Law and Diplomacy, 1969, pp. 148–149.

15. Some additional descriptions of conflicts resulting from rationalization of international production facilities are provided in Adams and Kobayashi, *Japanese Business*, Chapter 13; and Roderick S. Deane, "Foreign Investment in New Zealand Manufacturing," doctoral dissertation, Victoria University of Wellington, 1967, vol. I, p. 86.

16. Although the normalized results showed similar patterns, they are not presented here, since we were not interested in the relative ranking of the policies.

17. Excluded were firms that were extractive in their orientation, that is, firms that had three or more subsidiaries engaged in extractive operations.

18. See *Chairman's Address* at the Annual General Meeting, The Broken Hill Proprietary Co., Ltd., South Melbourne, September 16, 1966.

19. See *Contract of Work between the Republic of Indonesia and P.T. Pacific Nikkel Indonesia,* March 17, 1969, Djakarta.

20. For a description of the affiliation, see the SEC Prospectuses of the Liberian Iron Ore Company (LIO), holding company for the Liberian American-Swedish Minerals Company (LAMCO).

21. The d'Arcy agreement for petroleum in 1901 covered most of Persia.

22. For a treatment of the role of size in inducing joint ventures in iron ore projects, see Donald R. Hakala, "The Iron Ore Industry: A Study of Shifts in Ownership and Control," *Quarterly Review of Economics and Business,* 9, no. 1 (Spring 1966): 45–51.

23. The preference of users for their own sources is indicated in John E. Tilton, "The Choice of Trading Partners: An Analysis of International Trade in Aluminum, Bauxite, Copper, Lead, Manganese, Tin, and Zinc," *Yale Economic Essays,* 6, no. 2 (Fall 1966). Sometimes the joint venture agreement provides a detailed definition of average cost and formulas for sharing output. See, for example, *LAMCO Joint Venture Agreement,* April 28, 1960, Monrovia, and Edith T. Penrose, "Vertical Integration with Joint Control of Raw Material Production," *Journal of Development Studies,* 1, no. 3 (April 1965): 251–268.

24. "Significant Corporate Moves," *Business International* (June 12, 1970).

25. The formal arrangements have varied considerably. Sharing of equity in an operation has been only one vehicle to enable the government to play an active role. Many of the "service contracts" have been much more like long-term management contracts, whereby the foreign firm has been given certain rights and payments for a fixed time period. Actual ownership of facilities has been entirely in the hands of the state firm. See, for example, the Indonesian petroleum "contracts of work," such as Production Sharing Contract between P.M. PERTANGAN Minjak National and Continental Overseas Oil Company, May 12, 1967. Some of the arrangements with rather autonomous state enterprises have required two contracts, one with the department for mines or natural resources, which resembles a traditional concession, and one with the state enterprise, which resembles a joint venture agreement between private parties. See, for example, the Chevron / Hanna concession agreement and the Hanna / IFI agreements for the mining of the Cerro Matoso Nickel deposits in Colombia, *Joint Venture Agreement between Instituto de Fomento Industrial y Compañia de Niquel Colombiano* (Hanna Mining Company), Bogotá, July 16, 1970.

26. William H. Gruber, Dileep Mehta, and Raymond Vernon, "The R&D Factor in International Trade and International Investment of U.S. Industries," *Journal of Political Economy,* 75, no. 1 (February 1967): 20–37.

27. Moore, *Brazil,* p. 149.

28. William Rogers, *Think* (New York: Stein and Day, 1969), p. 243.

29. "Rheem Manufacturing Company," Harvard Business School, Boston, ICH 4G150, ICR 164.

30. Conducted by Harvard MBA students under the authors' supervision.

31. Whatarangi Winiata, "United States Managerial Investment in Japan, 1950–65, An Interview Study," unpublished doctoral dissertation, University of Michigan, 1966. The data were not well controlled for differences in industries and time periods, but the strength of the relationship indicates that it might hold if the data were adjusted for industry, date of formation, etc.

32. Ashok Kapoor, "Foreign Collaborations in India: Problems and Prospects," *IDEA,* 9, no. 2 (Summer 1966): 213–258, and 9, no. 3 (Fall 1966): 349–387, provides a detailed description of similar arrangements in India.

33. Jack Baranson, "Technology Transfer Through the International Firm," *American Economic Review*, 60, 2 (May 1970), p. 437, mentions the increasing concern in less developed countries about payments for technology.

34. See Lloyd N. Cutler, *Joint Ventures with Foreign Business Associates, Investors, and Governments* (Dallas: Southwestern Legal Foundation, Institute on Private Investments Abroad, 1959), pp. 261–284.

35. Conducted by Louis T. Wells, Jr., as a part of a project for Harvard Development Advisory Service.

36. Deane, *New Zealand;* see also D. H. W. van Hilten, *Joint Ventures* (Deventer: Æ. E. Kluwer, 1968), p. 100.

37. "Goodyear vs. Goodrich Tussle in Netherlands Points up Pitfalls of Joint Ventures," *Business International*, 17, no. 22 (May 29, 1970).

38. See Baranson, "Technology Transfer,". p. 439.

39. Robert B. Stobaugh, Jr., "The Product Life Cycle, U.S. Exports and International Investment," unpublished doctoral dissertation, Harvard Business School, 1968.

NINE

1. Diversification is only occasionally mentioned in the literature as a variable that influences ownership. D. H. W. van Hilten, *Joint Ventures* (Deventer: Æ. E. Kluwer, 1968), p. 115, does provide some discussion of the relationships between diversification and use of local partners.

2. See, for example, Roderick S. Deane, "Foreign Investment in New Zealand Manufacturing," unpublished doctoral dissertation, Victoria University of Wellington, 1967, vol. I, p. 94. He ranked acquisition as the second most important explanation for local participation. Frequently, the original owner desires to retain an interest in the subsidiary.

3. Karen Bivens and Enid B. Lovell, *Joint Ventures with Foreign Partners* (New York: National Industrial Conference Board, 1966), p. 13.

4. In the mining class we placed all firms whose primary SIC was 326 or 333 (pottery and primary smelting and refining of nonferrous metals) and which had three or more extractive operations abroad.

5. Outside of Japan, Spain, Ceylon, India, Mexico, Pakistan and, of course, Canada.

6. John D. Daniel, "Recent Foreign Direct Manufacturing Investment in the United States: An Interview Study of the Decision Process," unpublished doctoral dissertation, University of Michigan, 1969, pp. 169–170.

7. For an analysis of strategy in the petroleum, copper, and aluminum industries, see Raymond Vernon, "Foreign Enterprise and Developing Nations in the Raw Materials Industries," *American Economic Review*, 60, 2 (May 1970).

8. See *Ibid.;* and Martin S. Brown and John Butler, *The Production, Marketing and Consumption of Copper and Aluminum* (New York: Praeger Publishing Company, 1968).

9. Hugo E. R. Uyterhoeven, "Foreign Entry and Joint Ventures," unpublished doctoral dissertation, Harvard Business School, 1963, p. III-48.

10. Deane, *New Zealand*, vol. 1, Chapter 4.

11. See Endel J. Kolde, *International Business Enterprise* (Englewood Cliffs: Prentice-Hall, 1968), p. 265.

12. Described in *Business Latin America* (July 30, 1970): 242–243.

13. Uyterhoeven, *Foreign Entry*, p. III-48.

14. A score of "5" or "6" was considered "important."

15. International Chamber of Commerce, *International Joint Business Ventures*

in Developing Countries, Report of the Commission on International Investments and Economic Development, December 1968, p. 11.

16. Wolfgang G. Friedmann and George Kalmanoff, eds., *Joint International Business Ventures* (New York: Columbia University Press, 1961), p. 175, for a discussion of the role of governments in contributing capital.

17. Of the sixteen, eleven were entered between 1960 and 1967. However, joint ventures with local governments are not entirely a recent phenomenon, as is evidenced by Mira Wilkins' description of the interests in 1915 of Standard Oil in a joint venture with the Chinese Government. See Mira Wilkins, *The Emergence of Multinational Enterprise—American Business Abroad from the Colonial Era to 1914* (Cambridge: Harvard University Press, 1970).

18. James W. C. Tomlinson, *The Joint Venture Process in International Business* (Cambridge: M.I.T. Press, 1970). For a description of several joint ventures with government partners see Wolfgang G. Friedmann and Jean-Pierre Béguin, *Joint International Business Ventures in Developing Countries: Case Studies and Analysis of Recent Trends* (New York: Columbia University Press, 1971), especially pp. 16–19.

19. See, for example, Deane, *New Zealand,* p. 77; Whatarangi Winiata, "United States Managerial Investment in Japan, 1950–1964: An Interview Study," unpublished doctoral dissertation, University of Michigan, 1966, Table 3-3, p. 68; and W. P. Hogan, "British Investment in Australian Manufacturing: The Technical Connection," *The Manchester School of Economics and Social Studies,* 35 (November 2, 1967): 141–142. Hogan, surprisingly, found the opposite results for British investment in Australia.

20. The effects of oligopoly structure on the strategy of the small firms are, perhaps, demonstrated by the fact that the differences in use of joint ventures by the small and large firms in an industry are greater if each industry in the sample is weighted equally. For entries between 1960 and 1967, joint ventures accounted for 41 percent of the manufacturing subsidiaries for the small firms, compared to 28 percent for the large firms, with equal weighting for each industry. The effect of the weighting is to count more heavily those industries that have a smaller number of firms. These are presumably the ones in which oligopoly responses are most likely to dominate.

21. William J. Baumol, *Business Behavior, Value, and Growth* (New York: Harcourt, Brace and World, 1967), pp. 28–29.

22. John Von Neumann and Oskar Morgenstern, *Theory of Games and Economic Behavior,* 3rd edition (Princeton: Princeton University Press, 1953); Yair Aharoni, *The Foreign Investment Decision Process* (Boston: Harvard Graduate School of Business Administration, Division of Research, 1966), calls a similar behavior the "bandwagon effect."

23. Frederick T. Knickerbocker, a doctoral candidate at the Harvard Business School, is currently testing similar hypotheses on the investment patterns of the firms in this study.

24. The current work of Sidney Robbins and Robert B. Stobaugh, Jr. on the financial patterns of multinational enterprises indicates that smaller firms use fewer sources of funds than do large firms. David Mermelstein, "Large Industrial Corporations and Asset Shares," *American Economic Review,* 59, no. 4, part 1 (September 1969): 537, indicated that smaller firms faced higher costs of capital than did larger firms.

25. On the management side, see Raymond Vernon, "Organization as a Scale Factor in the Growth of Firms," in Jesse W. Markham and Gustav F. Papanek, eds., *Industrial Organization and Economic Development* (Boston: Houghton Mifflin Company, 1970), pp. 47–66.

26. Robert B. Stobaugh, Jr., "Utilizing Technical Know-how in a Foreign Invest-

ment and Licensing Program," a paper delivered to Chemical Marketing Research Association, Houston, February 23, 1970, pp. 3–4; and Endel J. Kolde, *Enterprise*, p. 269, says: "A small firm with limited capital and management resources is more likely to seek strong foreign partners than is a large company operating a network of production facilities in numerous countries."

27. Helmut Giesecke, *Industrial Investments in Developing Countries* (Hamburg: Hamburg Archives of World Economy, 1963), p. 135.

28. Jack Baranson, *Technologies for Developing Economies* (New York: Praeger Publishing Company, 1969).

29. For evidence that relatively small firms have been productive in generating new products, see William S. Comanor, "Market Structure, Product Differentiation, and Industrial Research," *Quarterly Journal of Economics*, 81, no. 4 (November 1967): 639–657; and F. M. Scherer, "Research and Development Resource Allocation under Rivalry," *Quarterly Journal of Economics*, 81, no. 3 (August 1967): 359–394. See also, D. C. Mueller and John E. Tilton, "Research and Development Costs as a Barrier to Entry," *Canadian Journal of Economics*, 2, no. 4 (November 1969): 572–574. They contend that the small firm is at no disadvantage in the "innovation" and "imitation" stages for certain kinds of research and development. F. M. Scherer, in *Economic Concentration: Part 3, Concentration, Invention and Innovation*, Hearings before the Subcommittee on Anti-Trust and Monopoly of the Committee on the Judiciary, U.S. Senate, May and June 1965, indicates a threshhold for the firm of $100 million annual sales beyond which increased economies in R&D are rare. None of the firms in this study fell below this figure.

30. The fear of a competitor's preempting a market is described in Alexander Lamfalussy, *Investment and Growth in Mature Economies* (London: Macmillan and Company, 1961), pp. 103–113. And Scherer, "Research and Development Costs as a Barrier to Entry," *Economic Concentration*, p. 389, discusses the marketing problems of the small firm.

31. See Timken case, United States v. Timken Roller Bearing Co., 83F Supp. 284 (N.D. Ohio, 1949), modified, 341 US 593 (1951), and *Business International*'s report on the U.S. Justice Department's action in U.S. v. Glaxo Group, Ltd., and ICI; and U.S. v. Farbenfabriken Bayer, and Chemegron Corporation 15, no. 14 (April 5, 1968): 106. For the E.E.C. Commission's position, see "New E.E.C. Antitrust Decision," *Business International*, 15, no. 45 (November 8, 1968): 355. For a rather thorough analysis of the antitrust implication of joint ventures, see John C. Scott and Steven K. Yablonski, "Transnational Mergers and Joint Ventures Affecting American Exports," *The Antitrust Bulletin*, 14, no. 1 (Spring 1969), and Friedmann and Kalmanoff, *Ventures*, Chapter VII.

32. A comparison of a crude rank coding for relative size and one for foreign experience produced a positive coefficient of correlation significant at the 0.01 level.

TEN

1. The principal product line of the parent is identified on a three-digit SIC basis by the Department of Commerce.

2. See, for example, Alfred D. Chandler, Jr., "The Structure of American Industry in the Twentieth Century: A Historical Overview," *Business History Review*, 43, no. 3 (Autumn 1969): 275–281.

3. These were the firms that did not yet have an international division and firms that had an international division to which subsidiaries reported directly.

4. The questionnaire returns indicated a similar pattern. Joint ventures accounted for the largest percentage of overseas manufacturing output in the firms that

granted much autonomy to foreign subsidiaries and the smallest fraction of the area-organized enterprises.

5. Lawrence G. Franko, tentatively titled, *Joint Venture Survival in Multinational Corporations,* to be published by Praeger Publishing Company, New York. "Instability" was said to have existed if the holdings of the multinational enterprise crossed the 50 or 95 percent lines, if the interests of the multinational firm were sold, or if the venture was liquidated.

6. Since the propensities to enter joint ventures were calculated by the decade, only those changes in organizational structure that took place within two years of the beginning of a decade were included.

7. See also Wolfgang G. Friedmann and Jean-Pierre Béguin, *Joint International Business Ventures in Developing Countires: Case Studies and Analysis of Recent Trends* (New York: Columbia University Press, 1971), p. 367.

8. Apparently, a number of French investors in the Ivory Coast, however, have converted wholly owned facilities to joint ventures in recent years.

9. Some readers will wonder whether the relationships described earlier might not be a result of changes that have occurred over time rather than from strategy differences. For example, might not the increased availability of partners in recent years explain why small firms had more joint ventures than large firms? After all, they made most of their investments in recent years. To eliminate such possibilities, not only the total stock of subsidiaries as of 1966, but also the new entries by both classes of firms between 1960 and 1967 were compared. All the relationships were found to hold in both kinds of comparisons.

ELEVEN

1. Albert E. Safarian, "Country of Ownership and Performance of the Firm," *The Economic Record,* 44, no. 105 (March 1968): 83.

2. "An Act to Approve the Agreement for Establishment of Cement Factory and Clarifications and Amendment Thereto," Made between the Government of the Republic of Liberia and a Foreign Group of Investors Represented by Fouad Kjalifa, Monrovia, March 3, 1966, and March 24, 1966, p. 4.

3. "Agreement between the Government of the Republic of Indonesia and A. Soriano y Cia," Djakarta, 1969, pp. 28–29.

4. See, for example, Leland L. Johnson, "U.S. Private Investment in Latin America: Some Questions of National Policy," Memorandum RM-4029-ISA, prepared for The Office of the Assistant Secretary of Defense / International Security Affairs, The Rand Corporation, July 1965, p. 63; and Michael W. Gordon, "Joint Business Ventures in the Central American Common Market," *Vanderbilt Law Review,* 21 (1968): 318. For a sophisticated attack on the benefits to the host country of joint ventures, see Thomas Horst, "On the Benefits of the Domestic Minority Ownership of Foreign-Controlled Firms," *Discussion Paper* No. 176, Harvard Institute of Economic Research, Harvard University, Cambridge, February 1971.

5. See, for example, Lester B. Pearson, *Partners in Development* (New York: Praeger Publishing Company, 1969), p. 112.

6. Business International, "Pros and Cons of Joint Ventures Abroad," *Management Monographs,* no. 18 (New York: 1964), p. 4.

7. See "Detroit Moves In," *Economist,* 237, no. 6637 (November 7, 1970): 75–76.

TWELVE

1. The work of Robert B. Stobaugh, Jr., who has examined the financial patterns in the same firms in connection with the study of the Multinational Enterprise and the Nation State, provides this finding. His results will appear in *Money in the Multinational Enterprise: A Study of Financial Policy* (New York: Basic Books, Forthcoming).

2. Donald T. Brash, *American Investment in Australian Industry* (Cambridge: Harvard University Press, 1966), p. 77.

3. Whatarangi Winiata, "United States Managerial Investment in Japan, 1950–1964, An Interview Study," doctoral dissertation, University of Michigan, 1966. The data were not well controlled for differences in industries, but the strength of the relationship indicates that it might hold if more controls were applied. The data came from the period 1950–1964.

4. See, for example, Brash, *Australian Industry*, p. 248, and Reserve Bank of India. *Foreign Collaborations in Indian Industry* (Bombay, 1968).

5. Robert B. Stobaugh, Jr., see note 1. The much greater role of debt financing in joint ventures than in wholly owned subsidiaries is also evident in U.S. Department of Commerce, *U.S. Direct Investments Abroad, 1966, Part II: Investment Position, Financial and Operating Data* (Washington: Social and Economic Statistics Administration, Bureau of Economic Analysis, 1972), Group 2, BEA-SUP 72-01, Table 6.

6. Brash, *Australian Industry*, and Albert E. Safarian, "Country of Ownership and Performance of the Firm" *The Economic Record*, 44, no. 105 (March 1968): 85–86, and Albert E. Safarian, *Foreign Ownership of Canadian Industry* (Toronto: McGraw-Hill Company of Canada, Ltd., 1966), p. 262.

7. Melville H. Watkins, (Head of Task Force), *Foreign Ownership and the Structure of Canadian Industry*, Privy Council Office, Ottawa, January 1968, p. 220.

8. Brash, *Australian Industry*, p. 98.

9. Roderick S. Deane, "Foreign Investment in New Zealand Manufacturing," unpublished doctoral dissertation, Victoria University of Wellington, 1967, vol. 1, Chapter 4, p. 96.

10. For wholly owned subsidiaries, the foreign firm is free, except for government constraints, to use transfer prices, royalties, technical fees, etc., to shift profits to lower tax jurisdictions, to avoid exchange controls, or to reduce the recorded profitability of a particular subsidiary so that accusations of exploitation are less likely.

11. See also, Lloyd N. Cutler, "Joint Ventures with Foreign Business Associates, Investors and Governments," Southwestern Legal Foundation, Institute on Private Investments Abroad (Dallas, 1959), p. 276.

12. Deane, *New Zealand*.

13. *Ibid.*, p. 236. See also p. 95.

14. *Ibid.*, p. 95. See also Brash, *Australian Industry*; and W. P. Hogan, "British Investments in Australian Manufacturing: The Technical Connection," *Manchester School of Economics and Social Studies*, 35, no. 2 (May 1967): 145–146. The larger role of fees and royalties in the remissions of minority joint ventures is evident in Table 23 of U.S. Department of Commerce, *U.S. Direct Investments*.

15. Cutler, *Joint Ventures*, p. 264.

16. Mathew K. Kurian, *Impact of Foreign Capital on Indian Economy* (New Delhi: People's Publishing House, 1966), p. 303. For Latin American regulations, see *Business Latin American* (October 29, 1970): 348–349.

17. That commonly appearing royalty rates can be approximately equivalent to what might be remitted to the foreign parent through higher transfer prices is illustrated by a simple calculation. Take 4.2 percent as the typical percentage of sales

that a subsidiary spends with foreign affiliates for the purchase of materials and components—that is, the average for less developed countries as reported in Gary C. Hufbauer and F. Michael Adler, *Overseas Manufacturing Investment and the Balance of Payments,* Tax Policy Research Study, no. 1 (U.S. Treasury Department, Washington, D.C. 1965), p. 25. If the "overcharge" on transfer pricing was the 155 percent that appears for chemicals in Colombia, then the transfer of funds through pricing amounts to 2.5 percent of sales. This is not an uncommon rate for the payment of royalty.

18. See Reserve Bank of India, *Foreign Collaborations,* pp. 101, 106. Several of these points are dealt with in Wolfgang G. Friedmann and Jean-Pierre Béguin, *Joint International Business Ventures in Developing Countries: Case Studies and Analysis of Recent Trends* (New York: Columbia University Press, 1971), p. 370.

19. Brash, *Australian Industry,* p. 228.

20. Jose de la Torre, "Exports of Manufactured Goods from Foreign Developing Countries: Marketing Factors and the Role of Foreign Enterprise," unpublished doctoral dissertation, Harvard Business School, 1970.

21. Cutler, *Joint Ventures,* pp. 261–284, provides a lawyer's discussion of the need for agreement with partners, but the lack of need when control is in the corporate family.

22. Herbert May, *The Effects of United States and Other Foreign Investment in Latin America* (New York: The Council for Latin America, January 1970), pp. 34, 36, provided evidence of the importance of access to the multinational system's marketing network. Two-thirds of the exports of the U.S. subsidiaries in Latin America were sold through affiliated enterprises; Jose de la Torre, "Marketing Factors in Manufactured Exports from Developing Countries," in Louis T. Wells, Jr., ed., *Product Life Cycle and International Trade* (Boston, Harvard Graduate School of Business Administration, Division of Research, 1972) confirmed the importance of the foreign firm's marketing network in increasing the exports of manufacturers from Nicaragua and Colombia.

23. Brash, *Australian Industry,* p. 229, mentions this vehicle of control.

24. See, for example, *Ibid.,* p. 233.

25. Kurian, *Indian Economy,* p. 317.

26. "Significant Corporate Moves," *Business International,* 17, no. 25 (June 19, 1970): 199.

27. The issue of control of foreign investment, from the point of view of the host government, is developed much further in Raymond Vernon, *Sovereignty at Bay: The Multinational Spread of U.S. Enterprise* (New York: Basic Books, 1971).

28. Kurian, *Indian Economy,* pp. 110–111.

THIRTEEN

1. See *Business Latin America* (November 5, 1970): 353–355, and *Boletin de Comercio Exterior,* ANDI, Bogotá (November 13, 1970).

2. Raymond Vernon, "Private Long-term Foreign Investment in Latin America," paper written for Interamerican Committee on the Alliance for Progress, January 1967.

3. See, for example, Paul A. Goldberg and Charles P. Kindleberger, "Toward a GATT for Investment: A Proposal for Supervision of the International Corporation," *Law and Policy in International Business,* 2, no. 2 (Summer 1970): 295–326. A number of proposals are developed in some detail in Chapter 8 of Raymond Vernon, *Sovereignty at Bay: The Multinational Spread of U.S. Enterprise* (New York: Basic Books, 1971).

INDEX

advertising, *see* marketing

Aeronaves de Mexico: partner in joint venture, 136

aluminum industry: joint ventures, 118–119, 135

American Metals Climax: joint venture in Australian mineral resources, 119

AMF Corporation: combination of product and area assignments, 26

Andean Subregional Group, 178–179

antitrust: challenge to market allocation agreements, 141

area diversification, 48–62; management, 54–57; marketing orientation and, 54–57; production rationalization and, 58–62; technology and, 57–58

area divisions, 15 (*see also* regional groups); development of, 50–53; global structure based on, 26, 27; new products and, 57–58; product diversification and, 81

Armstrong Cork Company: autonomy of subsidiaries, 94

Australia: export restrictions in joint ventures, 164; joint ventures among extracting subsidiaries, 117, 118; joint ventures more likely to deal locally, 159, 163; larger proportion of know-how in joint ventures, 164; Mt. Newman project, 118; suspended payments by joint ventures, 160

banana industry: attempt to use advertising to reduce competition, 175–176

bauxite: joint ventures, 117, 119

Borden, Inc.: product diversification, 36

Brazil: royalty payments allowed only for joint ventures, 162

Bristol de Mexico: joint venture with principal customers as partners, 136

Broken Hill Proprietary Company: joint development of Australian iron ore resources, 117

Business International, 95, 119, 122, 154

Canada: dividend tax and local ownership of subsidiaries, 150; joint ventures among extracting subsidiaries, 117; joint ventures more likely to deal locally, 159, 163; U.S. subsidiaries treated as part of U.S. operations, 188; variability of dividends from wholly owned subsidiaries, 160

Caterpillar: shared responsibilities of management, 95

Celanese Corporation: attitude toward joint ventures, 99; shared responsibilities of management, 9

cement industry: subsidiaries serving single national market, 49

Central American Common Market, 136

Ceylon: Colgate's combination of foreign sales operation and joint ventures in manufacturing, 112–113; insistence on joint ventures, 105, 150; minority joint ventures, 151

chemical industry: joint ventures, 122, 136–137, 158

Chesebrough-Pond's, Inc.: regional coordination of marketing, 56

Chile: local partners condemned by political opinion, 167

Chrysler Corporation, 138